The Scattered Family

The Scattered Family

Parenting, African Migrants, and Global Inequality

CATI COE

The University of Chicago Press
Chicago and London

Cati Coe is associate professor of anthropology at Rutgers Universtiy. She is the author of *Dilemmas of Culture in African Schools: Youth, Nationalism, and the Transformation of Knowledge*, also published by the University of Chicago Press.

The University of Chicago Press, Chicago 60637
The University of Chicago Press, Ltd., London
© 2014 by The University of Chicago
All rights reserved. Published 2014.
Printed in the United States of America

23 22 21 20 19 18 17 16 15 14   1 2 3 4 5

ISBN-13: 978-0-226-07224-1 (cloth)
ISBN-13: 978-0-226-07238-8 (paper)
ISBN-13: 978-0-226-07241-8 (e-book)
DOI: 10.7208/chicago/9780226072418.001.0001

Library of Congress Cataloging-in-Publication Data

Coe, Cati, author.
    The scattered family : parenting, African migrants, and global inequality /
Cati Coe.
        pages   cm
    Includes bibliographical references and index.
    ISBN 978-0-226-07224-1 (cloth : alkaline paper)
    ISBN 978-0-226-07238-8 (paperback : alkaline paper)
    ISBN 978-0-226-07241-8 (e-book)
    1. Foreign workers, Ghanaian—United States.   2. Families—Ghana.
3. Children of foreign workers.   4. Foreign workers' families.
5. Transnationalism—Social aspects.   I. Title.
HQ696.8.C64 2014
306.85—dc23

                                                                2013008861

♾ This paper meets the requirements of ANSI/NISO Z39.48-1992
(Permanence of Paper).

CONTENTS

ACKNOWLEDGMENTS

This book has benefited from the support of many people and institutions. The support came in numerous forms: through advice, providing me with a place to stay, trudging with me up and down the hills of Akropong, listening to recordings and transcribing them, reading my work and commenting on it, and giving me the financial resources to make it all happen.

First and foremost, I am so grateful to all my informants and their families in Ghana and the United States for letting me know about their lives and experiences. Two individuals in particular focused my attention on this line of research eight years ago, when I had only a vague notion of what I might be doing. Several Ghanaian churches on the East Coast welcomed me.

Kweku Aryeh, Joe Banson, and Margaret Rose Tettey helped immensely with my research in Akropong, helping me conduct interviews and focus group discussions, come up with questions, and guide the research itself. Kweku Aryeh walked with me for days on end in the hot sun without complaint so that we might make contact with as many households as possible. Through Kwesi Yankah's aid, Rogers Krobea Asante, Bright Nkrumah, and Emmanuel Ofori Amo were stalwarts in the frustrating and slow task of transcribing the many recordings. They helped me realize how much Akuapem people used Asante Twi. Later, Joe Banson and Margaret Rose Tettey helped me translate the more opaque bits of the transcriptions. Without all their efforts, this work could not have been completed. The home of Kwame and Mrs. Adu-Bediako in Akropong provided a calm place for thought and reflection after busy days of interviews and interpretation.

Earlier versions of these chapters were presented at different conferences and workshops, and I am grateful to many colleagues for their thoughts in response and in subsequent conversations: Erdmute Alber, Caroline Bledsoe, Deborah Boehm, Joanna Dreby, Esther Goody, Michelle Gilbert, Valentina Mazzucato, William Murphy, Catrien Notermans, Rachel Reynolds, Carola Suárez-Orozco, Sjaak van der Geest, and Ann Whitehead.

Emmanuel Ayesu, Carol Brandt, Vibiana Bowman Cvetokovic, Mary Ebeling, Inma Garcia-Sanchez, Kathy Howard, and Rachel Reynolds gave me feedback and encouragement on initial drafts of this manuscript. Jon Landau, an immigration lawyer in Philadelphia, made sure that my presentation of US immigration law was accurate. The most extensive commentary on the manuscript came from my mother and father, Robert P. Coe and Jane Meleney Coe, who know Ghana well from living there in the late 1960s and early 1980s, and Cheryl Shipman, who approached my writing with a keen eye for inconsistency and confusion. Three anonymous reviewers provided extremely helpful and thoughtful comments. To all of you, I am thankful for your suggestions regarding theoretical clarity, organization, and gaps in information.

This research was financially supported by numerous organizations: from the first by my home institution of Rutgers University, through the Research Council and the Childhood Studies Center, which paid for short trips to Ghana, Basel, and Northwestern University, where the Polly Hill Papers are located. Later stages of research were supported by the National Science Foundation and the Wenner-Gren Foundation for Anthropological Research, which allowed me to live in Ghana for five months in 2008 and for the follow-up fieldwork in 2009.

From the bottom of my heart, I am grateful to all of you for the contribution you have made to this work. May I be able to support you in some way in the future.

A Scattering of Families

Port Authority bus terminal in New York City can be a dark and scary place, but it can also be exciting, as it is a crossroads of people with different pasts and trajectories. As I was standing in line for a long-distance bus one summer, a striking middle-aged woman in an outfit made of African cloth stepped into line behind me. Because I had spent time in Ghana, a small country in West Africa, I was intrigued. I greeted her and learned, to my delight, that she was from Ghana. We chatted while we waited for the bus and sat together after it arrived, glad for each other's company on the long ride.

Vivacious, outgoing, and a lively storyteller, Irene told me about her life during our bus ride that afternoon and evening. I learned that she had lived in the United States for over twenty years and was a US citizen. She had worked for the past eight years as a live-in home health aide, a job in which she lived with frail elderly people in their homes for days or months at a time, helping them with cooking, grocery shopping, clothes washing, and other housework until they recovered or needed more extensive care. Irene had just returned from a trip to Ghana and was now on her way to a job in Massachusetts. Although she would have liked to recuperate a little bit more after her trip, she was concerned that if she did not take this position, the agency that had called her would not contact her again.[1] She was feeling trepidation about the new job: would the elderly woman to whose house she was traveling be nice or want her to be working all the time? Would the woman be racist or angry, feelings exacerbated by dementia or pain, as Irene had experienced in some situations in the past? Would Irene have her own room or would she have to sleep on a cot in the living room? Would she stay for a long time, or would the woman improve or decline rapidly? Irene tended to go far afield for her jobs, to suburbs and rural areas five or six hours away from her home in central New Jersey. Because she did not know if she would be able to buy ingredients for the Ghanaian dishes she liked or international phone cards in the neighborhood to which she was traveling, she had brought some of these items in her bags.

One of the reasons Irene brought phone cards was because in the spring she had given birth to a baby boy. After recovering for a short time from the birth, she spent nine weeks in Ghana with her family. When she came back to the United States, she left her baby behind with her parents, who were also looking after her two older children, a boy of thirteen and a girl of six, also born in the United States.[2] She told me in a later conversation:

> As much as it is hard, but at times it is the best way because you know they are with family, and secondly, they will be well taken care of, and you will also get the chance to go to work here and come back with the mind, that, "Okay, I don't have to worry about how my baby was taken care of."

She was not abandoning her children; rather, she called her children and parents in Ghana for long chats once a week and was able to visit them every two or three years. In fact, she saw herself as providing the best care for them she could.

As an immigrant, Irene is not unusual in being separated from her children. Contemporary flows of international migration are fueling particular kinds of family arrangements in which families are scattered and living in different countries. Spouses can be separated and a child can live apart from one or more parents and one or more siblings for several years. It can be hard to find statistics of this phenomenon, but those that exist suggest it is common for the children of immigrants to be separated from their parents for a period of time. One study based on interviews with 385 adolescents born in China, Central America, the Dominican Republic, Haiti, and Mexico and now living in the United States found that 85 percent of them had been separated from one or both of their parents for two years or more (Suárez-Orozco, Todorova, and Louie 2002). A larger survey of 8,573 US-based immigrants who had just received permanent residency (a green card) and their children found that 31 percent of children who themselves immigrated had been separated from at least one parent for two years or more (Gindling and Poggio 2008).[3] A study by Hirokazu Yoshikawa (2011) found that many Chinese immigrants in New York City sent their infants to China for grandparents to raise. Suggesting a similar phenomenon among Ghanaian immigrants, in 2008, children under the age of fifteen represented only 7 percent of the Ghanaian-born population in the United States, whereas they constituted 20 percent of the total US population and (for 2009) 36 percent of the total population in Ghana (UNESCO Institute for Statistics n.d.).[4] Although some of the children of Ghanaian immigrants are US-born and therefore do not show up within the Ghanaian-born statistics, Irene's and other immigrant parents' stories indicate there are US-born children sent to be raised in Ghana and Ghanaian-born children who will eventually join their parents in the United States who are not represented in the US figures. Whether the higher (85 percent) or lower (31 percent) numbers pertain, it is clear that this phenomenon is common, and common enough that we need to better understand why it is occurring and what its effects are on families, children, and their communities abroad and in the United States. These family members may eventually be reunited, whether those "left behind" join the migrant abroad or the migrant returns home, but they may also be more permanently separated, through divorce, premature death, or irreparably damaged relationships.

While the scattering of families among nonimmigrants is increasingly occurring through a decrease in stable marriages and an increase in blended households, family separations among international migrants are primarily driven by a particular contradiction: it has become easier to move money and goods across national borders over the past forty years, but a similar freedom for the mobility for people is not available. As Saskia Sassen (2006) argues, although economies are increasingly untethered from the nation—buffeted by domestic unrest in oil-producing countries and bank failure in the European Union, for example—politics are still or perhaps even increasingly bounded to the nation-state, putting public pressure on the easing of immigration restrictions.

Yet a mobile labor force is encouraged, in part by the mobility of finance and the increasing ease of transportation that allow for the flow of goods and capital. Foreign investments in, say, a factory generate connections and networks that enable people to migrate abroad (Arcelin 1983; Sassen 1998; Weiner 1987), as well as encouraging migration within a country to work in new forms of employment. Furthermore, conditions for making poorer countries attractive to foreign investment imposed by international financial institutions have resulted in those nations' disinvestment in social welfare, causing the middle class—the primary beneficiaries of most state support in poorer countries—to want to migrate to maintain their middle-class standards of living (Parreñas 2004; Reynolds 2002). Finally, labor-intensive sectors in destination countries that are hard to mechanize—such as fruit and vegetable farming and health care—have found immigrants attractive as a cheap and compliant labor force (Sassen 1998; Waldinger and Lichter 2003).

Because of conditions at home and their imaginings of abroad, many people want to migrate, and some are successful at doing so, using their networks (Glick Schiller, Basch, and Blanc-Szanton 1992). However, it is hard to migrate to the United States because US immigration laws do not recognize that supposedly unskilled migrants have employment opportunities, favoring family reunification and scarce technical skills as rationales for migrants' residence and work in the United States. Myron Weiner has commented, "U.S. legal immigration is largely independent of the demands of the labor market" because two-thirds of it occurs through family reunification (1998, 12). Despite the prominence of family reunification as a route to legally living and working in the United States, it is difficult to migrate as a family unit. Spouses, siblings, and parents and children may be separated from one another for many years as they gather together the funds and documents for applications and wait for them to be approved.

This reason was not significant for Irene's separation from her children, since she had become a citizen over her long years of living in the United States, and her children, born in the United States, were also citizens. However, her salary and working conditions as a home health aide—a poorly paid and labor-intensive occupation—made raising them in the United States difficult. Thus another reason driving the scattering of families is that wages in the sectors where immigrants work do not always support a family in the United States but are sufficient to support dependents in the home country with a lower cost of living.

Family separation is one consequence of the general difficulties migrants face in navigating immigration laws and making a living in destination countries. Contemporary arrangements between global capital and national governments are creating a new kind of family: one in which separated family members are connected emotionally and are in communication with one another, like Irene, but are "divided by borders," in the words of Joanna Dreby (2010), who has studied separated families in Mexico and the United States.

That many people are moving between countries is widely recognized. In destination countries, such awareness is fueling anger and fear: of being physically invaded, of having a national heritage diluted, of being economically displaced. In sending countries, migration generates fantasies and hopes of a better life, an abroad as "paradise," in the words of one Chinese migrant (Fong 2011). But that families are scattered by such migration is less commonly recognized, particularly by social service agencies and governments in destination countries. The press and governments in migrant-sending countries tend to be more aware of the children left behind than those in destination countries, some blaming mothers for their love of money and fearing youth delinquency (Parreñas 2004; Rae Espinoza 2011).

Given the paucity of public rhetoric on this topic, families are largely left on their own to figure it out. They respond by adapting their existing beliefs, practices, and resources of family life—I call this their repertoire—to their migration experience, checking in with their network of friends and relatives to help them evaluate their options and decisions. These repertoires are a set of cultural resources or frameworks—ways of speaking, thinking, and feeling about family—that mobilize material resources and people in ways that are considered normal and natural. Repertoires help organize the vastness of what people think, feel, and experience. Sometimes certain aspects of repertoire are brought to consciousness and attention, and a new language is used to articulate and share that conscious understanding with others. Repertoires provide interpretations by which people can evaluate a situation and be prompted to particular emotions like love and anger (Hochschild 2003; Reddy 2001). I'll give a fuller explanation of what I mean by *repertoire* below, but for now, this may suffice as a working definition.

What I want to suggest is that the repertoire of migrants and their families affects how they separate and how they feel about their separation. The level of suffering and pain that separation creates for families varies, because they, as individuals in touch with others grappling with similar problems, creatively enact their repertoire of family life in the situations they encounter. Some migrants have repertoires in which separation is normal and natural because of a long history of migration in their communities; others find they need to construct new ideals and ideologies to justify the transformation of their roles, causing tension and conflict within their families, because these ideals are not fully accepted by all involved. This book, then, is about the problems migrants and their families confront and the feelings that emerge in these situations, which they interpret and respond to through the frameworks available through their repertoires of family life. This book specifically examines how Ghanaian immigrants and their families adapt their repertoires to the parent-child separation a parent's international migration causes.

The experiences of Ghanaians, like other West African immigrants, can illuminate the variation and complexity in people's responses to the scattering of migrant families. West Africans have long been mobile, engaging in long-distance and trans-Saharan trade across different ecological zones, from the Atlantic Coast to the Sahel to the Mediterranean Sea, for hundreds, if not thousands, of years. Myths and historical legends of kingdoms, such as the oral epic Sundiata (Niane 1965), document the movements of people and the significance of hunters who roamed far and wide, gaining knowledge and founding new settlements. Such movement continued after borders were erected by European powers as they carved out spheres of influence and dominion across West Africa, borders that often cut across families, trade linkages, and sometimes kingdoms (e.g., Odotei 2003). Family traditions in West Africa have been shaped by long histories of migration and of women's work, in which relations can be sustained across long distances. Irene draws on this repertoire when she talks matter-of-factly about her children in Ghana and relies so readily on her parents to raise her children.

At the same time, Irene thinks carefully about how to raise her children. The responsibility of parenthood weighs heavily on her as she feels that her actions will have enormous consequences on her children's future. She described an early morning with her newborn baby in Ghana, when the two of them were alone together.

> And this came into my mind like, this little thing, his life depends on me. Whatever I do, it's either going to make him good or make him bad. So it's up to me to make good decisions to give him the best I can. . . . I was just crying. I said, God, please give me the strength and give me the wisdom to be able, you know, to raise my kids the best way I know how.

Although she brings her repertoire of family life to bear on this problem, her actions leave her feeling uncertain. Some parents I interviewed, similarly anxious, hoped this book would be a parenting manual in the American self-help tradition, recommending whether children should be raised in Ghana or the United States, and, if in Ghana, for how long and to what age.

From my conversations with Ghanaian immigrant parents and their children, I did not gain a clear sense of what advice to give, given the variation in people's experiences with their children and my own personal unease in giving advice about other people's complex situations. Instead, what I learned is how Ghanaians are adapting their repertoires of family life in a search for solutions to the problems they face. In essence, the problem they and other immigrants face is that they are a mobile labor force simultaneously encouraged to migrate by job opportunities, social networks, and images of a desired future and discouraged from full political and social belonging in the countries to which they migrate by immigration laws and lack of social supports for raising children.

This set of contradictory pressures around the mobility of labor has been significant in the expansion of capitalism, as I discuss in the next section. This discussion further complicates any advice I might give Ghanaian immigrant parents, because it illustrates that their parenting decisions affect not only them and their children, but that wider contemporary relationships between political power and economic capital have shaped their decisions, the topic to which I now turn. Some readers may wish to skip or skim the remainder of the introduction, which lays out the theoretical underpinnings of my argument, and proceed to chapter 1.

Capitalism, Migration, and Families

Marxist anthropologists have argued that capitalist growth has been fueled by the continuous incorporation of new workers.[5] Sometimes this is accomplished through the movement of people into areas where capitalist production is ongoing, as in the urban migrations of the agriculturally dispossessed during the Industrial Revolution in England, the trade in slaves and indentured servants in the production of cash crops in the New World, or the migration of people from poor and middle-income countries to wealthy economies today. At other times, it occurs through the movement of capital to new lands, such as American capital investment in Southeast Asia in the 1970s. What makes new workers so significant for profit is that employers can avoid the full expenses of the labor they employ and thus pay a worker a lower wage.

The full cost of a worker comprises the expenses of maintaining a worker across his or her lifetime, including periods when he or she is unable to work, for instance, during childhood, illness, disability, and old age. In childhood, furthermore, a person receives the social and emotional training and the sustenance for physical growth and strength necessary for future labor participation. Employers in the United States pay the costs of workers' maintenance across the life course indirectly through, on the one hand, state mechanisms of redistribution and, on the other, reciprocal exchanges within families. An employer makes social security contributions and pays taxes on their profits, funds that are given to the state to, among other things, provide education, training, and health services. Employers also pay indirectly for the next generation of labor by paying their employees "a family wage" that is sufficient to support the care of nonworking dependents. This family wage is redistributed through long-term reciprocities and the emotional obligations to others whom employees consider family.

Migrants are a less costly source of labor because most migrants migrate when they are already adult and in the prime of their working lives (ages twenty to forty-five). Other governments to which an employer in the destination country does not pay taxes supported their care and education as children. Furthermore, if a migrant's children and elderly parents are left in the country of origin, given differences in the cost of living between the two countries based on the exchange rate between the respective currencies, then a family wage to support these dependents can be lower. By hiring migrants at this lower wage, capitalist enterprises are better able to offer goods and services at a lower cost and thus compete with other companies across the city or world. That a migrant comes in the prime of his or her life and that his or her dependents do not come with the migrant is critical to the displacement of the costs of reproduction to migrants' families, on the one hand, and to migrant-sending countries, on the other.

Transnationalism is key to this process. What is meant by this term is that although the standard conception, on which US immigration law and schooling rhetoric is based (Hamann and Zúñiga 2011), is that migrants are immigrants who have permanently left one country to become residents and potentially citizens of another; many contemporary migrants have hopes and dreams bound up in networks that cross borders.[6] Irene, for instance, moves from one elderly person's house to another in situations that lack stability, but she remains connected to those she is close to—her children and parents in Ghana, her friends in the United States and Ghana, and her siblings in Germany—by cell phone on evenings and weekends. Irene's emotional life is entwined with people and events far from the people and events that make up her day-to-day existence: the shopping in new locales, the isolation of rural or suburban neighborhoods, the elderly person she is caring for, and their relatives who occasionally call or stop by. Irene longs to live in Ghana but cannot see how to support everyone, including herself, should she return for good. She seeks advice from friends on potential investment and business deals in Ghana but worries about the risks. In the meantime, she makes do: going to Ghana for weeks at a time when she has amassed some savings and returning to the United States when her money is exhausted to begin the cycle of working and saving again. Her children, while not migrants themselves, are also living transnationally, with some of their emotional life connected to their mother living in the United States, and their future hopes pinned on joining her, even as they live and go to school in Ghana. As Georges E. Fouron and Nina Glick Schiller (2002) note, even those who do not migrate participate in social fields that cross borders.

While a relatively recently coined term, *transnationalism* was also characteristic of previous generations of immigrants who wanted to return to their homelands after a period of successful migration and retained ties to their loved ones in the home countries (Foner 2005). Even those who migrate internally within a country remain connected to their home regions in translocal, if not transnational, ways. Strategies Ghanaians use to raise their children, for instance of sending their children back to the place of origin, have also been used by American rural-to-urban migrants, such as African-Americans during the Great Migration (1910–30). Claude Brown, in his gripping autobiography *Manchild in the Promised Land* (1965) about his childhood in Harlem in the 1950s, described how his parents, recent transplants, sent him, at the age of eleven, to live with his grandparents in North Carolina for a year because his mother was so concerned about his bad behavior, influenced by his associates in Harlem. Bebe Moore Campbell (1989) described growing up in Philadelphia in the 1960s with her mother and maternal grandmother, but much of her emotional life was fixed not on them, but on her father, with whom she spent summers in North Carolina after her parents' separation. Translocality, in the sense of maintaining connections to people in more than one place, is not solely a phenomenon that occurs across national borders.

Migration and translocality—key to the scattering of families without their dissolution—are spurred in part by people's desire to seek the resources they need across their own life course and those of the people they care for. Anthropological research has shown that concerns about paying for children's schooling (Boehm et al. 2011) or concerns about a parent's health care (Empez Vidal 2011) can prompt migration. Because these resources are not available locally, people manage their connections to multiple places to access them: in the case of Claude Brown's parents, for example, work was available in New York City, but protection for their son from the dangers of the street was not, and so they sent him to North Carolina for a year of his adolescence.

Work conditions and state welfare policies in destination areas may increase migrants' translocal connections. A study of Zambian urban migrants found that a weak formal welfare system and low wages encouraged them to maintain their ties to their hometowns as a kind of insurance policy in hard times (Ferguson 1999). Rural kin could provide access to a means of livelihood—such as farmland or housing—for urban workers in case of illness, disability, or retirement. Similarly, transnationalism becomes a survival strategy for immigrant families who mobilize the different opportunities available in different locales through their kin and nonkin connections (Schmalzbauer 2004). In the case of Ghanaians, as I explore in chapter 4, one reason Ghanaians like Irene send their babies and young children, born in the United States, back to Ghana is the lack of affordable, high-quality day care in the United States and the low wages in the jobs most available to them, insufficient for health care and day care. The lack of social supports for young children in the United States, in comparison to what is available to them in Ghana, in part through their remittances, makes raising children in Ghana attractive.

The state is involved in the scattering of families of contemporary migrants in at least two ways: it regulates the movement of migrant workers and their kin, and it is involved in the redistribution of funds to provide a safety net to care for workers across their lifetimes. States play a key role by determining the extent of social welfare for workers and nonworkers—dependent children, the disabled, and the elderly. Over time, states have assumed some responsibility for care, through the provision of public education for children, and of health services for the elderly and disabled. However, those priorities are in competition with keeping banks afloat or maintaining a country's bond ratings and ability to borrow funds (Katz 2001; Sassen 2006). Under the rationale of a smaller state, some countries are turning over their care functions to the market and decreasing their care obligations (Rose 1999). Scholars in Latin America, Britain, and the United States, countries that have increasingly experienced these kinds of policies since the 1980s, have called them *neoliberal* because the philosophical underpinnings of these policies are indebted to the liberal political philosophy of Adam Smith in which the freedom of the individual to enter into private contracts (in the marketplace) is given paramount importance. *Liberal* in this sense does not refer to the way this term is used in American political discourse, as the opposite of *conservative*. (In fact, these policies to roll back the state are considered politically conservative by observers.) Although neoliberalism is usually considered to be about the paring back of the state, it in fact is about organizing the state according to the logic of the market (Burchell 1996). The state continues to exist and is needed to actively constitute a space for market forces (Burchell 1996; Clarke 2002; Ong 1999). Thus even when the state funds public-care functions, they are increasingly provided through the private market, such as Medicare benefit plans being offered by private insurance companies or private management companies running public schools. The privatization of care is often—

although not always—accompanied by a decrease in the state's obligation to provide care across the life course, a decrease justified by the greater efficiencies attributed to the market.

For example, in Ghana, international migration to other areas in the subregion increased as a result of the economically difficult and politically unstable period of the 1970s and 1980s and structural adjustment programs by the World Bank and the International Monetary Fund during the 1980s. Structural adjustment programs weakened the Ghanaian government's ability to provide needed services, enhanced the export-oriented segments of the economy that did not necessarily create many options for economic mobility, and resulted in a decline in living standards for middle-class professionals and civil servants, thus generating desire among the educated and skilled middle-class to migrate. International and regional migration increased as Ghanaians traveled to Nigeria and Libya at first (Twum-Baah, Nabila, and Aryee 1995), but now every country in the world that is economically better off is a potential destination—from the United Kingdom and Europe to Australia, South Africa, Israel, Japan, the Caribbean, and the United States. Statistician K. A. Twum-Baah (2005) estimates that with a population of twenty-one million Ghanaians resident in Ghana, another 1.5 million, about 7 percent of the population, are outside the country; the estimate by the World Bank (2011), in contrast, is 3.4 percent.

Immigration laws in the country of migration also play a role in scattering families. While global economic integration attracts people across national borders, concepts of national sovereignty and nationalism govern immigration laws (Sassen 1996) and make such movement difficult. Guestworker programs are explicit in giving short-term contracts to able-bodied adults and separating workers from their dependents, as Cindy Hahamovitch (2011) has illustrated in her history of Jamaican guestworker programs in the United States. Here I suggest the US immigration system practically generates some of the same conditions, particularly the separation of workers from their families, similar to the guestworker programs Hahamovitch describes. Thus translocality—in particular, that family members are scattered geographically but remain connected emotionally—is fueled not solely by immigration laws but also by the lack of support for care across the life course generated by a combination of state policies and market forces, which encourages people to migrate and, once they have migrated, to turn to family at home for help.

In part because of the reliance on family to provide care across the course of workers' full lives, Marxist anthropologists have argued that non-capitalist institutions and forms of exchange not only coexist with capitalism, but also that capitalism relies on noncapitalist, sentiment-driven economic exchanges for the maintenance and reproduction of its labor force (Godelier 1977; Griffith 1985; Meillassoux 1981). The central procedure of capitalism is the conversion of products or services to a commodity that can be exchanged in the market (Sewell 2005). Families, on the other hand, distribute economic resources through exchanges governed by emotional feeling, on alternative circuits of valuation and circulation, rather than by markets (Folbre 2001, 2008; Sahlins 2004; Zelizer 2005). Because these circuits operate according to a different logic than financial booms and busts, they can serve as a safety net for individuals.

Furthermore, families are important for the maintenance of economic life, particularly in the maintenance and renewal of its labor force (Burawoy 1976). As noted above, families prepare young people indirectly for work through forms of care, by creating routines, teaching particular kinds of interpersonal and emotional communication, and helping children grow physically strong and healthy through providing food, housing, and health care. Thus capitalist economies rely on the emotional attachments parent-child relations generate and the unpaid labor of women within families (Meillassoux 1981).

This formulation of the relationship between capitalism and the family has led some historians and sociologists to argue that changes in the structures of economic and political relations require new kinds of families. For instance, historians have argued that the reason industrial capitalism arose earliest in England was due to its reliance on the nuclear family and individualism. In the words of Jack Goody, a critic of this approach, "it has been argued that the small, elementary family is particularly adapted to capitalist activity, enabling people to move to seek work where it is to be found and to accumulate for themselves alone" (2000, 133). However, the vast literature on the history of the European family does not support this view, instead showing that small, elementary families were not as common as initially believed and not more pronounced in England than other parts of Europe (Kertzer and Barbagli 2001; see also the discussion in Moore 1988). In a similar vein, sociologists have argued that late modernity creates a particular kind of person: self-reflexive, anxious, cut off from commitments to family and homeland, and creating new identities based on particular tastes and lifestyle interests (Giddens 1991). Going even further, Eva Illouz (2007) has argued, "the making of capitalism went hand and hand with the making of an intensely specialized emotional culture" in which workers became self-aware of their emotional lives (4). These formulations are too teleological, positing causal relationships in which capitalism has great power. William Reddy (2001) has argued, more flexibly, that "any enduring political regime must establish as an essential element a normative order for emotions, an 'emotional regime,'" such as fear about safety and security following 9/11 (124). However, as he discusses, an emotional regime can be strict or loose in its expectations about emotional expressions, it may cohere only around particular institutions or events, and not all political subjects may necessarily accept it. Scholars have therefore posited a relationship between a political or economic arrangement and the emotional life of individuals and families, although scholars vary in their thinking of how close the articulation is.

Some of this scholarship about the fit between an emotional culture and a particular kind of political-economic arrangement seems useful for understanding contemporary global capitalism, in which certain family structures seem advantageous. Some scholars, delighting in the irony, have argued that although the development of capitalism is attributed in part to the nuclear family, the scattered, extended family seems better suited to the increased mobility of labor in a global economy, particularly for entrepreneurs and captains of industry (Goody 2000; Jones 1992). For instance, a set of Chinese brothers, linked to a patriarch, can establish international branches of a family firm, drawing on a sense of trust inculcated through loyalty to the patrilineage (Ong 1999). A mounting body of scholarship further undermines the argument that the nuclear family is central to capitalism by showing that the regulation of contemporary labor migration encourages the separation of the nuclear family (recent examples include Boehm 2012 and Dreby 2010). Such demands for transnational migrant labor would seemingly require normative emotional regimes that enable close kin to live for long periods of time away from one another, at the same time as they have sufficient feeling for one another that adult migrants continue to support their parents, siblings, and children back home.

However, based on my research on Ghanaian transnational families, I argue that it does not make sense to think about contemporary global capitalism as requiring a particular emotional regime for it to endure in time.[7] Global capitalism is a diffuse and not coordinated set of activities generated by multiple actors and is not accompanied by a single discourse—a repeated pattern of statements—about family life and the emotions people should feel within families. Because capitalism is based on a simple principle—the convertibility of an object of value to a commodity that can be exchanged—capitalism travels easily, but unevenly, demonstrating highly dynamic and changeable characteristics (Sewell 2005). Economic structures are loosely, rather than tightly, integrated with family life. Economics and families seem to have their own, somewhat autonomous, cultural logics (Sewell 2005; see also Goody 2000). As a result, many forms of kinship are amenable to global capitalism (Goody 2000), and there is not a dominant form that is most suited to capitalism. For instance, West African trade networks—based on familial and fictive kin ties established through shared ethnic identity—are easily extendable to New York City and Paris (Stoller 2002). "Structures of feeling" do not necessarily correspond to economic structures (or vice versa), but rather have emergent and dominant threads, which create possibilities for change, including greater (or less) articulation between economic demands and a person's emotional life (Williams 1982). Henrietta Moore, summarizing feminist literature on the topic, argues, "While it is undoubtedly true that capitalism has transformed the process of production, reproduction, and consumption in societies, it has not done so simply in accordance with the needs of capital. These processes of transformation have been equally determined by the existing forms of production, reproduction, and consumption; in other words, by the existing forms of kinship and gender relations" (1988, 116).

Following Moore's attention to existing forms of social life, what I argue is that transnational migrants manage the contradictions generated by the state and global capitalism's mobilization of resources through their repertoires of parenting, kinship, and gender. In light of these issues, I want to develop the concept of repertoire more fully and consider the consequences of this concept for the study of migration and family life.

Repertoires of Family Life

My understanding of repertoire derives principally from the work of Ulf Hannerz (1969) and Ann Swidler (2001). These scholars of social life consider culture to be a tool kit that people apply to particular situations, patching together various ideas and resources to solve a problem they are currently facing. In the words of Ulf Hannerz, "whether or not an individual will adopt a culturally suggested mode of action may be taken to depend to a great extent on its relevance to his situation" (1969, 193). This understanding of culture as a tool kit emphasizes the flexibility of culture while maintaining that it organizes people's actions and possibilities. Ann Swidler argues that a cultural repertoire provides scenarios and narratives into which one can imaginatively place oneself and the other participants, somewhat along the lines of George Herbert Mead. Applying a repertoire is about making analogies: what is this situation most like?

Some aspects of repertoire are captured by the term *habitus*, proposed first by Marcel Mauss (2006) in 1935 and further developed by Pierre Bourdieu (1977). Habitus, in Mauss's conception, is comprised of the everyday routines or bodily techniques of a person such as the habit of brushing one's teeth or style of walking. Inculcated through previous experiences, these habits and routines are embedded in the body, a set of tastes and dispositions perhaps not even available to a person's consciousness, although Bourdieu thinks the habitus may be available to consciousness or undergirded by ideals discussed more explicitly within a community (like honor). For Bourdieu, the habitus is "the cultivated disposition, inscribed in the body schema and in the schemas of thought," that disposes a person to act a particular way in a situation (1977, 15). The habitus is "a system of lasting, transposable dispositions which, integrating past experiences, functions at every moment as a *matrix of perceptions, appreciations, and actions* and makes possible the achievement of infinitely diversified tasks, thanks to analogical transfers of schemes, permitting the solution of similarly shaped problems" (82–83, his italics). There is then some overlap with repertoire, in the sense that the habitus disposes people to act in a certain way but is flexible enough to be applied, through analogy, to new situations people face.

The past experience that looms largest for Bourdieu is the family of one's birth or childhood. Through the family, the habitus is inextricably linked to class position, because every family has a class position within society (Bourdieu and Passeron 1990). Because the habitus of a person indicates his or her social class origin in an unequal society, not all dispositions or tastes, not all ways of seeing and acting, are equally valued. Thus the habitus confers *cultural capital*, or symbolic, social investments that pay off in terms of a person's access to status, wealth, and power (or whatever is valued). For example, the way one speaks (which may be unconscious) signals a particular class position. If valued, it may be taken as a sign of intelligence and good upbringing, which may confer upon the speaker rewards that lead to status, such as good grades or approval.

Although the habitus is a very similar concept to repertoire, I prefer *repertoire* to *habitus* for three reasons. First, repertoire signals a multiplicity of cultural resources and frameworks, a body or collection of practices, knowledge, and beliefs that allows people to imagine what is possible, expect certain things, and value certain goals rather than the primacy of frameworks laid down through experiences in the family of origin. Some theorists, and Bourdieu himself, have recognized that the habitus is multiple in the way that repertoire is. Jay MacLeod, for instance, in his study of adolescent boys growing up in a public housing complex, reworked the notion of the habitus, considering it to be multiply layered, constituted not simply through the boys' family life, but structured through the boys' subsequent experiences with peers and school (1995, 137–38). However, the concept of the habitus still tends to focus attention on the "first" set of dispositions acquired through the family, which I think repertoire avoids.

Second, the habitus emphasizes bodily and unconscious dispositions, an important point to make, but which slights the moments when such dispositions become visible and discussed. As Jean and John Comaroff (1991) have argued, the historical moments when something commonsensical becomes the subject of commentary and when topics of debate become naturalized into bodily responses and reactions are important, because they signal change.

These two differences contribute to my third reason for preferring repertoire to the habitus, which is that the habitus seems more resistant to historical analysis, or an exploration of how it changes through time, both within the course of a person's life course and across generations. Repertoire is open to revision, reshuffling, and reflection. Some theorists have pushed Bourdieu's concept of the habitus in these directions.

Clearly, there is much overlap between the habitus and repertoire, and the concept of repertoire, as I illustrate in my description of its characteristics below, draws on the work of many anthropologists, sociologists, and historians. In the discussion below, I aim to systematize various theoretical strands through the concept of repertoire, because I find it so useful to understanding what I learned from my interactions with Ghanaian immigrant parents and their children.

Repertoire as Multiple

People develop their cultural frameworks through becoming aware of others' repertoires in the process of interacting with them, mainly through observation of others' behavior (including observing what they say) rather than explicit instruction. "By participating in social processes, every individual learns beliefs, values, and modes of action which are shared by others . . . the beliefs and the values may be only inferred to be shared by others, on the basis of overt behavior" (Hannerz 1969, 191). People's actions, as the enactment of their repertoire, provide implicit information to others about what they consider to be an appropriate response to a particular situation. Through their participation in diverse, but particular, social fields and relations, people develop multiple cultural frameworks as part of their repertoire (Olwig 2007).

As noted above, repertoire implies an additive process in which cultural frameworks acquired earlier do not disappear entirely. Instead of a new framework completely replacing an older framework, the older framework is not performed as often, or continues in some way, such as in a narrower section of society, or in another field of activity. From her work in Nepal, Laura Ahearn (2001) shows how "newer" ideals of love and personal compatibility coexist with "older" notions that marriage is determined by fate. For example, a Nepalese woman mixes the two idioms of fate and choice in explaining her marriage: "We didn't dislike each other enough to break up. This is my fate, I said, see? . . . Well, for myself it was written that I would marry; if it hadn't been, I would have left him, see?" (110). Ulf Hannerz (1969) similarly describes how members of an African-American, low-income neighborhood in the United States are familiar with "ghetto" *and* mainstream values: "Ghetto dwellers tend to have some familiarity with mainstream modes of action, although they may not know them in detail and although in many cases their inability to practice them makes them unskilled in their performance" (191). James Ferguson (1999) has similarly noted that urban migrants in Zambia have available to them two oppositional identities and cultural styles—village-oriented and city-oriented. Although migrants enact either one style-identity or the other, they are familiar with both.

Repertoire is widely used in sociolinguistics to designate the different ways of speaking (or registers), appropriate for different contexts, which people learn to use in conjunction with nonlinguistic signs (such as dress or stance) and which give people emblems of identity. Basil Bernstein (2000) uses repertoire to signal an individual possession in distinction to the reservoir of cultural resources available in the community as a whole, a distinction I do not make. He is interested in how social practices of isolation and exclusion lead to differences in individual repertoires. Folklore scholarship also uses repertoire to designate the expressive genres a person can produce or with which he or she is familiar, as well as knowledge of the contexts for their production. Repertoire as I am using it refers not only to expressive genres or speech but also to larger cultural frameworks that help direct people's actions, but like its use in sociolinguistics and folklore, it implies a multiplicity of resources with which people become variably familiar, through the particular social fields in which they participate, and which are available for their use in those social worlds.

Repertoires as Habitual and Conscious

The degree to which people debate, analyze, and reflect on their repertoire varies. Some ways of thinking, speaking, and acting in a repertoire can be so obvious as to be beyond verbalization, in that people apply aspects of their repertoire without thinking about them or without questioning why they do so. These might include bodily practices, like attending to balance (Geurts 2002), but can also involve forms of socializing and problem solving. Margery Wolf (1972) argues that women's repertoire of family life in Taiwan is

> below the level of consciousness. Mothers do not tell their about-to-be mar-
> ried daughters how to establish themselves in village society so that they
> may have some protection from an oppressive family situation, nor do they
> warn them to gather their children into an exclusive circle under their own
> control. But girls grow up in village society and see their mothers and sisters-
> in-law settling their differences to keep them from a public airing or present-
> ing them for the women's community to judge. Their mothers have created
> around them the meaningful unit in their fathers' households, and when
> they [the daughters] are desperately lonely and unhappy in the households
> of their husbands, what they long for is what they have lost. (41)

In other words, women passed on knowledge about how to create a supportive community in a village of strangers without articulating or discussing their techniques. Instead, daughters had observed such strategies in the course of growing up, and when they needed such knowledge in their own periods of loneliness, they were able to enact it. What is learned through habitual routines may be enacted through habitual routines, without discussion or reflection. In this dimension, repertoire is like the habitus.

However, other aspects of a repertoire may be talked about and subject to evaluation and reflection. Family life may be the topic of political discussion or debate, for instance, about absent fathers, single mothers, or gay families. Sometimes the debate occurs through hidden or encoded forms of dissent that a dominated group uses (Radner 1993; Scott 1985). Generally, people have greater consciousness of their repertoire when they are absorbing a new skill or mode of action, when they have to actively retrain their bodies or learn a way of doing something, which, as it becomes more habitual, will be less necessary to bring to awareness to enact (Reddy 2001).

Repertoires of family life tend to include both more conscious and less conscious aspects. They are composed of habitual family practices and relationships, and the obligations and expectations for the distribution of resources within families, as well as the idioms and discourses that people use to reflect on and evaluate those obligations and relationships.

Repertoire as Enacted

Another important feature about repertoire is that it implies performance, use, and enactment. Diana Taylor, in her study of performance in the Americas (2003), contrasts the ephemeral repertoire of embodied practice with the enduring material of the archive, which separates the source of knowledge from the knower. Her opposition is particularly useful in understanding the colonial history of the Americas, in which the colonizing project discredited indigenous repertoires of performance. I follow her in emphasizing the ways that repertoires are transmitted as "live, embodied actions in the here and now to a live audience" (24), and that they constitute a form of knowledge, memory, and interpretation.

However, a person only enacts some of his or her repertoire in the world. A repertoire can contain other possibilities for action that are declined, for whatever reason, including personal history, or as people reflect on their actions and situations (Godelier 1986; Swidler 2001). People may know more than they enact or be aware of greater possibilities of action than they believe is right to do. For example, they probably know that family arrangements exist other than their own; some may decide that those relationships are abhorrent, while others may hold them in abeyance but find at a later moment that they become more attractive possibilities. Furthermore, the articulated ideology of family life may not always correspond to its enacted and practical arrangements (Moore 1988); for instance, women's income-generating work may be necessary for the survival of a Puerto Rican cane-grower's household, but is described only as "helping" (Mintz 1960).

When enacted, cultural frameworks are put into use in a particular situation to help interpret what is going on (as in Goffman's notion of "frame" [1986]) and guide subsequent action. Cultural frameworks provide people with goals in relation to such action and help them understand their emotional responses to such situations. However, one cultural framework may be insufficient to justify or explain a particular emotion, causing another cultural framework within the repertoire to be mobilized (Swidler 2001), hence the combination of fate and choice in the example of Nepalese marriage given above. The friction between the cultural framework and the "balky world" (Sewell 2005, 179) in which it is mobilized is one of the causes of changes in a person's repertoire. A repertoire is creative, flexible, and adaptable, because it has to be applied to a situation that is not exactly similar to the situations that have come before.

Repertoires and Power

Because cultural frameworks are mobilized in relation to a particular situation, and because they develop through interactions with others, people may enact different aspects of a shared repertoire in light of their particular position. People—as gendered and aged, and with different social positions—not only have different experiences of family life but also their experiences from particular social positions give them different agendas and different interpretations of a situation (Ortner 2006). For instance, Margery Wolf (1972) argued that women in Taiwan defined *family* differently from men. Although men defined family as extending through the generations through the male line, women delineated it as a contemporary group based on the children of a mother, the uterine family. Women's notion of family did not always conflict with that of men, since men are born and raised in the uterine family, but neither were they completely identical. Women had a different understanding of kinship because they had different interests and were afforded different positions in the family. However, although men and women have different understandings of family, they are aware, at some level, of the other's definition of family. People are therefore aware of more than they may enact, but as they change social position, that wider awareness and knowledge is available for them to put to use. For instance, children, as they age and have children of their own, may begin to enact cultural frameworks associated with their parents of which they were previously simply aware.

Because certain cultural frameworks are associated with particular groups of people, a repertoire has dimensions of power and status. Some frameworks and modes of acting and speaking may be more highly valued than others. Gaining greater familiarity with those valued frameworks may be blocked through lack of participation in the networks in which they are enacted. Furthermore, some frameworks may be better suited to a particular economic or legal arrangement than others, thus capturing more social and economic resources. Some people may therefore find pleasure or happiness as they put into practice their sense of what is normal and right; others may find that it is difficult to do so and are frustrated that they cannot, for instance, earn money and live together, resulting in adjustments to their notion of family.

Often particular family arrangements, such as single motherhood, are associated with class positions and status, and are stigmatized or valued as a result. In Taiwan, a patrilineal family is formally recognized, but the uterine family is not. In southern Ghana, sending one's children to live in another household is associated with poverty or other troubles. The differences in the status and power that are associated with particular cultural frameworks and the way they confer a particular identity mean that people may self-consciously discard or work to enact particular cultural frameworks, bringing some to the front stage and putting others in the back room of their repertoire. It is still available to them, but dusty and unused; a person may have more difficulty enacting that particular cultural framework with ease.

Furthermore, not all cultural frameworks are acknowledged as valued and legitimate by those who hold power and resources according to different cultural frameworks. For instance, many of the family practices that Ghanaians consider normal and natural are not acknowledged by US immigration law, which prioritizes different kinds of family arrangements and a different understanding of family. As Deborah Boehm (2012) notes, "one primary way that the state divides families is through its definitions of 'family' itself, constructs that delineate and regulate kinship relations" (60). Such differences in definitions of families result in pain on the part of Ghanaians, because they cannot enact their methods of raising children. Ghanaian families and US immigration authorities experience pressure to change to accommodate their expectations and understandings to one another. I will return to the reforms to US immigration law that Ghanaians might desire in the conclusion.

Repertoires Can Be Reshuffled

Because a repertoire is applied to a world in which other people enact their own repertoires, a particular performance may fail or succeed, leading a person to revise his or her cultural frameworks. Furthermore, people accommodate to one another in their interactions with one another, drawing on their sense of others' repertoires, speaking in different ways and acting differently in relation to people positioned differently, in the process expanding and changing their own repertoire (Hannerz 1969).

The enactment of a cultural framework through a mode of action is risky. Some situations are new, requiring an adaptation of an existing interpretation or narrative to that situation through analogy, making the enactment of a repertoire even chancier. I follow Sewell in much of this discussion, using repertoire in place of his "cultural schema." Like Bourdieu's sense of the habitus being applied analogically to different situation, Sewell argues that cultural schemas can be transposed; in other words, "they can be applied to a wide and not fully predictable range of cases outside the context in which they are initially learned" (2005, 141). Or, in the words of Ulf Hannerz, "It is not at all certain that one has been exposed to detailed solutions to the very complicated kinds of situations one may be confronted with, so certainly there must always be much innovation in individual adaptations" (1969, 186).

As people transpose their cultural frameworks into the world, they may well encounter frustrations or setbacks—Sewell gives the examples of a joke that may backfire or a crop that may fail. A person's repertoire is an artifact of other people's failures and successes as they applied their repertoires to particular situations. Some situations may even be too difficult to find a good solution for (Coe and Nastasi 2006). These failures or frustrations may cause people to reshuffle their repertoire, putting some pieces on the back burner and adding new ones. There are limits to this reshuffling: people can only imagine what is possible through their experiences and interactions, and some frameworks may be more valued or more denigrated than others, leading to consequences for the actor's status when he or she uses one strategy rather than another.

The act of transposing one's repertoire to a new resistant situation causes repertoires to shift slightly or abruptly, whether consciously or not. Vietnamese refugees in the United States, who were separated from kin in the process of fleeing war, expanded the criteria for inclusion in the family circle to friends and distant relatives who were critical to the economic survival of households (Kibria 1993). Such expansion of kinship networks among Vietnamese immigrants was undergirded by an often-discussed value about the significance of kin as an economic safety net, but was otherwise not commented on as new and different. Thus change may occur not only through more visible dramatic turning points and revolutions but also through more "everyday ruptures" (Coe et al. 2011) or "obscure evolutions punctured and punctuated by crises" (Phillips 2011, 26), as people creatively extend their cultural frameworks into situations and experience the results. They may even downplay the sense of change to justify their actions and normalize the situation, particularly when the transposition of a framework—creating "fictive kin"—works well.

When the transposition of a framework does not solve the problem, the reshuffling of a repertoire does not generate satisfaction and a sense of ease, but uncertainty and ambivalence. Ulrich Beck (1992; 1999) and Anthony Giddens (2000) consider the sense of risk to be a critical part of the modern self, shorn of its "traditional" roots. My work suggests, rather, that the sense of risk comes from the transposition of one's repertoire into a new domain and not knowing what the outcome of one's actions will be. Because parenting is a long-term project and does not always generate positive outcomes, many Ghanaian immigrant parents, like Irene, feel uncertainty about whether their actions will be successful and are constantly evaluating their choices.

Swidler argues that cultural changes happen through institutions explicitly organizing a new worldview or set of values that direct action and generate meaning, what is often called "ideological work" (1986, 278). Although such institutional involvement frequently does allow for change to be more widely recognized and spread more rapidly, as I found in my previous work (Coe 2005), I am also aware that change can happen in a variety of ways, without the involvement of organized groups promoting a specific view of the world. At minimum, for change to happen, habitual aspects of one's repertoire have to be brought to greater consciousness, as Jean and John Comaroff (1991) suggest. Raymond Williams discusses this process, in which feelings and thoughts are confused and unarticulated, manifesting themselves as "an unease, stress, a displacement, a latency: the moment of conscious comparison has not yet come, often not yet coming" (1977, 130). Jean and John Comaroff describe the same process:

> It is the realm of partial recognition, of inchoate awareness, of ambiguous perception, and, sometimes, of creative tension: that liminal space of human experience in which people discern acts and facts but cannot or do not order them into narrative descriptions or even into articulate conceptions of the world; in which signs and events are observed, but in a hazy, translucent light; in which individuals or groups know that something is happening to them but find it difficult to put their fingers on quite what it is. (1991, 29)

Such uneasiness, since it is a negative emotion, may be suppressed, but psychologists have found that suppression is usually unsuccessful in the long term (Wegner and Smart 1997).

People may then begin to try to make such "unease" coherent and organized, finding new language to use when talking about such feelings. In
other words, they do their own ideological work to understand and organize their experience, which they sense as chaotic or stressful. People tend
to order their experiences by creating hierarchies, comparisons, and dichotomies: "that was the way of the past, this is now," or "we do this, they do
that" (Sewell 2005). For instance, as we will see among Ghanaian immigrants, international migrants' frustrations about their parenting practices
make them more conscious of their repertoire. As a result, they codify and
essentialize their repertoire, despite its dynamism, through language highlighting cultural and national differences. For instance, in conversation
with a Ghanaian immigrant raising his two children in the United States,
he told me that Ghanaians knew how to raise their children despite the
country's poverty, implying that Americans did not, despite their country's
wealth.

> Ghana de, ahia yɛn, yenni sika. Ghana yɛ poor country, Third World, but ye-
> tumi tetew nkwadaa no.
> In Ghana, we are poor and don't have money. Ghana is a poor Third World
> country, but we know how to raise children.[8]

This codification and fixing of qualities as characteristic and enduring of
certain groups of people is derived from Ghanaians' interactions and observations at work (often involving care work and observations of others'
intimate lives), conversations within their social networks, and media representations. As a result of their migration experiences, Ghanaian immigrants engage in a nationalization of parenting practices by emphasizing
hard and fast boundaries between America and Ghana (Erickson 1987;
Malkki 1995).

These ways of speaking about families in "national ways" are then
shared within their social networks, helping others make sense of their
vague unease and giving it voice. "Recurrent kinds of statements about the
facts and evaluations of life are obviously important in cultural sharing"
(Hannerz 1969, 188). Migrant networks are critical for such cultural sharing and the insertion of new ways of speaking and acting into migrants'
repertoires. Much of this sharing occurs through talk, on the phone or in
person, and during community events such as funerals, church functions,
and weddings. Migrants articulate and evaluate their expectations of family
life, for themselves and to others in their networks, in response to their desire to make sense of their frustrations in transposing their cultural frame-

works. Although the talk may be criticized as gossip (Dreby 2006; Menjívar and Agadjanian 2007), it is critical to the reinforcement and reshuffling of migrants' repertoire.

This conceptualization of national differences leads Ghanaian immigrant parents, like other immigrant parents (Gibson 1988; Portes and Rumbaut 2001; Zhou and Bankston 1998), particularly other Black immigrant parents (Waters 1999), to try to insulate their children from becoming American, whether through sending them back to Ghana or giving them exposure to the Ghanaian immigrant community in the United States. The recent "Tiger Mom" controversy is a slightly different manifestation of this immigrant parenting strategy (Chua 2011).

The scholarship on migration has long been concerned with culture and cultural change through the lens of immigrant assimilation or acculturation to a new society. In the assimilation model, culture is viewed in quite binary and rigid ways: an immigrant either holds onto family traditions or family norms and values, or assimilates into American society. Earlier scholarship on migrant families focused on tensions and conflicts between the less assimilated first generation and the more assimilated second generation. As the scholarship on immigrant families has grown, the model based on assimilation has gradually grown more nuanced. To name just a few examples, Margaret Gibson (1988), Mary Waters (1999), JoAnn D'Alisera (2004), and Philip Kasinitz and his colleagues (2008) have shown how some immigrant parents try to recreate aspects of their home communities in the United States in an attempt to ensure their children's success in school and beyond: economic success in the United States (one kind of assimilation) may be supported by selective, not wholesale, cultural assimilation to "American life." Still, I would argue that notions of acculturation and assimilation—even when rendered more complex by recent scholarship—do not capture the flexibility and pragmatism of migrant families in their use of cultural resources. Many studies of this phenomenon can seem reductive and static, essentializing cultures in the same way that some migrants do. The concept of repertoire provides a less binary and more complex explanation than that of assimilation for immigrants' self-conscious reflections on their strategies. It allows us to see how migrants are adapting and adopting, adding to rather than replacing cultural frameworks. Even though some migrants may organize their experience and repertoire reshufflings according to rigid national binaries, scholars should not adopt migrants' essentializing renderings of their repertoires as their own analysis. The degree to which people verbalize and objectify their repertoire is the result of interactions they have had over time, to normalize certain practices or expectations and, conversely, as they bring them to consciousness and make them subject to outright negotiation.

Repertoires of Transnational Families

Because repertoires are products of the experiences through which people have enacted them, migrants have different repertoires of family life at their disposal to adapt, refine, and select. There are a growing number of studies of African migrants in the United States. Some illustrate the transposition of African trade networks (Stoller 2002) or religious communities (D'Alisera 2004; Kane 2011) to the United States, highlighting continuity. Others reveal more conflict and rupture, particularly around marriage and gender relations (Babou 2008; Holtzman 2000; Manuh 1998). None so far have focused exclusively on family life, although relations with spouses, children, and siblings are such important parts of immigrants' lives that these studies do provide information on these topics within the larger context of work and migration experiences. These studies show that some of what I offer from the experiences of Ghanaian immigrants has resonance with African migrants more generally; specific comparisons are noted throughout the book.

There is a much more extensive literature on separated children in the scholarship on migration from other regions. Studies of separated children and parents from Mexico, Central America, and the Philippines describe the pain that children and migrant mothers, in particular, feel about their situation: migration disrupts their expectations about family life and ideal mothers' roles (Hondagneu-Sotelo 1994; Parreñas 2001, 2004; Schmalzbauer 2004). Some mothers try to rework what being a good mother means, such as identifying themselves as a provider rather than a nurturer. But these reformulations do not always stick, causing pain for children who feel unloved or neglected. For instance, a Mexican mother in the United States whose children were in Mexico expressed how she could not be a good mother simply by remitting to her children. She said, "You can't give love through money"; rather, love "required an emotional presence and communication with a child" (Hondagneu-Sotelo and Avila 1997, 563–64). Some scholars have argued that this lack of love causes disruption in children's schooling, difficult relationships with their parents and caregivers, and attempts to join their parents across the border, as witnessed by the harrowing attempts by child migrants from Central America to cross Mexico and the U.S.-Mexico border (Heidbrink forthcoming; Nazario 2006).

Other research shows that globalization does not necessarily disrupt family structures. For instance, Heather Rae-Espinoza (2011) argues that most children of Ecuadorian immigrants who stay behind tend to normalize their situation, by representing their caregivers as their parents in school and among their peers. Jennifer Hirsch's nuanced work (2003) argues that the expectations of love in marriage are changing not because of Mexican migration, but due to a larger generational shift in marital expectations occurring in both Mexico and the United States. Karen Fog Olwig (1999) makes the strongest critique of the existing literature by arguing that children's suffering is based on their expectations of care. The Saint Kitts and Nevis children she interviewed had expectations of households that could be maintained across long distances and in which children often circulated through different households. Because flexible family arrangements were considered normal, the children left behind did not necessarily feel emotional pain at separation from migrant mothers. Jessaca Leinaweaver (2008) also notes that well-established traditions of fostering in Ayacucho, Peru, enable parents to migrate internationally. Although the literature on transnational children from Central America and the Philippines tends to emphasize the yearning children have for the migrant parent, particularly the mother, and the problems that result from their separation, my research supports the conclusions of Olwig (1999) and Suárez-Orozco and her colleagues (2002) who argue that cultural expectations, particularly interpretations of parent-child separation as normal or unusual, are highly significant in influencing children's responses to a parent's migration. As Henrietta Moore reminds us, "The concept of 'mother' in any society may not be constructed through maternal love, daily childcare or physical proximity" (1988, 26). Differing conceptions of care and motherhood result in transnational families from different regions, communities, and class backgrounds expressing different emotions about mother-child separation as they creatively enact their family repertoire in the world.

Several features of the repertoires of many Ghanaian migrants make the separation of parents and children through transnational migration less disruptive and more normal to them. One is a distributed notion of parenting, common in West Africa, in which many different people, not only the biological or social parents, can be involved in the care of a child. As a result, many children circulate among households, known as "fostering" in the literature on West Africa and "child shifting" in the Caribbean (e.g., Forde 2011; Soto 1987). By circulating through various households, children develop an extensive network of relationships that can help them develop into adulthood, but which may simultaneously exploit them (e.g., Alber forthcoming; Amselle 1971; Bledsoe 1990). Bruce Whitehouse (2009) has noted fosterage's role in the migration of Malians to Brazzaville, Congo. The second characteristic is a recognition of the materiality of care, in which a person's distribution of his or her resources is taken as his or her level of affection for others, unlike in the United States, where the distribution of material resources between family members is downplayed (Folbre 2001, 2008; Zelizer 1985, 2005). As a result of a public discourse of how care is demonstrated through material exchanges, reliability of remittances, rather than presence, can characterize a good parent (Tetteh 2008).

However, other aspects of the repertoire of Ghanaian migrants are frustrated by transnational migration, resulting in compromises and heartache. One is that children have tended to circulate to live with wealthier relatives living in places with access to valued education and "civilization." In the contemporary world, this means those living abroad rather than in Ghana. But transnational migrants have trouble bringing their own children, much less the children of their siblings, to live with them in the United States. In response, international migrants are extending some kinds of fosterage that have supported working, migrant mothers but not other kinds that have moved children to new locales to gain familiarity with modes of behavior associated with the educated middle class and to access opportunities for high-status education or training in a skilled craft. Secondly, while children live separately from their parents, or husbands from their wives, within Ghana, they still visit them. In contrast, separation and abandonment are more pronounced for international migrants because of the cost of commercial airfare and immigration restrictions on tourist visas, as I have discussed more extensively elsewhere (Coe 2011b). Lastly, many contemporary Ghanaians are increasingly ambivalent about child fosterage arrangements, at a time when transnational migrants seem to be reinvigorating these practices. The urban middle class, in particular, would prefer to "live together in one's own house" with the idiom of emotional closeness or love: they are willing to foster-in nieces and nephews, but are less willing to send their own children to live elsewhere. The idiom of "living together" drives migrants' dreams of having their own house, built through remittances, where their family can live, even if it means living apart temporarily. This idiom is also a means by which migrants and their loved ones can critique and express their sorrow about being scattered. This book illustrates how Ghanaian migrants' repertoires, particularly their practices and ideologies of distributed parenting, are used in their transnational migration, but are also challenged by it, resulting in reshuffling and change.

Furthermore, I will show that such reshuffling of repertoires is ongoing. Some aspects of contemporary migrants' repertoires gained legitimacy during earlier periods of Ghanaians' involvement with global capital through cocoa farming and other export crops. Very few studies of transnational family life examine the history of family life or compare it to the family arrangements of rural-urban migrants; Jennifer Hirsch's excellent study (2003) is a notable exception. This lacuna occurs despite the fact that in many parts of the world international migration is largely preceded by internal migration to factories and farms and larger economic changes such as industrialization or the development of export agriculture (Sassen 1998; Trager 2005). Internal migration has also been increasing rapidly alongside international migration and is a much more widespread phenomenon. By examining an earlier period of internal migration, as well as comparing the child-care arrangements of transnational families to those of contemporary migrants within Ghana, I show in a more careful way what makes transnational migration new and disruptive for Ghanaians. My work suggests that globalization—as "a single system of connection, through capital and commodities markets, information flows, and imagined landscapes"—is neither a new phenomenon characterized by radically different dynamics nor a smooth extension of rural-urban migration (Cooper 2001, 189; see also Appadurai 1996; Eriksen 2003; Guarnizo and Smith 1998). Some of the newness of transnational migration stems from how it channels the flows of resources that are so crucial to the care and raising of children. Supporting other scholarship on the global chains of care work (Ehrenreich and Hochschild 2002), my research suggests that international migration is distributing the work of caring to dependent relatives in poorer countries.

As a result of transposing their repertoire to cope with transnational migration, Ghanaian migrants are expanding and deepening some aspects of their repertoire and changing others. Contemporary global capitalism is therefore generating changes in family life and emotional regimes, not in a unitary or even way, but as migrants creatively use their repertoires as they encounter the possibilities and constraints generated by neoliberalizing, sovereign states increasingly dependent on mobile and fickle flows of capital.

Studying Family Life and Migration

I had been aware of the many Ghanaians living and working in the United States from my early days in graduate school in the mid-1990s when I began to study Twi, one of the many languages of Ghana. My Twi teacher was also the pastor of a local Ghanaian church, which I occasionally attended to practice hearing and speaking Twi. After my dissertation fieldwork, on the teaching of national culture in Ghana's schools, I continued attending the church to keep up with my Twi, which was growing increasingly rusty with disuse. As my relationships with people in the church grew, I considered doing a project examining how their children adjusted to schools in the United States. When I discussed this idea with my friend, the pastor, he gently explained that although I saw many adults in the church, their children were not necessarily living with them, but rather were in Ghana. A few weeks later, I met Irene as I have described, and I decided this topic was so intriguing I had to pursue it: why did Ghanaian immigrants raise their children in Ghana and how did they feel about it?

From contacts in the church, beginning in 2004, I interviewed some parents about their migration and parenting choices. I also spoke to the children of migrant parents and the children's caregivers, which I was able to do in visits to Ghana in 2006 and 2008. In 2006 I had discussions with students at three secondary schools and a junior-secondary school, one in Akuapem in the Eastern Region and three in Kumasi, the second largest city in Ghana with over a million people. Located in the Ashanti Region, it serves as a major trading nexus between the coast and the north of Ghana.

Figure 1. Downtown Kumasi. Photo by author.

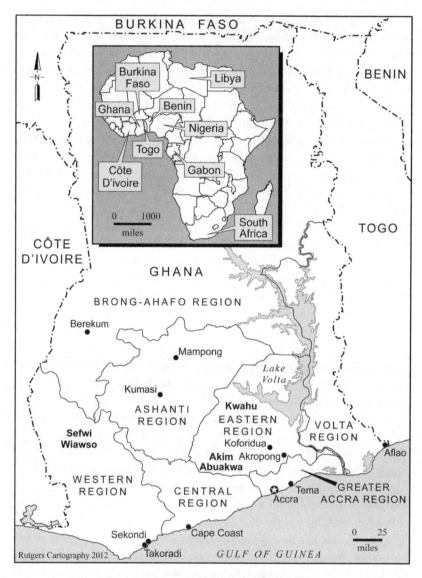

Map 1. Ghana and Africa. Map by Michael Siegel.

I visited the students' foster parents where possible and then made contact with those parents who were living in the United States, interviewing them over the phone or visiting them for the day if they lived on the East Coast—most lived between Virginia and Massachusetts.[9] In some cases, I had a chance to attend church with them as well.

I was struck by how the interviews and visits with strangers seemed to go much better and be more open than those with church members I had known for some time. My explanation for this fact was the church community's concern about gossip, which I'll discuss in greater depth in chapter 5. Despite my promise of confidentiality, those who were active in the church community were concerned about airing what they saw as their children's or family's dirty laundry. In contrast, those who saw me come briefly into their lives to talk to or visit with them seemed far more willing to share their experiences because I had few or no contacts with other people in their local Ghanaian immigrant community. Even though I did not obtain as many interviews from the church as I expected, I learned a great deal from my participation in the church community, from the services, youth group meetings, and informal conversations during celebrations and parties held in the church. To protect people's privacy, all names given in the book are pseudonyms and identifying information has been omitted.

From these interviews with those affected by international migration, I then sought to understand more purposefully the differences in child-raising arrangements between international migrants and migrants within Ghana (called internal migrants). To that end I conducted a household survey in the town of Akropong in Akuapem in 2008, visiting 220 households with Kweku Aryeh, a young man from the town, and interviewing ninety-three foster parents and the eighty children over the age of eight they were fostering. Interviews with foster parents, as with parents abroad, focused not only on their experiences of raising children but also on their own childhoods, to understand historical changes in child-raising arrangements. While the foster parents and children were living in Akropong at the time, not all of them considered Akropong their hometown. Most were Akan and from somewhere in the Eastern Region. The exceptions were Ga, Ewe, and Frafra, the latter from northern Ghana. Thirty of the foster parents were fostering a child of a migrant abroad. Forty-five of the children interviewed also came to discussions that were organized in their neighborhoods. Although I participated in these discussions, they were led by other members of my research team: Joe Banson, a church elder who had grown up in the town, and Margaret Rose Tettey, a teacher from the town. Finally, six of these children's parents who were living in the United States were contacted and interviewed on the phone or in person. I was able to interview three other triads of parents, children, and foster parents living outside Akropong. The interviews and discussions were recorded, transcribed, and translated.

All in all, I conducted thirty-eight interviews with parents in the United States (ten of which were joint interviews with the husband and wife, twenty-eight with only one parent). I spoke to seventy-one children of migrant parents in group discussions or in interviews. The young people ranged in age from eight to twenty-five, with an average age of sixteen, and their parents were in a wide range of countries, from Japan and Italy to Nigeria, with the United Kingdom and the United States the most common destinations. Most of these young people were in Ghana, but five had recently immigrated to the United States; the latter's average age was slightly older, at nineteen years. I also spoke to fifty-three fostered children whose parents were living in Ghana, twenty-seven foster parents of children of international migrants, and fifty-six foster parents of children with parents living elsewhere in Ghana. Between those three groups, there were twenty-one parent-child pairs and six parent-child-foster-parent triads who were able to reflect on the same situation from different perspectives.

With the exception of one family, all of my informants came from southern Ghana. The overwhelming majority were Akan, from the Ashanti or Eastern Regions. A few had family connections to other countries in the West African region, such as Togo and Nigeria. Illustrating the prevalence of migration in the subregion, one woman identified sometimes as a Ghanaian and sometimes, in the presence of her Togolese husband, as Togolese. One girl was living in Ghana with her uncle but her father in the United States was from Togo. Another woman who identified as Ghanaian had a Nigerian father and a Ghanaian mother. Raised in Ghana and married to a Ghanaian, she went to university in Nigeria because of the greater ease of college access.

Two-thirds of the international migrant parents had resided in urban locales, such as Kumasi, Accra, or the neighboring port city of Tema, prior to their migration. For Ghanaians, they were quite highly educated; 20 percent had a university degree. In Ghana they had worked as market women, teachers, civil servants, electricians, and mechanics. The median length of their stay in the United States had been six years, with two-thirds having lived ten years or fewer in the United States, with a range of one to thirty-five years. Reflecting the prevalence of health-care employment among Ghanaians seen in national surveys, of the forty-six parents whose US employment characteristics were obtained, fourteen worked in the health-care field (30 percent): four as nurse's aides, three as home health aides, and the remaining seven in other occupations within the health-care field. Fifteen parents (or 39 percent of all parents interviewed) had children living solely in Ghana, fourteen parents (37 percent) had children living only in the United States, and nine parents (24 percent) had children living in both places.

The interviews and discussions generated a lot of talk and opinions on marriage, migration (internal and international), and reciprocal exchanges between children, parents, and foster parents. They also generated evaluations of different kinds of fostering arrangements and how these had changed over time. In our interviews, some conducted in English and some in Twi, according to the preference of the participant, I sought to learn more about the experience of separation and what shaped their emotional response to familial separation. My relationship with some of those I interviewed continued, as with Irene; with others, the interview was the end of our in-depth conversations. In 2008, Kweku Aryeh and I followed up with those I had initially met in Akropong in 2006.

Through interviews, I was missing the more subtle and deep dynamics of family life, which I might have learned through living with a family, as Margaret Trawick (1990) and Lila Abu-Lughod (1986) did, or by following a family network over time, as Karen Fog Olwig (2007) and Greta Gilbertson (2009) have done. Annette Lareau and other members of her research team were able to combine observations with interviews with twelve families by staying overnight and spending periods of time with them on several short visits (Lareau 2003). Becoming part of a household seemed less fruitful when families were scattered across different households. Furthermore, those in the United States were very busy, and being more a part of their family lives would have been more disruptive than shorter interviews. I did stay briefly (for a weekend and a week respectively) with two families while migrant mothers, one of whom was Irene, were in Ghana for an extended stay. I also stayed overnight with two families in the United States for the purpose of attending a ceremony that lasted late into the night. I was aware that through interviews I was getting the more verbalized aspects of people's repertoire of family life.

Talk, however, is an important part of people's repertoire. Language is conventional—we learn what to say and how to say it through our interactions with others. Talk can be habitual as well as subject to more self-conscious debate and training. The term *discourse* refers to the conventionality and patterning of talk in which specific vocabulary, expressions, and style are associated with the topic of speech. Expressions of emotions are also conventional, as people try to translate a host of thoughts about an experience through the words commonly in use in their world. In speaking about emotion, people may change the nature of the experience for themselves: an expression of sorrow may heighten the sense of grief, or mitigate it; or someone may realize that, in fact, she is more angry than sad (Reddy 2001). As a result, in our interviews I learned what people thought was appropriate to express to me and perhaps express to themselves. Having done interviews with many Ghanaians before, I was aware of how people could relate their feelings with considerable indirection, describing their own experiences through stories about friends, for instance.[10] Or people might hint at disappointments, which, when queried, would be elaborated. I felt as if the interviews let me listen in to forms of talk that my informants normally shared with their relations or friends. Thus through interviews I heard their discourses—their patterned ways of speaking—about migration, US immigration policy, marriage, child raising, and appropriate reciprocal relations between generations. Other observations from participating in Ghanaian immigrant community life in the United States and in everyday life in Ghana helped round out my data dependent on discourse.

I'll begin with an overview of some of the significant features of Ghanaian migrants' repertoires and show how these features are a historical product of previous migrations and movements within Ghana. I'll turn then to US immigration law and the ways it thwarts Ghanaian migrants' repertoire of raising their children, and how Ghanaian parents respond. The next four chapters examine how migrant parents, their children, and the foster parents of the children extend and revise their repertoires as they respond to their separations.

By using Ghanaians as a case example, I hope to show that although global capitalism and the state have generated conditions that promote the separation of families, migrants and their kin respond to these conditions differently, because they creatively enact their repertoire of family life in the situations they encounter. There is not a straightforward fit between a particular economic or political structure and a family form. Instead, the degree of articulation, or the lack thereof, is generated by people's creative enactment of their repertoires in situations shaped by political and social mobilizations of ideas and resources.

ONE

A History of Family Reciprocities

Material Exchanges between the Generations in Akuapem

A van (or *trotro*) traveling from Accra to the Akuapem hills first hurtles across the Accra plains and then slows down as it climbs the escarpment through a series of twists and turns in the road. On the top of the ridge, it travels through town after town and I learned to recognize a pattern in the housing types that allowed me to see when we had left one town and entered another. At the center of town are low, one-story houses built around an inner courtyard and made of plastered mud-brick. Bedrooms in rectangular blocks enclose a central courtyard that forms the main living area, where "arbitrations occur, cooking is done, children play, stories are told, and family celebrations and funerals are held" (Pellow 2002, 31). The bedrooms are tiny and dark, with a window or two and shutters to close for privacy and security. They function as places to sleep and to store goods, but most activities occur outside, in the courtyard. Such houses are family houses, with extended family members laying claim to different rooms.

A little farther out from the center there are imposing two-story houses primarily built by migrants from Akuapem who made their fortunes through cocoa farming or trading in the first half of the twentieth century. These houses show a grand face to the street: on the ground floor, they have elaborate steps leading to a covered porch with columns, and often a second-floor covered porch from which residents can watch passers-by. Behind this imposing facade is often a courtyard with one-story blocks of bedrooms, as in more traditional housing types. Many people live in these large houses—sometimes descendants of the original owner, sometimes renters—but because they are jointly owned, house repairs and maintenance are delayed, with no one person wanting to take responsibility—a tragedy of the commons.

Finally, on the outskirts of the same towns, remittances from abroad

Figure 2. Courtyard of a compound house in Akropong. Photo by author.

are funding the building of newer mansions. Harder to see behind their enclosing walls, they gleam with their white paint and glass windows. The newer houses are organized around the model of a detached bungalow with a garage, smaller quarters for household help, and a garden full of ornamental plants, all surrounded by a high wall, imitating the housing provided for senior-level colonial and postcolonial civil servants.

During a focus group discussion in Akropong, a thirteen-year-old boy drew a modern Ghanaian house, painstakingly depicting the critical features: fans, hanging light bulbs, light switches on the wall, screens and windows, and furniture. A kitchen across the courtyard contained a stove, a light switch, and a kettle. A sitting room had many chairs, a television set, and a picture hanging on the wall. These rooms were surrounded by a courtyard with flowering potted plants. The artist commented, "εyε fε," or it is beautiful. Although he labeled the drawing "U.S.A.," it corresponded more to the ideal of a Ghanaian house than an American one, but illustrated how he saw abroad as having all the amenities desired of a new house in Ghana.

These different houses are a visual symbol of the historical depth of migration in Akuapem and the connections migrants maintain to their hometowns, for even if they have gone away, they plan to build a home here. They also illustrate how what is now old was once new, and that

Figure 3. A new house in progress on the outskirts of Akropong. Photo by author.

Figure 4. A boy's drawing of an ideal house, titled "U.S.A." The drawing portrays several rooms with chairs, tables, electric fixtures hanging from the ceiling, television sets, and screened windows. One of the rooms is a kitchen with a stove; a pot sits on one of the burners. The courtyard contains two well-trimmed plants in pots.

what glitters today in the sun may fade and become shabby beside the new houses to come.

Perhaps harder to recognize, at first glance, is that the houses—both new and old—are symbols of love and affection, made to honor and house a loved one. The man who built the house in which I stayed in 2006 and 2007 had named the house after his mother, a fact I understood better after Paul, a thirteen-year-old boy, told me that he would like to build his grandmother a house when he grew up. Paul said,

> *Me nso anka mɛtɔ asaase na masi dan ama no, na mayɛ biibi a ɛwɔmu ama no, na matɔ kaa ne ade ade ama no.*
> I would like to buy land and build a house for her, to do something good for her, to buy a car and other things for her.

Paul dreamed of being able to do this for his grandmother because she had taken care of him in his childhood. As his desire suggests, gifts of material goods express love and care: his grandmother has taken care of him, and he would like to take care of her by giving her a house, a car, and other items. The understanding that affection can be expressed through the provision of food, clothing, and education, rather than through copresence (such as through attending soccer games or tending to a sick child) means that migrant parents can be good parents even when they are not living with their children. As I have discussed more thoroughly elsewhere (Coe 2011c), they can even be better parents—because of their increased earnings—than those who stay.

Because parents and children in Ghanaian transnational families use exchanges of material goods, in part, to evaluate the quality of their relationship, this chapter will focus on the history of this aspect of their repertoires, illustrating how it changed over time. In particular, I show that during the development of cocoa in Akuapem, when a cash economy was rapidly expanding, relations between adults and young people who were kin were dominated by discussions of debt. Young people became obligated to those who had paid for their medical care, expenses, or debts, obligations that included the carer's rights to control their labor and residence, to receive payments when they married (in the case of girls), and to use them to raise capital to buy land, as I will explain below. Those rights helped adults obtain capital and labor at a particular transition in the cocoa economy, as slavery was declining and before the farms produced enough profits to pay workers. I argue that exchanges between young people and their kin that centered on debt changed, over time, to become reciprocities of care as they are understood in transnational families today.[1]

Many studies of transnational family life have argued that transnational migration generates challenges to existing kinship repertoires. Most of these studies have focused on the marital bond as the source of conflict when gender roles and household labor are redefined in transnational households, but a few also examine how children of migrant mothers experience the loss of maternal affection and feel shortchanged when a mother migrates (Hondagneu-Sotelo and Avila 1997; Parreñas 2004; Suárez-Orozco, Todorova, and Louie 2002; Wolf 1997). Lacking in this line of research is an appreciation of how kinship repertoires disrupted by contemporary transnational migration have been produced and negotiated historically in contexts of previous instability, including the migrations of previous generations. Kinship repertoires challenged by transnational migration today may be composed of repertoires previously reformulated in response to changing economic conditions at a particular historical moment.

Studies of globalization and transnational migration are surprisingly ahistorical and highlight the newness of the phenomenon. For instance, such scholarship rarely references earlier research on internal migration, although many transnational migrants first migrated to a city or factory before going overseas (Sassen 1998; Trager 2005). Nancy Foner (2005) has challenged the ahistoricity of the literature on transnational migration by carefully documenting how transnational life and networks also characterized earlier generations of immigrants to the United States, including a longing to return and participation in political activities in the home country, despite the greater difficulties and expense of long-distance travel and communication compared to today. Jennifer Hirsch (2002) has similarly shown that not all changes in transnational families are caused by transnational migration: changes in marital expectations among Mexican migrant men and women are occurring among younger nonmigrants as well, representing a generational change about the conjoining of love and marriage. Other nuanced studies show that transnational migration results in both continuity *and* change, in gender roles and family structures (Gamburd 2000; Glenn 1983; Olwig 2007; Rae-Espinoza 2011). A sense of the historical background helps to reveal what is, in fact, new and challenging about contemporary contexts of migration for transnational families. It also highlights how "tradition" is made up of recompositions of material that is both old and new as people flexibly deploy their repertoires.

In this chapter, I describe how contemporary ideas of the materiality of care are constructed from previous debt-care exchanges between kin. These exchanges were modeled on pawning relationships that became more significant as slavery declined. Just as slavery in Akuapem increased to support the oil palm industry in the mid-nineteenth century, so pawning and debt-care exchanges in the early twentieth century were significant in establishing the cocoa farms from whose profits the grand houses in Akuapem were built. This history illustrates how Ghanaian families adapted their repertoires to respond to local opportunities and constraints generated by a long and changing engagement with global trade.

I focus on one area of southern Ghana in this discussion. Although this examination of the history of Akuapem kinship repertoires does not represent that of all Ghanaian migrants in the United States, most international migrants from Ghana do come from areas of southern Ghana, and many features of kinship I discuss here will be familiar to other Akan-speaking peoples.

In representing change over time, one has to choose where to begin. Such a decision implies that the era that came before was more stable and enduring than what occurred thereafter, even though changes were occurring in that earlier period also. I begin with a discussion of kinship prior to cocoa, recognizing, where possible, that one could go even further back in time and document how this period too consisted of adaptations of repertoires inherited from the past.

Akuapem Kinship before Cocoa

Akuapem is a traditional kingdom, comprising seventeen towns along a ridge and their satellite villages in the valleys below, about an hour's travel from Accra, in what is now the Eastern Region of southern Ghana. The ridge made the area somewhat inaccessible in comparison to other parts of southern Ghana, so Akuapem was settled only in the fifteenth or sixteenth century.[2] The first settlers spoke variants of the Guan language, made their living through farming, and were ruled by shrine priests. Kin were organized as lineages descended through their fathers from a common male ancestor, known as a patrilineage, which was further divided into smaller "houses."[3] From the middle of the seventeenth century on, the Guans in the area were dominated politically by various Akan states that sought to control the trade in gold and slaves to the European forts on the coast (Kwamena-Poh 1973). People from these Akan states came to live in Akuapem and spoke different dialects of Twi (or Akan). They brought with them a new political system, in which the political leaders or chiefs were

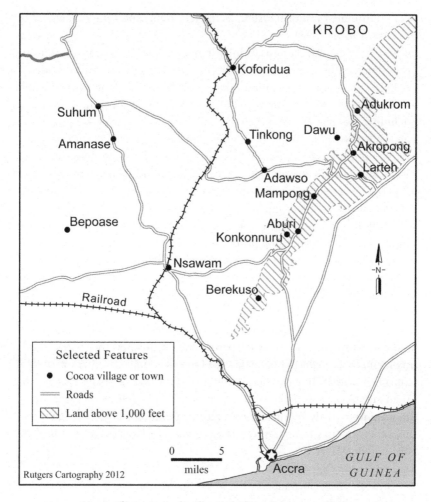

Map 2. The towns on the Akuapem ridge and the cocoa villages
in the valleys to the west. Map by Michael Siegel.

members of royal families and not religious specialists.[4] The Akan settlers
and rulers were members of matriclans (or *abusua*). Matriclans, formed
through common descent from a female ancestor, had been important
in the transition from hunting to farming in the forest regions of southern Ghana, but lost their social significance to smaller lineages and even
smaller "houses" (Wilks 1993). Through Akan domination, the Guan people learned Twi and incorporated Twi loan words into their Guan dialects.
They began to imitate the Akan style of chiefship, organized hierarchically
on the model of an army's battle formation, and became part of the new

Akan-dominated political system as the left, right, and center wings (*Nifa*, *Benkum*, and *Adonten*) of the army. However, they maintained their own unique festivals and patterns of inheritance. Shrine priests continued to be important for the Guan but generally were no longer the political leaders.[5]

Both Guan and Akan families were organized around the corporate unit of the "house," which comprised all descendants of a common ancestor, including the living, the dead, and the unborn. A "house" was not a building, although there might be houses and land associated with a house, nor was it a household, but rather a corporate understanding or name for closer kin. Houses distributed economic gains and losses across a group of people, evening out inequality between house members and reducing individual risk to economic loss, famine, or other crises (Douglas 1971). The head of the house (*abusuapanyin*), an elder member of the family, was responsible for safeguarding property belonging to the house and using it to help the house as a corporate body, such as helping members get out of debt or paying for members' burials. The head of the house was also responsible for arbitrating disputes and maintaining the religious rituals that were necessary for good relations with the house members who had died and become ancestors (Rattray 1969). The house helped bury its members and chose inheritors for their property. In a patrilineage, the successor to a man who died ought to be the deceased man's younger brother or paternal cousin; in a matrilineage, his sister's son.[6] However, perhaps because the Akan and Guan have lived with one another for four hundred years or so, they are not strictly patrilineal or matrilineal but also acknowledge ties to the other parent's family. An anthropologist of Akuapem, David Brokensha, noted:

> There are many aberrations, such as the "patrilineal" Guan allowing children to inherit . . . from their mothers, or the "matrilineal" Akim [or Akan] indulging in testatentory [or inheritance] disposition in favor of sons [as opposed to sisters' sons, as would be usual among matrilineal people]. It would perhaps be better not to think of "systems" being either patrilineal or matrilineal, but of using "double-descent" [kinship through the mother *and* father], with a strong emphasis on one side or the other. (1972, 78; see also Middleton 1979 and Hardiman 2003)

Wealthy men in matrilineages in Akuapem tried to provide in their lifetimes for their sons as well as their sisters' children, just as wealthy men in patrilineages also tried to provide for their sisters' sons (Hill 1958; Johnson 1972). In partially acknowledging both maternal and paternal sides of the family, their repertoires so clearly composite, Akuapem people are somewhat unusual in southern Ghana, where identification with either the maternal or paternal line is much more pronounced.

In the mid-twentieth century, house bonds were more important than conjugal bonds. Husbands and wives were from different houses. They did not always live together, particularly at the beginning of their relationship when each might reside in a building belonging to their own corporate house (Brokensha 1972). Children might live with their parents, if they lived together; with one or the other parent, if they lived apart; or with other house members, such as a grandmother, a woman in the house of an older generation (called a mother), a slightly older man in the same generation (known as a brother), or the family head, whether or not their parents lived together. Furthermore, in a society where polygamy was common, cowives and their children might live apart from one another and their husband-in-common to reduce tension and jealousy. Children, like other people, were first and foremost members of the corporate house, and they circulated through different households as they and others pleased. Children were particularly valued because they could help a house continue into the future and grow in size; they also enabled their parents to become respected elders and ancestors.

Although husbands, wives, and children might not live together, husbands and wives did cooperate in food production, as has been documented in the extensive literature on the Asante in the eighteenth and nineteenth centuries. Husbands and wives each had access to land through their respective lineages, and they helped one another on their individual farms, without establishing joint property or rights to the other's lineage land. The unit of production, composed of a husband and wife and their dependents, was therefore smaller than the unit of distribution, the house (Douglas 1971). Marriage was a relationship maintained by the exchange of ongoing reciprocal obligations and responsibilities: "Asante men had the right to call on the labor of their wives and expected them to provide a broad range of domestic services, including fetching water, cooking, cleaning, and looking after children. In turn, women expected to receive from their husbands care or maintenance, in the form of meat, clothing, and food crops" (Allman and Tashjian 2000, 62). Under such circumstances, a wife's refusal to cook for her husband or a man's delaying providing his wife with clothing was a serious sign of unhappiness in the marriage and could be cause for divorce (Allman and Tashjian 2000, 13; Austin 2005).

To judge by contemporary West African farmers, children probably began to contribute to household production at an early age, in part to relieve their mothers' work. They might start contributing as baby-minders from the age of six or seven, allowing the mothers of toddlers to go to farm (Gottlieb 2004). They might begin helping with the smaller tasks on the farm, such as weeding (Polak 2012), and take on full responsibility for the domestic tasks of cooking, fetching water, and sweeping by the age of ten or twelve (Reynolds 1991). Thus children were important contributors to the domestic household, with the value of children's labor increasing as they aged. As they grew, boys were expected to live with their fathers or maternal uncles. Children worked for those they lived with and received in return their daily food, whatever medical care they might need, occasional gifts of clothing, and the promise of help in the future.

In the nineteenth and early twentieth centuries, conjugal work units were supplemented by two kinds of bonded people whom individuals and houses acquired: slaves and pawns.[7] The Basel Mission, which set up mission stations and schools in several Akuapem towns from 1835 onward, became fascinated with trying to understand Akuapem practices of slavery and pawning, not simply for humanitarian reasons, but also because it relied on these practices (or variants of them) to meet its own labor needs (Haenger 2000) and to fill its new schools.

Slavery became important in Akuapem because of the cultivation of oil palm and its refinement into palm oil, which greased machines in British factories (McPhee 1926). Akuapem chiefs and large-scale plantation owners had begun cultivating oil palm in the valleys below the ridge in the 1830s (Haenger 2000; Johnson 1972). Slaves were important for this export crop because of its intense labor needs, particularly in its refinement and transportation (by head load) to the coast (McPhee 1926, 30–36; Sutton 1983). Because of its involvement in oil palm agriculture, Akuapem became a destination for traders who brought slaves from outside: northerners, and around 1869 captured Ewe refugees fleeing an Asante invasion (Getz 2004; Gilbert 1995; Haenger 2000; Jenkins 1970b). Because slaves were stripped of their family membership through their sale, they lacked the protection and identity that a house offered. As a result, they were "freely disposable unpersons" (Haenger 2000, 57): they could be sacrificed at the funeral of a member of the owner's house or sold if they were disobedient or infertile.[8] Owners generally gave slaves their own land to work, requiring that they work for the owner two days a week.[9] In the 1840s, slaves lived in villages near the oil palm plantations, while owners moved between the towns on the ridge and their various plantations to oversee the work. The slaves grew their own food and perhaps some oil palm for their own sale and tended the owner's oil palm farms (Haenger 2000; Jenkins

1970b; Johnson 1972). Because slaves had no house, the children of slaves became incorporated into the owner's house as quasi-relatives and could inherit in the absence of other descendants (Haenger 2000).

Pawning was a different kind of bondage in which a person served as security for a loan by living and working for the lender until the debt was repaid. Pawning was generally conducted between houses whereby the head of one house pawned one or more of its members to another house (Austin 2005, 142). For example, a head of a house might need money to pay the costs for a house member's funeral. In the absence of other forms of credit, he or she would go to a wealthy person and ask for a loan. As security that the loan would be repaid, the debtor would give the lender a junior member of his or her house, who would return home when the loan was repaid. During the time that the loan was outstanding, the pawn would live with and work for the lender like other members of his or her household. Akuapem heads of houses pawned their junior members, particularly adolescents and young adults, to other Akuapem people they knew. The familiarity offered protection on both sides of the exchange: the creditor was assured that the debtor would want to redeem the pawn and thus was more likely to repay the loan, while the debtor was assured that the creditor would not abuse the pawn in the interim. Although slaves in Akuapem mainly worked in farm villages at a distance from the major towns, pawns were more associated with domestic work, probably because of their smaller numbers. During this period of residence and labor, the creditor was responsible for feeding and clothing the pawn. The pawn was obligated to stay with the lender until the debt was repaid, unlike unpawned children who could move between residences, building up their store of reciprocal relationships through their labor. Sometimes pawns ran away from the lenders, forcing repayment of the debt or their replacement by another relative.

A person could only pawn or sell into slavery another person over whom they had the right to do so: heads of houses could pawn members of the house to pay debts house members incurred; chiefs could pawn their subjects who owed them court fees; slave owners could pawn their slaves or their children by slave wives; people could also pawn themselves to pay their own debts. When the Basel missionaries were summoned to the chief's court to help with a case regarding a child's death in 1864, they heard the proverb "Ɔba sɛ, ose na wɔwɔ mmusua," which they took to mean, as was written in a marginal note to a description of the case: "the child resembles the father, but he has relations (the father can't sell the child without the relations of the mother) the rel[ation]s have more to say than the f[ather])" (Basel Mission Archives, D-20.4, May 20, 1864, p. 177). Their explanation suggests that members of a matrilineal house had more control over selling or pawning a child than did the father, who was not one of the child's maternal relations.

If a house were in trouble, the elders of that house would first consider pawning a female house member who was married. They would approach her husband to see if he would be willing to give them a loan.[10] If not, the house head would be able to pawn their relative to someone else and thereby end the marriage. Husbands appreciated wives who were their pawns or slaves because they gained more rights to the labor of these wives and their children, those rights transferred to them by the woman's house through the exchange of money in sale or loan. In Asante, "historically, compared to marriage with free women, slavery and pawning offered free Asante men opportunities to acquire more wives and children, at lower cost, and/or additional property rights over wives and children" (Austin 2005, 175). Only those men who had children with a slave wife had rights to pawn or sell their children.

These were the kinship and household repertoires in Akuapem in the late nineteenth century prior to the coming of cocoa. People belonged to their houses ("their relations" as in the quote above), which provided them with an identity, access to resources such as land, and protection from debts and abuse. Conjugal ties were dependent on reciprocal exchanges between husbands and wives, who formed the basic unit of production helped by a host of dependents—children, younger siblings of the spouses, other members of their respective houses, pawns, and slaves.

Men stretched the reciprocal exchanges that were part of their kinship and household repertoire to gain access to capital and labor and establish cocoa farms. These reciprocal exchanges were significant in expanding export agriculture because they operated according to a different dynamic than capitalism. As Marshall Sahlins argues, "The family—with its unpaid labors, its allocation of work and resources by solidary social relations, its flows of values from the haves to the have-nots, in brief, its kinship economy, not to mention the emotions associated with all this—the family is structurally an anticapitalist system" (2004, 147). Men relied on kin relations that did not depend on strict cash exchanges in order to gain access to capital in an increasingly monetized economy.

In the process, kin relations became more commodified, but not fully so. The commodification occurred through the language and practice of debt pawning, in which control of another's labor and residence were dependent on cash payments. In other words, reciprocal kin exchanges were used to acquire labor and capital to take advantage of new economic opportunities, resulting in those relationships looking like those between debtor and pawn. For instance, conflicts emerged in court cases over the meaning of marriage payments and child support: did marriage payments signify a marriage or rather a loan in which a woman became a pawn who had to work for her husband? Did maintaining a child or adolescent—paying for his or her medical care, expenses, and debts—give men rights to pawn that child, use his or her labor power, and, in the case of a girl, accept her future marriage payment? Marriage payments increasingly became seen as putting a woman in her husband's debt, which entitled him to control over her and their children's residence, and hence their labor. People creatively drew on their repertoires to take advantage of new economic opportunities, in the process changing their repertoires. Sometimes, their different perspectives on and interests in these changes brought them into conflict and landed them in court.

The Changing Family Obligations of Akuapem Cocoa Migrants, 1905–30

Information about the changing family obligations of Akuapem cocoa migrants comes from three sources: court records from towns in Akuapem in the National Archives and Eastern Regional Archives in Ghana; oral histories Polly Hill conducted among Akuapem cocoa farmers; and Basel Mission sources, mainly letters and reports from the European missionaries and articles by African Christians and ministers in a monthly Twi-language newsletter, *Kristofo Sɛnkekafo*. Court cases as a form of data highlight and may exaggerate the conflicts that existed among families during the cocoa boom. Oral histories and contemporary observations by missionaries and African Christians round out the picture by providing information about families who negotiated similar issues without going to court.

Mobility and migration were common in Akuapem in the late nineteenth and early twentieth centuries, for men, women, and children. One man from the town of Larteh in Akuapem told Polly Hill in 1960, "The Larteh people traveled much before cocoa-time. To Accra, Sekondi, Cape Coast, to the north as carriers, hammock-carriers, load-carriers. . . . Before cocoa they traded in rubber in Akim Abuakwa and Ashanti and there was coffee locally; maize was sold to our neighbours who had none" (Hill 1963, 205). Oil palm, as noted earlier, was grown in plantations away from the hometowns. A few people the Basel Mission trained as skilled craftsmen traveled throughout West Africa; one, Tetteh Quarshie, was credited with bringing cocoa to Akuapem, although there were several pathways by which cocoa was introduced and promoted in Ghana (Hill 1963; Kwamena-Poh 1973).

The profits from these migrations were plowed into acquiring land for cocoa farms. The first cocoa farms were established in 1879, and when they ran out of land nearby, around 1892, Akuapem farmers began migrating farther to the west to acquire new land. The cocoa boom peaked around 1900 in Akuapem. "Soon after 1900 it had become shameful, in some of the larger Akwapim [Akuapem] towns, not to have bought a land [for cocoa]: 'people were laughing because we were so late,'" said a farmer from the Akuapem town of Mampong in 1960, who had failed to buy land before 1902 or thereabouts (Hill 1963, 182). "Everybody wants land for cocoa plantations," reported the Basel Mission's yearbook, *Jahresbericht der Basler Mission*, in 1908 (quoted in Debrunner 1967, 255). In the first decade of the twentieth century, African Christians and missionaries reported that the towns on the Akuapem ridge tended to be deserted—quiet and overgrown with weeds—because people were staying near their cocoa farms farther to the west (Ofori 1907).[11] The colonial economy of the late nineteenth and early twentieth centuries prompted travel not only because of cocoa, but also to the inland city of Kumasi for trade or to the coastal city of Sekondi to work on the railway. Men and women from Akuapem also migrated to nearby cities and towns to trade as part of the growing informal, urban sector, itself fueled by the trading and transportation of cocoa.

As Jean Allman and Victoria Tashjian (2000) have argued, in Asante, cocoa growing "took root so firmly because it fit so well into preexisting patterns of production and exchange" (6). At the same time, it prompted changes in family life because it gave "a broad range of rural commoners access to cash and the cash economy" (5). Akuapem sources support these scholars' conclusions drawn from their detailed research in Asante. Cocoa put two pressures on previous modes of production. One was that men needed capital with which to purchase land in areas where they were strangers and did not have lineage connections. However, they did not need much capital, because migrant farmers only needed enough for an initial share in a down payment, since the land was bought jointly with others and final payments delayed for decades (Hill 1963). One source of funds was the pawning of relatives—particularly for those in patrilineages, their own children. The second pressure point concerned labor: as slaves became scarce, and pawns more difficult to acquire, men turned increasingly to their wives and children as a source of labor.

Polly Hill's interviews with elderly Akuapem cocoa farmers in the late

1950s show that many of those in patrilineages raised the capital to buy land in the early twentieth century through the pawning of their children, siblings, or paternal nephews, although others used profits from palm oil production, the rubber trade, or their earnings from trade or crafts work (Hill 1958). Children and young adults were particularly popular as pawns because they were junior members of families with few rights and because their status could be hidden from colonial officials who equated pawning with slavery. A presbyter and storekeeper from the Guan (and patrilineal) town of Larteh told Polly Hill that his father had bought land farther to the west in 1906 by pledging his children (Interview with E. R. Lattey, the Polly Hill Papers, Box 4, Folder 7). Kwame Adu, an old man from the Guan town of Mampong, told her how he had been pawned when his father bought land, sometime before 1903 (Interview with Kwame Adu, the Polly Hill Papers, Box 19, Folder 6a). He reported: "'After my father had bought the land he was a bit short of money' so he had to go to a certain [man] for a loan of five pounds" for which Adu himself was pawned, serving the lender for five years before the debt could be repaid. Because the lender had promised to help with the construction of the Presbyterian Church in Mampong, part of Adu's service to him included building the church.[12] "Pawning is common," said a witness from the double-descent town of Berekuso (Hill 1963, 211–12) in a court case in 1907 (*Rex v. Osaku*, January 15, 1907, SCT 2/5/16). Sometimes children in patrilineal houses wanted to be pawned, knowing that it would result in greater wealth for their families. For instance, in 1958, E. O. Walker remembered from his childhood in the early twentieth century in Larteh that he did not want to go to school so that he could instead be pledged to help his parents buy land (Notes on the Manuscript Book by James Lawrence Tete, the Polly Hill Papers, Box 4, Folder 7).

Some cocoa farmers had access to slave descendants and pawns to help them work. A farmer who jumped into the cocoa boom early, Kofi Pare, a man from the Akan town of Aburi, brought five laborers to work a large plot of land in 1896. These men were "indebted" Fanti and Aburi people—Polly Hill explains—"which is to suggest that they were similar to servants and pawns" but who "'stayed with him as sons'" (Visit to Kofi Pare, May 18, 1959, the Polly Hill Papers, Box 3, Folder 2). However, in the absence of slaves and pawns to work for them, some men turned to actual sons (and daughters and wives) as labor, as also happened among Asante cocoa farmers in the 1930s and 1940s (Allman and Tashjian 2000). In fact, cocoa farmers wanted many wives, so that they and their children could work the fields (Kaye 1962, 19). One Christian writer to *Kristofo Sɛnkekafo* in 1916 from the village of Nsakye (near Aburi) made the connection between slavery and marriage explicit, saying that while slavery has been abolished, wives work very hard and are therefore like slaves (Ɔsabo 1916).

The significance of wives' and children's labor meant that many lived near the cocoa farms. One woman from the Guan town of Mampong told Polly Hill that "when her husband went to Amanase [where his cocoa farm was located] she went too (or anyway at a very early stage) with the children" (Mampong, the Polly Hill Papers, Box 19, Folder 6a). A Basel missionary, Josef Mohr, reported in 1906 that "the rush into the Akropong Middle School"—a boys' school—had "noticeably slackened, because the parents now prefer to take their sons with them on the farms" farther to the west rather than keep them in school in towns on the ridge (quoted in Hill 1963, 227). A man might well stay with his wife and children near his farm plot, but a man with cocoa farms in multiple locations tended to move between his farms to oversee their management. Because people from the Guan town of Larteh had bought land in many places, "the people were therefore accustomed to the notion of buying land and also to the notion of 'living in more than one place at one and the same time'" (Hill 1958, 8). Many Larteh women were left in charge of farms during their husband's absence, which could be quite frequent if he was the owner of many lands (Hill 1958). If a man had multiple wives, he might place a wife at each farm. One man from Akropong, eighty-one years old in 1958, had seven wives and seventeen children living on most of his lands and divorced a wife who refused to stay at one farm to look after it for him (Interview with Okra Kwame Donkor, age eighty-one, in Akropong, April 5, 1958, the Polly Hill Papers, Box 5, Folder 1; see also Hill 1963, 201). Thus cocoa farming accompanied a set of more intense expectations between husbands and wives and between fathers and their children, but these expectations did not necessarily entail living together in one household, or in living together in a household in which nuclear family members were the only residents.

Men justified controlling women's and children's labor because with the expansion of the cash economy, marriage payments increased, as did the costs of raising children. Basel missionaries had noted that gifts were given to mark a marriage in Akuapem in 1875 (Jenkins 1970a), but marriage payments increased sharply in the late nineteenth and early twentieth centuries, fueled in part by the cocoa boom. A minister from Akuapem, Nathanael Asare, described in 1917 how marriage payments could be sixty, eighty, or even a hundred pounds without distinction for whether a man was rich or poor, much higher than the amount of a loan for which a pawn served as security (Asare 1917; see also Amoa 1907 and Interview with Kwame Adu, February 24, 1960, the Polly Hill Papers, Box 19, Folder 6a).[13] As a result, the meaning of marriage payments changed. As occurred in Asante, through marriage payments, a husband attempted to control the labor and residence of his wife and children as if they were his pawns.

This tension between whether a relationship was marriage or pawnship was the subject of many court cases in Akuapem in the early twentieth century.[14] In case after case, men claimed that the money they gave women was a marriage payment, and women claimed it was just a loan. One of the things at stake in such conflicts was the woman's place of residence. Because she worked where she lived, a man's control over her labor was implied when he asked her to live with him or live near his farm. When she left her hometown to live with him on his farm, she lost family support such as access to her own land and was more dependent on her husband; she contributed to his accumulation but had less opportunity to build her own. As an example among many, in 1915, a Christian produce buyer from the Guan town of Dawu wanted to take a young woman he considered his wife on a trip to Akyem, to the farmlands to the west, but her father refused to let him take her until the full marriage payment had been paid. The produce buyer had paid twenty pounds of the thirty-five-pound debt the woman's family owed, which he considered the marriage payment, and he had maintained the young woman through school (*Albert J. Chum v. Asare Kwame*, November 1, 1915, ECRG 16/1/20). Perhaps because he had paid her school fees for four years, the court agreed with him that he was in fact married to the young woman and had the right to travel with her over the objections of her father.

Relations between adults and their children continued to be reciprocal, but following the trend in marital relationships were based increasingly on cash payments and forms of debt. Fathers had various obligations to their children's continuing care: they paid for children's debts and helped them in court cases, paid for their maintenance or provided food, paid their medical expenses when they were sick, and helped their sons get land and marry. As the case above suggests, children's care became increasingly expensive as schooling became more popular. In repayment for such expenses, fathers had rights to their children's labor and their daughter's marriage payments, an increasingly important source of capital for men, and thus increasingly disputed. Parental care became a debt the young person incurred, which gave the adult providing care certain rights over the young person. As Stefano Boni argues, in the Sefwi Wiawso district, "whoever catered for the child (paid debts, maintenance, medical expenses) was often recognized as having privileged rights over the youngster" (2001, 27). When multiple adults provided care, those rights could be disputed.

Through cocoa, relations between men and their children and between husbands and wives became more oriented toward debt. Although relations between adults and children and between husbands and wives had been based on reciprocal exchanges prior to cocoa, the cocoa boom led to the commodification of those relations, with the payment of cash (particularly in the form of debt) allowing for greater control over a person's labor and residence, even though that control was often contested.

This history illustrates how participation in export agriculture and an increasingly cash economy changed the reciprocities between men and women, and between adults and children. Nonwage labor provided through family relations was used in the beginning stages of the cocoa industry in southern Ghana. Capitalist forms of production such as wage labor and using land as collateral for loans only emerged in the 1910s, once the land became valuable, with mature cocoa trees, and the farms were producing enough cocoa to pay laborers from the harvest (Austin 1987, 275–76; see also Hill 1963, 17). Noncapitalist forms of labor and social life helped subsidize capitalist modes of production, even though in the process they became more commodified.

This history also shows that repertoires of kinship have changed over time, through the actions of numerous people as they strove to generate new understandings of appropriate reciprocities. Families responded to the increased flow of and need for cash the cocoa boom occasioned by drawing on the resources and relationships available to them, prompting changes in their expectations and obligations for significant relationships. As people put pressure on one another, expecting more or giving less, stresses and strains resulted. Sometimes changes in family life occur imperceptibly and slowly, and sometimes quite rapidly, as we see during the cocoa boom. Whatever their speed, the changes are built on the past, as people use the resources and relationships available to them to adjust to new situations.

Debts between Kin Today

Over the course of the twentieth century, there were two major transformations in the obligations between the generations. One was that the exchanges became more long term than they had been in the past. Secondly, these exchanges shifted in favor of children: parents were obligated to give more to raise a child. As the value of cocoa farms and agriculture in general dwindled, senior family members had less to offer junior members in return for their service. Senior members of a family lost control over junior members as the resources they controlled became less valuable. Children's obligations to reciprocate became more elastic, conditional on a child's affection for his or her caregiver and his or her future economic success, rather than predicated on direct debt exchange. Because of these changes, mutual obligations between parents and children are less commodified today than they were a hundred years ago.[15]

As Jean Allman and Victoria Tashjian (2000) note in their book about changes in Asante family life, new expectations that fathers pay for their children's schooling changed the reciprocities between parents and children in dramatic ways. Formal education increased the cost of raising children, not only because of school fees but also because children went to school rather than working on family farms. Furthermore, schooling was only part of what was necessary for a child to be launched into adulthood and making a living. Girls sought apprenticeships as seamstresses and bakers after they completed school, for which fees and equipment were required. They needed capital to start their businesses when they had completed their training. Children previously had immediately returned some of what they had been given through their household labor. When a child went to school, despite being able to contribute to domestic labor around school hours, a child's return of the exchange was, for the most part, pushed off to a later date. Because he or she had been to school, the hope became that he or she would become educated and be able to support his or her parents in their old age.

Material care that passes from caregiver to child is seen in Akuapem today as an "entrustment," a term Parker Shipton (2007) coined, in which being cared for creates a responsibility for a person to reciprocate in the future. "Entrustment implies an obligation, but not necessarily an obligation to repay like with like, as a loan might imply. Whether an entrustment or transfer is returnable in kind or in radically different form—be it economic, political, symbolic, or some mixture of these—is a matter of cultural context and strategy" (11). Through such entrustments, child care is intimately related to elder care. Gabriel, a migrant in the United States mourning his recently deceased mother whose funeral he had been unable to attend in Ghana, advised me to have children because, "When you are old, you want to have children, who can look after you." Likewise, a minister in a Ghanaian church in the United States blessed a couple and their children on their tenth wedding anniversary, saying that their three children were "an investment." He told the congregation, "When the parents are old, their children will take care of them. Hopefully, their children will become 'somebody'"—important people who are respected and wealthy and thus able to care for them.

Adults who care for children—whether their own or other people's children—hope that these children will grow up *to want to* and be successful enough *to be able to* reciprocate in the future. Both characteristics are necessary for reciprocity. Parents are therefore as concerned about a child's character—humility, responsiveness to discipline, and respect for elders as part of the child's repertoire—as a child's educational success in ensuring a child's future ability and willingness to repay the metaphorical debt of care. I return to how parents abroad try to enact this set of goals in chapter 5.

Entrustment is bedeviled by doubt and uncertainty. A caregiver helps children, but it is not clear that he or she will be helped in return. Many parents and foster parents take a philosophical approach: they stressed over and over to me that they did not expect anything from the child they were caring for, nor would they demand anything from the child, but rather if the child felt like helping them, then such help would be welcome. Mr. Yirenkyi, taking care of his grandson whose father was abroad, said,

> Ɛnyɛ awofo no na edemand, but ɛsɛ sɛ wo ara wohwɛ sɛ, "ɛnyɛ me maame anaa me papa anaa obi a, anka baabi a midui no anka merennu hɔ." Enti wo a wohwɛ a, obi yɛ wo papa a woda no so ase (saa na mɛfa no nen) but ɛnyɛ sɛ ɛyɛ nhyɛso sɛ, mede wo aba sɛɛ, wo wɔ Aburokyiri enti ɔsram biara mena me sei. NO! Ɛno de enye! Na sɛ ɔyɛ ɔbadwema paa de a, a ɔdwene kɔ akyiri de a, otu ne nan koraa a, ose, "Ei! Mepaa ara na ɛnnɛ matumi ahyɛ mpaboa yi? Manso dae sɛ, menya mpaboa. Na hena na ɔmaa minyaa mpaboa yi?"
>
> The parents should not demand help, but rather, you yourself [as the child] should look at the situation and see, "If not for my mother or father or someone else, I would not have achieved what I have." So if you look at your life, you thank your father (at least that's my opinion). But it is not an obligation that I brought you into the world, so if you are abroad, you have to send me such-and-such. NO! As for that, it is not right! But if the person is wise and thoughtful, when he or she takes a single step, he or she will think, "Hey! Am I really wearing these shoes? I never dreamt of even having shoes. So who helped me get these shoes?"

Because the contractual agreement of direct exchange and repayment of care is muted, I would argue that these reciprocities are not commodified. Reciprocity, at its best, is based on voluntary contributions, made out of love and gratitude, as one woman in her sixties expressed to me. As a child, she had stayed with her grandmother in Akropong while her mother traveled for work to Nsawam, a nearby commercial town on the railway line. She said that she loved her grandmother more than her mother,

> *efiseε me nena na metenaa no hɔ ara na ɔhwε me kosi berε a ɔyε aberewa. Enti ɔyε aberewa na me nso mehwε no a kosi berε ko ara.*
> because I lived with my grandmother and she looked after me until she was an old woman. So when she was an old woman, I in turn looked after her.

One documented change in elder care is that a child is increasingly able to justify his lack of care for an elderly parent on the lack of payments the parent provided in the past for the child's care, particularly for the child's schooling and medicine (Aboderin 2004; van der Geest 2002). Because fathers are usually both wealthier—and thus more able to care—and more negligent in their responsibilities to their children than are mothers, Sjaak van der Geest (2002) argues that elderly fathers are more likely to be neglected by their children than are elderly mothers in southern Ghana. In my own research, some adult children of elderly fathers have been cajoled or scolded into providing them with financial support, even though those children felt neglected by their fathers as young people, with their school fees or apprenticeship training paid for through their mothers' backbreaking work. I have also encountered adult children taking care of elderly parents to whom they did not feel close. One elderly woman had not been raised by her mother, but in her middle age she had told her elderly mother to come join her in the family house in Akropong so that she could take care of her. Her siblings—particularly those abroad—have helped by sending remittances to support both mother and daughter.

In general, the reciprocities between parents (or foster parents) and children focus on material exchanges, exchanges made across the life spans of the children and parents, the one provided for in childhood providing for the other in his or her old age. In contrast, in the period of cocoa, fathers' and other men's material help, particularly the paying of debt, was rewarded with the children's direct and immediate service. Children's service might also pay off for them in the long term, through their access to land, and fathers might earn money from their daughters' marriage payments. However, in general, the exchange was more immediate, and more commodified, in the past than it is in the present, although echoes of it remain in the language of "investment."

Conclusion

A repertoire in which parental obligations are defined as material care has implications for how young people respond to a parent's migration abroad.[16] For example, Kwabena, a fifteen-year-old boy whose mother was abroad, said that although his mother's elder sister provided day-to-day care, he was happy his mother was in the United Kingdom because:

> *Obetumi de nneɛma abrɛ yɛn ne ade. Ɛhɔnom asetena no ye kakra sɛn ehanom de no, enti sɛ onya biribi a na anka watumi de abrɛ yɛn.*
> She is able to bring me and my aunt things. Life there is better than life here, so if she gets some money, she can bring it to us.

He told us that she brought clothes, shoes, and money, and that he was not at all unhappy that she was far away. Similarly, a girl whose father lived and worked in Accra and visited her and her sister on the weekends emphasized the gifts he brought her in her drawing.

She drew him bringing her a dress, a book bag for school, and a bag with a notebook, pencil, and eraser placed inside. He is at the center of

Figure 5. A girl's drawing of her father bringing school supplies and clothing as a gift to her.

the picture, the objects he is bringing in orbit around him. The materials for school are highlighted through the bright colors she used. Her drawing thus illustrates what fathers are expected to provide for their children. Such provision of material support is understood to be dependent on a person's ability to give as well as his or her willingness to share available resources with intimates.

Some research on transnational families has argued that migration facilitates the commodification of love because migrant parents attempt to replace emotional intimacy with material goods and remittances. For example, in her study of Honduran transnational families, Leah Schmalzbauer (2004) describes a father who "tries to maintain a connection with his son by sending him toys. Yet, although his son has developed a new love of video games and motorcycles, he still does not understand where or who his father is" (1324–25). A Mexican transnational mother commented, "You can't give love through money"; rather, love "required an emotional presence and communication with a child" (Hondagneu-Sotelo and Avila 1997, 563–64). A Filipino domestic worker in Rome commented on her childhood experience when her mother was a domestic worker in the United States: "If a child wants material goods, they also want maternal love" (Parreñas 2001, 376). Yet other Filipino children of transnational migrants accept commodities, rather than affection, as the most tangible reassurance of their parents' love (Parreñas 2002). The literature on transnational migration from Mexico, Central America, and Southeast Asia suggests that migrants and their children understand motherly love to be maintained through emotional intimacy, communication, and living together, for which the flow of gifts and remittances serves as an imperfect replacement when parents migrate transnationally.

These arguments that transnational families are unsuccessfully replacing love with material goods depend on a discursive and cognitive split of emotions and material resources that is particularly salient in the West. For example, Sharon Hays describes the ideals of the American model of intensive parenting as: "Children should be valued not for the material gains they might bring to their parents but for their goodness, innocence, and inherently loving nature—all of which mark their distance from the corrupt, outside world" (Hays 1996, 125). However, in practice, intimate and economic relations are deeply intertwined. For instance, Peter Stearns and Mark Knapp (1993) have argued that Victorian notions of familial love were bolstered by economic changes that allowed property owners to make the physical home a more pleasant place and central locale, as well as by competitive market relationships that made men turn to emotional support at home. Laura Rebhun points out from her work in Brazil, "kin-ship, friendship, and partnership all combine economic and emotional aspects as people demonstrate love through sharing, and through sharing obtain the goods and services upon which their lives depend. Sharing may be accomplished fairly and equally, or it may be coerced, unfair, unequal, and exploitative" (1999, 210). Furthermore, Rebhun points out, emotion—such as attachment, loyalty, compassion, anger, jealousy, and mistrust—can affect how material resources are distributed and shared among peo-ple. A family's care of children has significant economic costs, requiring commitments that might be undercut by straightforward market concep-tions about investment and exchange (Folbre 2008). Rather than putting economics and intimacy into separate domains or subsuming intimate re-lations to economic ones, Viviana Zelizer (2005) argues that we need to understand how intimate relations and economic transactions intertwine, in inheritance, divorce proceedings, and paid care giving, for example (see also Strathern 1985). As Allison Pugh (2009) has discussed in relation to children's consumption in the United States, a parent can show affection and attachment through providing a child with the consumer goods that give the child dignity among his or her peers.

In the case of Ghana, the logic of care outlined in this chapter empha-sizes the materiality of care between parent and child. The provision of shoes, clothing, houses, and school bags is important in and of itself. In ad-dition, it serves as a signal of emotional depth and closeness between giver and receiver. It creates relations of indebtedness, or entrustment over a life-time, which a child may repay when he or she attains maturity. Although the distribution and sharing of material resources is central to all intimate relations, the economic underpinnings of emotional relationships tend to get downplayed or ignored in the West and in other countries. In Ghana, to the contrary, children are more likely to understand material care as a sign of love, consider it as an obligation they would like to reciprocate, and can praise or criticize a relationship on the basis of economic exchanges, as I shall explore further in chapter 7. This discourse does not result from the commodification of intimacy within transnational families, as scholarship in other regions suggests might be happening, but rather from a repertoire in which material exchanges are central to parent-child relationships.

TWO

Distributed Parenting in the Twentieth Century

The reciprocities of care described in the last chapter depend on a temporal understanding of care. Lifetimes have a certain rhythm, from the dependency of infancy and childhood, to adult roles generating income and children, to elderhood as a time of weakness and sickness. Care flows between people at different stages in their life courses, when they are at different moments of vulnerability and ability. An often-quoted Twi proverb expresses this sense, metaphorically drawing on a person's teeth as a physical sign of age. Mr. Yirenkyi, an elderly man in Ghana, quoted the proverb to me in this way:

> Sɛ wo maame anaa wo papa anaa obi a hwɛ wo na wo se yi aba de a, edu baabi hwɛ no na wei [pointing to his teeth] no ntutu.
> If your mother or father or someone looks after you while your teeth are coming in, look after him or her when his or her teeth are falling out.

A major aspect of giving and receiving care appropriately is attending to the movement of one's own life course in relation to others' chronologies. Individuals, each in their own course and pace of development and decline, in their mutuality of being, feel empathy for one another and have a stake in one another's well-being (Joseph 1994; Sahlins 2010, 2011). People's lifetimes are knitted with multiple others in which differences in personal positions and capacities create possibilities for support, and previously received care and love create the desire to do so. Flows of care can therefore be flexible and temporary, changing in relation to new circumstances, as Catrien Notermans (forthcoming) notes in her research in Cameroon.

The understanding that care is given when one can give and when the other needs it not only affects the timing of care, but also allows such caring to be distributed among many people, according to need and capability. A retired teacher in Akropong expressed his thinking about parenting by quoting a local proverb.

nyɛ ɔbaakofo na ɔyɛn mmofra.
It is not one person who raises a child.

He then translated the proverb into English, "Not one person, [or] one family, takes care of the total education of a child." He supported his point by saying that in schools there were many different teachers, who each taught a different subject.

A Presbyterian minister spoke similarly. He and his wife were taking care of her brother's son, David, because her brother, David's father, was deceased.

Onipa baako biara no, nnipa bebree na ɔbɛboa no ansa na watumi anyin. . . . Enti sɛ obi pɛ sɛ yeboa no a, yɛhwɛ a, yɛhwɛ yɛn sikasɛm na yebetumi aboa no a, na yaboa no akosi baabi, na obi nso atoa so aboa no. Na ɔno nso baa a, na waboa obi. Saa ara na nkakrakakra—Tesɛ efie a yɛwɔ mu yi, mmofra nketewa a ɛwɔ mu ne ade, ɔno sua ade wie a, na wadan ne ho teacher na ɔne wɔn atena ase na wakyerɛ wɔn ade. no nso osua ade ne ɔnte ase a, ɔwɔ problem a, na ɔde aba na yɛakyerɛ no.
Many people help each individual to grow up. . . . So if someone wants us to help, we look at our financial situation and if we can help, then we help them to a certain place, and then someone else takes over. When that person grows up, he will also help someone. That's how we do things. Little by little [we help one another]—Like in this house, with the little children here, when [David] finishes studying, he becomes a teacher, sitting with and teaching them. Or if he has a problem understanding his studies, he brings it to us and we teach him.

These statements reveal how two highly educated people justify the distribution of care for children. Their metaphors, drawing on images of school organization and peer help with homework, are a way of talking about the distribution of children's care that is in the repertoires of many people in southern Ghana. There are several points to be made from their statements. One is that multiple people provide care: children need many different kinds of experiences and expertise, not all of which only one or two people (their parents) can provide. Therefore, and this is the second point, care is flexible and temporary: different people do their bit as they are able and then others take over ("help them to a certain place and someone else takes over"). Care can therefore be temporary: if the situation changes— for instance, if a caregiver becomes sick or needs to travel to find work—a child can be passed along to someone in a better situation to help. Care is almost conceived as a chain in which the child is passed between people who each do what is within their abilities. Third, care is responsive to the care receiver's needs and the caregiver's abilities, changing across their lifetimes and in relation to the larger social, political, and economic environment. For example, David, a teenage boy, can help the younger children in his household, his aunt's children, with their schoolwork. Finally, the possibility emerges that care does not have to be reciprocated immediately or to the caregiver in his or her old age, but rather can be reciprocated by caring for someone else, further along in time ("when that person grows up, he will also help someone"). What is not expressed in these statements is that the caregiver gains respect for being a morally upright person in using his or her resources to care for others.

These care relationships are less like permanent adoption and more like fostering, in American terms: children maintain their relationships with and legal connection to their parents, even as they live with and develop reciprocal relationships with others. The relationship is informal, without legal documents signed. It is called *fosterage* in the anthropological literature of West Africa, and I use that term here. But because the sharing of care for children is so normal in Akuapem, there is no equivalent Twi word for the practice.

This chapter describes how this repertoire of distributing care changed over the course of the twentieth century, drawing on oral histories that I conducted in 2008 with eighty current foster parents—overwhelmingly women—ranging in age from twenty-four to eighty-three years from the town of Akropong, as well as ethnographic and qualitative research on children and fosterage from other towns in Akuapem and elsewhere in southern Ghana from the 1960s and 1970s. The combination of my interviews and other studies indicates that the reasons for children living with people other than their parents have changed over time. Fosterage in the past occurred for a wide variety of reasons, from a child's need for schooling or apprenticeship to a woman's need for domestic help or companionship, in which she asked a grandchild or younger sibling to come live with her.[1] These reasons meant that rates of fosterage increased with the child's age, as a child went to school or was able to help a woman with her household work. Fosterage also enabled mothers to migrate for work, and they would leave behind their small children with their mothers.

The more diverse reasons used for fosterage in the past have today become more restricted, as something that one would only do in crisis or if one were poor. The changes in the ideology surrounding fosterage have left fostered children in a more vulnerable position. Because of the spread of ideals of raising one's own children the educated, urban middle class promoted, fosterage is increasingly stigmatized. The middle-class ideologies that underpin this shift are not considered Western, distinguished from an African, "traditional" practice of fosterage; rather, these differences in ideals of family arrangements are associated with a middle-class lifestyle and Christianity (Fortes 1971; Oppong 1974). Mark Liechty (2003) argues that the middle class in Nepal is a group less defined by its relations to the means of production than by its ability to consume, a definition that applies also to the Ghanaian middle class. Made up of teachers, bureaucrats, retail entrepreneurs, independent artisans, and the like, they are at one step removed from both capitalists and laborers. As a result, they focus on particular modes of consumption to mark themselves.[2] Liechty suggests that "class culture is always a work-in-progress, a perpetual social construction that is as fundamentally bound to the 'concrete' of economic resources as it is to the cultural practices of people who jointly negotiate their social identities" (Liechty 2003, 4). He does not, however, discuss family practices in the construction of class cultures—although others in the United States have (e.g., Lareau 2003)—but instead focuses on media, consumption, and youth culture. Although the ideology of raising one's own children marks middle-class and educated status, it has spread beyond that class. These class ideals create a contradiction for Ghanaians abroad, who mainly come from the educated, urban middle class in Ghanaian society, but for whom fosterage helps resolve certain problems of women's work, women's migration within Ghana, and unequal access to social and economic resources, as fosterage did for their mothers and grandmothers before them.

With the spread of swollen shoot disease, which devastated cocoa trees in the 1930s, there were sharp declines in the returns from cocoa, and cocoa farmers became less prosperous than they had been previously (Brokensha 1966). Furthermore, government programs after independence in March 1957 continued colonial policies that promoted the welfare of urban areas over rural localities, such that urban centers became more prosperous and had better access to services and facilities than villages. These inequalities promoted migration to commercial and metropolitan centers. People drew on their repertoire of distributing children to deal with the increasing importance of schooling, women's migration, the growth of a middle class, and income inequality between rural and urban residents, themes I discuss in turn.

The prevalence of children living with neither their mother nor father has not changed much, hovering around 20 percent of children nationally for the past forty years, and around 50 percent in Akuapem until recently (see tables 1 and 2).[3]

My explanation of why the rates of fostering are higher in Akuapem than in Ghana as a whole is due to the Akuapem research being based solely on schoolchildren: many schoolchildren were fostered in Akuapem because of the area's schools, which were highly respected until the early 2000s, and some research has suggested that fostered children were more likely to go to school than not fostered children (Isiugo-Abanihe 1983).[4] With the exception of one study (Klomegah 2000), surveys quite consistently show that rates of fosterage increase with age. For example, in the 2008 Demographic and Health Survey, 8.0 percent of children aged 0–4 were fostered; 17.3 percent aged 5–9 years; 22.3 percent aged 10–14 years; and 25.4 percent aged 15–17 years (Ghana Statistical Service, Ghana Health Service, and ICF Macro 2009). The 1971 figures in table 1 are only for children under ten, and the figure for older children was likely much higher.

Table 1. Percentages of children fostered in Ghana, 1971–2008

	1971, children under 10 years (1)	1991, proportion of children of female heads of households under the age of 40 years being fostered (2)	1998, children under 15 years (3)	2008, children under 18 years (4)
Children living with neither their mother nor father	19%	25.6%	15.7%	16.1%

Sources:
(1) From the 1971 supplement of the 1970 census, based on surveys of about 5 percent of the population, or 427,966 people; this percentage is no doubt low because only children under ten are included (Isiugo-Abanihe 1983).
(2) From the 1991 Migration Research Study that surveyed 969 female-headed households (Nyarko 1995). This rate of fostering is probably high because female heads of households were more likely to foster their children out than women in male-headed households.
(3) From the Ghana Demographic and Health Survey 1998, a survey of 4,843 women age 15–49 and 1,546 men age 15–59 across Ghana (Ghana Statistical Service 1998).
(4) From the Ghana Demographic and Health Survey 2008, survey of 4,916 women age 15–49 and 4,916 men age 15–59 in 12,323 households across Ghana (Ghana Statistical Service, Ghana Health Service, and ICF Macro 2009).

Table 2. Percentages of children fostered in Akuapem, 1963–2005

	1963, Larteh, Akuapem, schoolchildren (1)	1971, Konkonnuru, Akuapem, schoolchildren (2)	1996, Akuapem North district, schoolchildren (3)	2005, Akropong, Akuapem, schoolchildren (4)
Children living with neither their mother nor father	63.4%	41%	52%	25%

Sources:
(1) From a survey of 690 schoolchildren, or 40 percent of all schoolchildren in primary and middle schools in Larteh (Brokensha 1966).
(2) From a survey on the sleeping arrangements of 61 schoolchildren; the eating arrangements are similar, but not exactly the same (Hardiman 2003).
(3) From a survey of 212 students in three junior-secondary schools in Larteh, Akropong, and Abiriw and in one primary school in Akropong (Ghana National Commission on Children 1997).
(4) From my survey of 1,182 students in three primary and three junior-secondary schools, Akropong, Akuapem, July 2005, out of seven primary and five junior-secondary schools in Akropong.

Fosterage for Schooling and Training

One of the reasons a parent might send a child to live with another person is for schooling or to train the child to work hard and learn how to do housework. In fact, someone who is not a parent is seen as better at disciplining a child because he or she is not swayed by affection for the child and because the child will be more respectful of someone less familiar. Educated people—such as teachers and nurses—were (and continue to be) favored as foster parents, because they—through their disciplined routines, education, and understanding of "modern life"—were seen as being able to provide a particular kind of training for children and adolescents that uneducated or poorly educated parents could not. Educated persons' association as ideal foster parents continued a long-standing practice of the Basel missionaries in Akropong, who took schoolboys into their houses to be domestic servants from the 1840s onward (Coe 2005; Haenger 2000). As with the training European missionaries and African pastors provided, training by educated people in the late twentieth century was seen as helping a child become educated and middle class; fosterage was a way to change a child's repertoire and increase his or her cultural capital.

Akuapem has long been associated with education, with higher rates of education earlier than many other parts of southern Ghana. For example, according to the 1960 census, among those older than fifteen years, 71 percent of males and 40 percent of females in Larteh had at least some education, compared to national figures of 29 percent and 11 percent respectively (cited in Brokensha 1966, 242–43). In the late nineteenth and early twentieth centuries, the missions trained skilled craftsmen and artisans in addition to teachers, pastors, and nurses. Educated people were respected in Akuapem and elsewhere in southern Ghana (Brokensha 1966); they served as brokers of international commercial trade and were chosen for secure, high-status jobs as civil servants. In Akuapem people's discourse, education made one "modern" and "civilized": tidy in one's personal and household appearance, literate, Christian, attentive to schedule and time, and polite and respectful in one's demeanor. Civilization is designated by the Twi term *anibuei*, literally "one's eyes are opened," a term associated with the West but which has become localized as the description above suggests. Fosterage was a strategy to help one's child become upwardly mobile through education, Christianity, and the performance of disciplined behavior associated with a mission education.

A good friend, a relatively uneducated woman in her sixties, expressed some of the reasons more commonly used in the past in her discussion with me about fosterage.

Me idea *ne sɛ, ebia, na* mother *no pe sɛ ne ba no kɔ baabi na ɔkɔ hu* changes, *sɛ wote ase? Na osua ade yɛ, papa, ebia ɔpɛ sɛ osua nhoma. yɛ bia na ɔte* teacher-*ni bi nkyɛn,* time *wɔ hɔ a wode bɛyɛ w'ade bewie, wowɔ* time *a wobesua ade. Ebi wɔ hɔ a, ɔwɔ* mother *no nkyɛn a, onsua ade, ɔnyɛ hwɛɛ, ɔbɛkɔ abɔnten akɔ goru kɛkɛ. Enti sɛ ɔwɔ obi nkyɛn de a, obesua ade papa, obesua fie ade yɛ, obesua ade nso, wuhu? wɔ* time *a ɔde bɛyɛ n'ade. Na ɔwɔ* mother *no nkyɛn a, ommua* mother *no, onsuro no, ɔnyɛ ne hwee. Enti ɔtee no sɛ gyae saa de yi yɛ anaa yɛ saa ade yi a, ɔrennyɛ, na ɔwɔ obi nkyɛn de a, osuro, ɔbɛyɛ!*

My thought is that, perhaps, the mother wants her child to go somewhere and experience different things, you see? Like learning housework very well, or perhaps she wants the child to be educated. So perhaps she[5] goes to live with a teacher, and when she finishes her chores, she has a scheduled time to study. In some cases, a child living with her mother doesn't study and doesn't do anything [in terms of household work], but just goes out in the street to play. But if she lives with someone else, she will learn to do the right thing: she will learn how to do housework, and she will also study. She has a schedule to do these things, but if she is living with the mother, she doesn't respond to her mother's requests, she is not shy with her mother,[6] she doesn't do anything for her mother, so if her mother tells her to stop this or do that, she won't do it. But if she is living with someone else, because she feels shy of the person, she will do it!

Because children might not always listen to their own parents, because of the familiarity and affection between them, some people in Akropong, particularly older people, felt that someone other than a parent could better educate or discipline children. Another woman of about the same age (fifty-nine years) similarly felt that someone who was educated could give a child an understanding of some of the "civilized" or "modern" ways of doing housework and behavior. She attributes her son's appropriate demeanor today to his staying with a female teacher when he was younger.

Oow kyerɛ sɛ, wahu sɛ, sɛ wo ba nso tena obi nkyɛn a otumi nya anibue foforɔ bi ka n'abrabɔ ho. Sɛ wahu nea mekyerɛ no? Yiw. Efi sɛ ebia ɔwɔ me nkyɛn a, sɛnea respect a ebia obenya wɔ me nkyɛn no, ɔwɔ obi nkyɛn a, obenya respect more than that, sɛ wahu? Mhm. ɛno nti nso me ba no sɛnea, ɔɔyɛ boy, nanso ɛfa sɛ saa rough, rough, a boys no yɛ no wonhu no sɛ—ɔmfa saa ekuw no mu koraa. You see, if your child lives with someone else, he will gain a bit more civilization in his way of behaving. Do you see what I am saying? Yes. Because if he was with me, he would be respectful all right, but he will become more respectful if he lives with someone else, you see? That is how it was for my child; he is a boy, but he isn't disrespectful ["rough rough"] like some other boys and he doesn't associate with those kinds of boys at all.

The teacher helped her son through to the end of secondary school and ultimately helped him find a job in Accra, a success story indeed.

In interviewing adults about their childhoods, a common reason to live with someone other than their mother or father had to do with geographical location rather than issues of discipline: their parents were farmers in a village without a school, and their relatives lived in town where there was one. Children had been fostered for this reason since the early twentieth century, as suggested by a court case in which an Akuapem young man was fostered with a man in Accra in order to go to school there (*Charles Amponsa for Ya Odi v. Adu Kumi*, April 29, 1919, ECRG 16/1/15).

Although in the early twentieth century children and wives lived in the farm villages to care for the cocoa farms and the interplanted food crops, by the mid-twentieth century children lived in town to attend school, in either the care of their mother, another relative, or a teacher, while the parents or fathers stayed at the farm village where there might be no primary or middle school. By the 1940s and 1950s, men deserted the towns on the Akuapem ridge and stayed mainly near their farms (Brokensha 1966; Kaye 1962, 153).[7] Some of these farm villages, like Tinkong, were located in the valleys below the towns on the Akuapem ridge and were only a few hours' walk away; others were farther to the west of the Eastern Region capital, Koforidua, and were several hours' travel by lorry (*trotro*), the means of public transportation. A thesis by W. Otu on child socialization in Larteh from 1955 reports, "Many of the parents in Larteh live for a greater part of the year in the villages where they farm. There are therefore many school-children who stay in the town with their aunts, grandmothers, teachers and other relatives and friends who occasionally receive substantial help from the parents of the children" (cited in Kaye 1962, 156). In 1963, among schoolchildren in Larteh, 28 percent said that their fathers lived in Larteh, 32 percent of fathers were in their farm villages, and 40 percent were in the cities or elsewhere (Brokensha 1966). During the cocoa boom when farmers could be relatively wealthy, the parents were the ones to pay their children's school fees while the foster parent in town took care of their daily expenses.

A seventy-nine-year-old pastor from Akropong whom I interviewed in 2008 (he was born circa 1931) recounted how he lived with his parents at their farm village until it came time for him to go to middle school in the 1940s, when he began living with various family friends in the nearest town, Suhum, located to the west beyond Koforidua, in the Eastern Region. Another seventy-nine-year-old, a daughter of Akuapem teachers living and working in a village in the Brong Ahafo Region to the north and west of Kumasi, lived with an Akuapem teacher in the nearby town of Berekum to go to middle school, visiting her parents in the village on weekends.[8] E. O. Walker, a Larteh resident, told Polly Hill, the geographer who doc-umented the Akuapem cocoa migration, in 1958 that the children who stayed in Larteh to go to school visited their fathers over the holidays, with the lorries full of children going to the farm villages at the end of term (Information given by E. O. Walker, October 7, 1958, the Polly Hill Papers, Box 4, Folder 7). Hill (1960) also noted that she met an Akropong farmer who lived in his farm village at Bepoase who was helped by his brother and his wife during the year, and his children joined him during school holidays to help out. Schooling thus curtailed children's labor in the farms and households of their fathers, although they contributed as they could.

As rates of schooling increased in the 1950s and 1960s, school fostering with nonrelatives continued to be significant among my Akuapem infor-mants. The Gold Coast gained internal self-government in 1951, winning full independence in 1957, under the leadership of Kwame Nkrumah and the Convention People's Party (CPP). The CPP government was determined to expedite the development of the country, and one of its first budgetary proposals concerned education. Under the Accelerated Development Plan for Education in 1951, which aimed to provide some schooling for every child, the 1950s were characterized by the rapid expansion of primary schooling, as tuition fees in primary schools were abolished (although textbooks and uniforms were still costly), and new classrooms and schools were built, bringing schools to rural areas. Across Ghana, over 132,000 children began their schooling in January 1952, more than twice the number of the previous year, and by 1957, the number of children in primary school nationally was double that of 1951 (McWilliam and Kwamena-Poh 1975, 83–84). In 1961 in the Akuapem town of Larteh, 86 percent of children of school-going age were enrolled in school (Brokensha 1966).[9] Fostering enabled children to live close to schools located in the towns, while parents (particularly fathers) remained closer to their farms in the villages.

As more middle schools were built in the villages during the 1960s, the practice of school fostering shifted, illustrating how practices available in people's repertoires did not completely disappear but rather that their meaning changed. It meant living with an older sibling or sibling of a parent who was willing to help with the costs of schooling, rather than living with someone who was located near a school. These reasons are of course difficult to disentangle. As the revenue from cocoa farming declined, farmers were increasingly poor in relation to others, while those who lived in a town were more likely to have a ready source of cash with which to pay school fees; they also lived near a school. Although earlier school fostering entailed the child's parents paying for most of the child's expenses, now the foster parent paid those costs. For instance, a fifty-eight-year-old grandmother (born ca. 1950) said in her childhood that she had lived with her mother's older sister in Akropong to go to school. Her childless aunt had a store in Akropong and paid her school fees and all the costs of her care. She took her aunt to be her mother, feeling more love for her than for her mother, but she visited her mother, a farmer in a village near the town of Suhum, on some of her school vacations and helped her farm.

Fostering as a strategy of child raising existed prior to the mid-twentieth century, but it was mobilized to help provide children over the age of six with an education, as Esther Goody (1982) has described, increasing children's movement into the households of relatives and nonkin. Fostered children were slightly more likely to be in school than nonfostered children in 1971 (Isiugo-Abanihe 1985). My older interviewees, in their late seventies, raised far from Akuapem in the 1940s, went to live with strangers for their schooling, because there were no relatives available; they relied on family friends and a teacher from Akuapem (a fellow national, so to speak). By the 1960s, as schooling became more widely available and more children were expected to go to school, children of that era—now in their fifties—went to live with relatives who would help pay for their schooling or launch them into a trade, and children would visit their parents on holidays, helping them on their farms. An older sister, an aunt, a maternal uncle, or an educated person such as a nurse, pastor, or teacher were all valued foster parents. Fostering for the purpose of proximity to school became less necessary; instead, economic necessity became more prominent.

Maternal Employment and Migration

In the 1960s and 1970s, an increasingly important reason for fosterage was to support women's work and migration. Work participation rates among Ghanaian women are high; in 1979–80, 92 percent of women who were married or had been married aged twenty-five to forty-nine were working, in farming or other occupations (Blanc and Lloyd 1994; Isiugo-Abanihe 1983). Similarly, in 2000 the labor participation rate for women over the age of fifteen in 2000 was 87 percent compared to 88 percent for men of the same age (Heintz 2005). Despite their high labor participation rates, women's poverty rates were much higher than working men's because of the informal commercial and agricultural sectors in which they mainly worked.

Women of all social classes were expected to work and have many children. In 1968 the fertility rate was an average of 7.1 births per woman, but by 1996 it had dropped to 4.6 births per woman (Ghana Statistical Service 2005; Gyimah 2006; United Nations 2003). Ghanaian women age fifteen to forty-nine expressed an interest in having between 3.8 and 5.4 children in 2003, with younger women having an interest in a fewer number of children than older women, and urban fewer than rural women (Ghana Statistical Service 2005).

The goals of fertility and making a living are not viewed as incompatible for women, as they sometimes have been in the United States (Moe and Shandy 2010). Instead, having children is perceived as a reason to work, because one needs to be able to feed one's children (Clark 2001). Women predominantly work in trade, skilled production (as seamstresses and food and beverage makers), and agriculture, all self-directed forms of work that allow mothers some flexibility. A tiny few work in formal employment, in which education is the primary criteria (6.2 percent of women in 2000; Amu n.d.). Despite their small numbers, the educated women employed in the formal sector loom disproportionately large in the literature on fosterage in Ghana. Because formal employment was a less flexible work environment and resulted in transfers across the country, women in formal employment relied on fosterage to coordinate their reproductive and productive lives.

Income-generating work for women, whether in the formal or informal economy, was associated with migration, particularly to urban areas. Towns in Ghana grew rapidly after World War II. There were far more economic and commercial opportunities available in the cities than there were in the villages, which became increasingly associated with poverty. "Poverty in Ghana," wrote a Ghanaian economist about the 1990s, "is essentially a rural phenomenon" (Vanderpuye-Orgle 2004, 12). Towns, on the other hand, were the symbol of civilization, modernity, and status. As in much of the Global South, development in Ghana has been quite uneven, with social services, infrastructure, and employment concentrated in urban areas, particularly in the capital city of Accra. The seat of government administration, Accra is also the site for the sole international airport in the country, is provided with port facilities through the nearby planned city of Tema, and contains approximately 50 percent of Ghana's commercial and industrial enterprises (Konadu-Agyemang 2001). Eighty-four percent of all foreign companies established in Ghana since 1983 are headquartered in the capital, Accra, because of its proximity to international transportation hubs, financial services, and government ministries (Pellow 2002). Nearly 70 percent of all senior-level public-sector jobs are located in Accra (Konadu-Agyemang 2001, 51). Because of the opportunities for work in the formal and informal commercial sector, cities in Ghana grew rapidly in the latter half of the twentieth century. Although it was clear that the towns were growing rapidly in the 1960s, one study reported, "this movement is only one part of the complex and apparently interrelated migration pattern in that country. In addition to the influx of people into the larger towns, there are extensive movements—both permanent and temporary—between rural areas, and considerable immigration from neighboring West African countries" (Transportation Center 1964, 1).

Drawing on the 1960 census and surveys he did in 1962, John Caldwell (1969) estimated that a third of the rural population in southern Ghana had taken part in some form of urban migration, with males, young adults (aged fifteen to twenty-four), and the more educated more mobile than their contemporaries. In 1960, 10 percent of those born in the Eastern Region went to Accra, the capital and the largest city in Ghana (Transportation Center 1964). In the Akuapem town of Aburi, "one household explained, 'Everyone is struggling for existence, and, since there are no jobs in the village, they should go into the big towns for jobs'" (Caldwell 1969, 90). Although the towns on the Akuapem ridge were decidedly not villages, they too lost their young people to the cities and other rural areas because of the scarce employment opportunities in Akuapem.

Migration was for work, for men and women. Because men tended to migrate first in the early days, migration led to spouses living apart, until women could join their husbands in town (Caldwell 1969). Although women in previous generations had migrated, as part of the cocoa migrations described in the last chapter, they had mainly done so for their husbands' sake, to work on their cocoa farms. However, in the 1960s and 1970s, women began to migrate by themselves: Lynne Brydon (1979) notes that although a previous generation of women from Avatime in the Volta Region migrated mainly to join their husbands, about half of the migrant women she surveyed in 1977 migrated primarily for work. From my data it seems that this change happened earlier for Akuapem women, given their educational levels and proximity to Accra. These work migrations were seen as a temporary sojourn: both male and female migrants sent remittances to their relatives in the hometown and hoped to return there to live out their days (Caldwell 1969).

In order to facilitate their labor migration, female migrants relied on two kinds of fosterage: grandmother fosterage of the child, and the fosterage of a child helper. Broader demographic studies show that migrant mothers—whether going to rural or urban areas—were slightly more involved in both fostering-in and fostering-out than those women who had not migrated (Blanc and Lloyd 1994; Isiugo-Abanihe 1983, 1985; Twum-Baah, Nabila, and Aryee 1995). Fostering-*out* often meant grandmother fostering; fostering-*in* meant acquiring a child or adolescent helper.

Grandmother Fosterage

Living with a grandmother was common for children across the generations, but for the older women I interviewed, raised in the 1940s and 1950s, the rationale given for doing so was providing assistance to the grandmother: housework, companionship, and errand-running. For these reasons, the child was usually old enough to help out around the house. One seventy-year-old woman was sent to live with her paternal grandmother in Akropong because her father had only brothers and they wanted a girl to help their mother. A sixty-eight-year-old woman went to live with her paternal grandmother, after whom she was named, so that she could be sent on errands. Both these women attribute their lack of or delayed start to schooling to being fostered with their grandmothers because their help was necessary for the household. Lynne Brydon (1979) describes a similar situation in Amedzofe in which children served as helpers of the elderly, helping maintain their independent households in old age, an important marker of dignity (van der Geest 1997).

Beginning for those in their fifties, raised in the 1960s and 1970s, grand-mother fostering became conceived as more of a help for the mother of the child than for the grandmother. Grandmother fostering allowed a young mother to seek work in an urban area because she could leave behind her child or children. Brydon saw this as a new form of fosterage in Amedzofe in the late 1970s, because such children were sent to live with the grandmother after weaning; they were much younger than the usual fostered children. Migrant women who used grandmother fostering were more likely to be young, unmarried, or separated. For example, a fifty-three-year-old woman described how she lived with her grandmother in Akropong as a child in the 1960s because her mother was working in the market town of Nsawam and had remarried, while her brother went to live with their father. Grand-mother fostering was also common among women who were transferred every few years because of their or their husbands' civil service employment, because they wanted their children to have a more stable living situation. A forty-seven-year-old nurse (born ca. 1961) described how her mother, then a young, unmarried woman, gave her to her grandmother after her birth. She stayed with her grandmother because her mother worked for the so-cial welfare department in Kumasi and was often sent to different stations across the country. She never knew her father, and in fact, her grandmother treated her as if she was her youngest, last-born child. A seventy-year-old woman (born ca. 1938) described how she was married to a soldier who was sent on transfers, and so their first two children stayed with her mother, probably during the 1960s. One woman in her thirties said she went to live with her grandmother because her father didn't look after his children. And a woman in her twenties stayed with her maternal grandmother because her mother went to work in Takoradi, a port city in the Western Region.

These oral statements indicating the prevalence of migrant mothers leaving their young children in the care of grandmothers support other studies of fostering among urban female migrants in West Africa in the 1960s and 1970s, by Lynne Brydon as already mentioned, Mona Etienne (1979) in Côte d'Ivoire, and Barry Isaac and Shelby Conrad (1982) among the Mende of Sierra Leone, and by later research by Caroline Bledsoe and Uche Isiugo-Abanihe (1989) in Sierra Leone and Céline Vandermeersch (2002) in Senegal.

The significance of grandmothers in helping their daughters' work continues today. One woman in her seventies taking care of five grandchildren in Akropong in 2008 explained why she did so.

> Sɛ, sɛbe, sɛɛ mewɔ hɔ a mewɔ ahooden yi de, na wo ba no wo a, ɛsɛ sɛ wutumi boa no kakra na ɔno nso, sɛ ɔkɔyɛ adwuma bi wɔ baabi koraa na watumi ayɛ biribi saa, na sɛ mmofra no wɔ ne nkyɛn a, ebia aban adwuma, ɔbɛkɔ adwuma, enti ɔbɛsɔre, ɔbɛhwɛ mmofra no ne ade no, na wayɛ late, enti ɔkɔ koraa adwuma no onnya no sɛnea ɛsɛ sɛ onya no. Me nso seisei, Onyame adom, menyɛɛ aberewa yi enti na ɛsɛ sɛ meboa mmofra no kakra, na ɔno nso tumi nya na kakra a, obenya no na ɔde aba.

> If my child has given birth and I am alive and able, I have to help her a little so that she can go out to work or find something to do. If not, I would have done wrong. If the children are with her, then if she is going to work, perhaps government work, then she will get up, get the children ready, and she will be late to work. Even if she makes it to work on time, she will be frazzled. By God's grace, I haven't become an old lady yet [in terms of her strength and health], and so I should help out with the children so she can get a little something to bring home.

As she suggests by the "little something," grandmothers are reliant on the remittances of these and other working children for their and their grandchildren's sustenance. Grandmothers are supported by remittances from a range of people, such as their brothers or other children, not just the parents of the children in their care.[10] Although their grown and working children would be obligated to help their mother in any case, they are prone to provide more assistance and more regularly if their mother is looking after one of their children. The parents of the children in the grandmother's care may visit more often, bringing cash and groceries whenever they come;[11] women also help with cooking and laundry on their visits. Grandmothers support the mothers to work, but they also secure their own livelihood, because the mother is likely to remit to them: "grannies mind small children in order to strengthen their links to the parents of the grandchildren" (Bledsoe and Isiugo-Abanihe 1989, 462; see also Brydon 1979). Fostering helps connect those who migrate to those who stay behind (Etienne 1979).

It is less clear whether the grandmother receives direct assistance from the fostered child. As infants and small children, the grandchildren cannot help their grandmothers, but as they grow, they can help with household chores and be a companion to the grandmother. However, some evidence suggests that grandmothers are associated with the care of babies, and that as children grow older, they go to live with their parents or other relatives. For instance, in Konkonnuru, an Akuapem village, in 1971, 34 percent of surveyed primary-school children were living with their grandmothers, but none from among the middle-school students surveyed, suggesting that grandmother fostering was more common among young children than among older children. As children got older, they were more likely to live with other relatives—a father's brother or mother's sister—and nonrelatives, who were found only among upper-primary and middle-school students (Hardiman 2003).[12] D. K. Fiawoo (1978) showed that in two communities he surveyed—Kaneshie, a neighborhood of Accra, and Mampong in the Ashanti Region—grandparent fostering constituted two-thirds of fosterage cases for children under the age of seven, but only 11 percent of those aged seven to fifteen years.

One of the reasons is that grandmothers are viewed as poor disciplinarians who spoil children. Thus they are viewed as appropriate caregivers for the early years of life but not as children grow up and require discipline. Because grandmothers are physically weaker than younger adults, people say older children and adolescents are not afraid of their threats of physical punishment. Furthermore, a grandmother may want to go to bed early, giving children the opportunity to roam about the streets late at night. In one junior-secondary school I visited in Akropong in 2005, a teacher scolded the students who lived with their grandmothers, taking it as an explanation for why they were not doing well in school. As an elderly woman grows too sick or weak to take care of small children, their other children—the grandchildren's aunts or uncles—might step in to take over the care of any grandchildren in her care. The attentive grown children of an elderly woman are attuned to the multiple timelines—of her abilities and needs, the needs of the children in her care, and their own financial situation—that might allow them to take over the care of all or some of those children as she grows older and weaker.

However, some children did stay with their grandmothers throughout their childhoods. Agnes Klingshirn (1964) studied eleven children in different households in Larteh, four of whom had come to live with their maternal grandmothers as babies and were still living with them, at the ages of five, seven, ten, and thirteen. In the last chapter, I quoted a fifty-three-year-old woman from Akropong who said that her grandmother looked after her until she was an adult, and then she in turn looked after her. Thus some children did remain long enough with their grandmothers to reciprocate their care. In general, grandmother fosterage built on older patterns of fosterage, but the reasons changed in the 1960s and 1970s to support younger women's migration and work. This resulted in a shift to a younger age of child fosterage. Through fosterage, some grandmothers received a companion and assistance with daily living, but primarily, they received economic and social support from the parents of the children they fostered.

Fostering a Helper

The second way that fosterage was used to help a mother's employment was when a woman who had migrated for work would take a child into her household to help with chores, including raising her own children. This strategy was more common among educated and married women who were formally employed and among women married to men in formal employment, but was also important for women who were traders, who appreciated having an assistant to hawk goods around town (Schildkrout 1973). All the Akropong women I interviewed who were in their forties or older and went as a helper to another household had gone to live with their older sisters and their husbands. For instance, a woman in her seventies had gone to live with her older sister and her husband, a policeman, who moved around frequently on transfers. A sixty-year-old woman described how, when she was about ten years old (around 1958), she went to help her older sister after her sister married and had a baby:

> Na meyɛ abɔfra kakra na me nua panyin no kɔware, na wɔn nso wɔkɔ akyin, ɔtontɔn ade nti na ɔwo a, na metu—na mete ne nykyɛn na meturuw ne ba no ma no na watumi akɔ guaso. Na meyɛ aduan ma mmɔfra no.
> When I was a little girl, my older sister got married. She was a trader and she took things around to sell, so when she gave birth, I carried—I lived with her and carried her baby on my back[13] so she could go to the market. I made food for the children at home.

Some of the girls who helped out their older sisters in this way were rewarded by having their school fees paid for or being sent to learn a trade, although that was not the case for this particular woman, to her life-long disappointment. A forty-eight-year-old woman (born ca. 1960) went to live with her older sister, a nurse, for twelve years, finishing middle and secondary school while staying with her. Describing her sister's reliance on her in the household, because of her sister's employment, she said that she helped prepare the meals of her sister's husband, something husbands usually insist that only their wives prepare. Thus young and teenage women

helped their older and adult sisters combine work and their household responsibilities, at the same time as their older, more educated sisters might
help them go to school.

The option of bringing a helper into the household was more expensive
for mothers than leaving their children in the hometown with a grandmother, because the cost of living in town was higher and housing space
scarcer. This second form of fostering to support mother's work was hard to
distinguish from children's domestic service. Maidservants, children living
with distant kin or nonkin, were common from the 1960s onward in educated households in Accra, and have featured prominently in West African
fiction about elite households (Goody 1966; Reynolds 2006; see also Moran 1992). One study from 1974 found that all twenty "educated" households in Accra surveyed had at least one maid (Bain 1974). The maids'
average age was 14.7 years, and only seventeen of the ninety-three maids
in these households were reported to be related to the father or mother. In
a survey of fifty fostered children in a middle-class neighborhood of Accra
in 2001, twelve (or 24 percent) were domestic servants (Ametefe 2001).
Children who are domestic servants today tend to be in their mid- to late
teens, having completed junior-secondary school (nine years of schooling).
These arrangements are associated with the child being treated differently
than other members of the household, such as getting cheaper food and
not sleeping in the same bed as the other children in the house, key images
of difference and separation. Domestic servants are asked to do the heavy
household work, such as the laundry or fetching water, and are worked
hard, from the early hours of the morning to late at night. They are vulnerable to sexual abuse by men in the household, and they may feel lonely
and isolated. The benefits of these arrangements for the child—wages or
further training—are seen as illusory or difficult to obtain, conditional on
abusive levels of service for several years. These arrangements reveal a transformation in fosterage that is occurring across West Africa, in which more
attenuated ties between foster parents, the child, and the child's parents
can lead to a child's maltreatment, in which the reciprocities of care are
manipulated and abused (Alber forthcoming; Argenti 2010).

Although domestic servants have a long history in elite and middle-
class, urban households, Akuapem children did not seem to participate in
this kind of domestic service until recently. Of those I interviewed in Akropong in 2008, only women younger than forty and from poor families
mentioned living with a nonrelative or distant relative in an urban area
during their childhoods, suggesting that the practice became more common in the 1990s. A thirty-four-year-old woman (b. 1975) lived with a

friend of her father's cousin for two years in Accra. A twenty-nine-year-old (b. 1979) worked for a teacher at a secondary school in Akropong for two years, and she used her pay to buy a sewing machine. A twenty-eight-year-old (b. 1980) went to live for four years with a child of a sibling of the head of the family—a distant relative—in the port city of Takoradi, until she got pregnant by a son in the household, at the age of seventeen. A twenty-seven-year-old woman worked for two nonrelatives in Accra, from the ages of eleven to seventeen (ca. 1992–98). That Akuapem young people began working as housemaids in the 1990s indicates the growing prosperity of the elite in urban areas during this time period.

Although reasons for fostering in the past were numerous—from discipline and schooling to companionship and service—the major reasons today highlight the class distinctions between the households of the birth and foster parents; a foster child is associated with domestic service. The reasons to foster-out a child today are also more negative—based on what a birth parent lacks—than in the past, when the reasons centered on what an alternative caregiver or household needed in the way of labor or could provide a child by way of better training or further schooling. These reasons also put foster children in a more vulnerable position, subject to abuse, which is then used to critique fosterage negatively as a practice. In my discussion about fosterage with an old friend, a woman in her fifties who sold used clothes in the market, she said:

> *Ɛfa kɛsɛ no yɛ ahokyerɛ na ɛma obi de ne ba kɔma obi sɛ ɔne no tena. Sɛ anka ɛnyɛ ahokyerɛ de a, ɛyɛ me sɛ obiara nni hɔ a, ɔbɛwo ne ba sɛ womfa no nkɔ ntena.*
>
> A major reason why someone sends his or her child to live with someone else is poverty. If there was no poverty, it seems to me that no one would give away a child he or she has born to live [elsewhere].[14]

She added that many cases of fostering in Abiriw, a smaller and poorer town that borders Akropong, occurred because the parents did not have work or because one parent had died. Her vehemence in this matter may have been because she herself was barely making ends meet as a single mother who was trying to put her daughters through secondary school, which, because of their boarding facilities, were more expensive than primary and junior-secondary school. Yet her general sense was reflected in the comments of others I met in Akropong. It is also borne out by data from Accra, collected by Elizabeth Ardayfio-Schandorf and Margaret Amissah (1996). In a survey of fifty fostered children in three Accra neighborhoods in 1994, they found that 88 percent of the surveyed fostered children came from low-income families, and only 12 percent from high-income families. Although not all the children were fostered in high-income households, low-income households tended to bring in fewer children—one child, rather than the two or three of high-income households.

Mr. Yirenkyi, a retired teacher in his seventies, added marital problems to the reasons why parents might send their children to live elsewhere, although he also highlighted financial issues as a cause.

Na εtɔ da bi a, na there are problems, problems in marriage, *enti na mmofra ebi kɔ ha. Afei ɔyε ebia, m'adwuma asee. Me* wife *nso ɔkɔ* retirement. *Yεn* last born *wɔ* SSS. *Yεn* pension *entumi mmoa yεn, enti se yεwɔ onua bi a, yεwɔ wɔfa bi a, yese kɔtena wɔfa hɔ eh.* At least *woprapra ne dan mu anɔpa biara a na ɔno nso wahwε wo.*

Once in a while, there are problems, such as problems in a marriage [divorce or separation], so that is why children are scattered. Maybe I have lost my job and my wife is retired, and our youngest child is in secondary school. Our pensions don't go far enough, so if there is a sibling or maternal uncle available, we can say [to the child], "Go stay with your uncle, so at least if you sweep his room [symbolic of all household chores] every morning, he will look after you."

Cati: *Wobedidi.*

You will eat.

Mr. Yirenkyi: *Afei eyε ebia.* These are helping hands, *enti na yεma yεn mma kɔtena baabi foforo, na εmom anka, ne* totally no, *eye se* parents *baanu bεyεn abofra no,* the way they want the child to grow. It is the most perfect way of rearing, caring for children.

Maybe so [in response to my comment]. They are helping hands, and so we let our children live elsewhere, but otherwise, really, it is better for the two parents to raise the child in the way they want the child to grow. It is the most perfect way of rearing or caring for children.

His statement reflects the sense that fosterage is associated with children moving from living with parents who are poorer, unmarried, less healthy, and in crisis to others who are healthier, wealthier, married, and in more stable circumstances, as is true of adoption and foster parenting in the United States. This does not mean that the woman or man who takes in a child is necessarily rich or does not have any troubles, just that he or she is slightly better off than the biological parent. Fosterage is more clearly tied to the distribution of wealth and power within and between families now.

As fostering has become associated with poverty or crisis, it has become increasingly stigmatized, first by those who were educated, but now increasingly across social strata in Akropong. As Mr. Yirenkyi said, fosterage has become the less favored option, resorted to when "the most perfect way of rearing children"—by the parents—is not possible. Perhaps this critique explains why surveys indicate that fosterage declined in Akuapem between 1998 and 2008.

Looking after One's Own

The discourse of the nuclear family—being raised by one's parents—has a long history in Akuapem because of the Basel Mission that arrived in Akuapem in the 1830s. Although Christians were more likely to live in nuclear family arrangements than non-Christians, it is doubtful that this arrangement was prevalent even among ministers and teachers. For instance, reflecting on marriage and migration in the Twi-language Basel Mission newspaper, *Kristofo Senkekafo*, an African Christian commented in 1895 that Christian men who traveled to seek work often left their wives and children behind (Oben 1895). He advised them to stay away no more than a month or two in their travels; if the trip lasted longer, then his wife and children should come with him to help in the work. Ministers and teachers were often peripatetic, moving from one mission station or school to another in the course of their careers, and would not always take along their wives and children (Kwamena-Poh 2005). Still, over the course of the twentieth century, the Christian discourse on the nuclear family became increasingly important. Because being educated meant becoming Christian, Christian discourse shaped educated people in Ghana.

Discourses about raising one's own children are not associated with the West in Akropong, but rather have been localized, connected, on the one hand, with powerful personal transformations and, on the other, with a sense of what is right, in the grand scheme of things. Jean Comaroff (1985) describes a process of symbolic bricolage as the Tshidi Tswana of southern Africa appropriated Christianity. The process of localization of Western ideals of the family has similarly occurred through syncretic bricolage in which various signs and elements of colonial everyday life, Christianity, and practices of distributing children were fused into a new middle-class identity. One ideological thread contributing to the discourse of the nuclear family is charismatic Christianity, an increasingly powerful force in Ghana since the 1970s and a bricolage of missionary Christianity and traditional religious practice. These new and popular forms of Christianity are particularly focused on rooting out the Devil's influence on people's lives. Because one way the Devil can affect a Christian is through his or her contact with less God-fearing relatives, many of the solutions prescribed by charismatic pastors involve separating Christians from their extended family members. "The aim of deliverance sessions is to turn people into individuals who are independent of and unaffected by family relations," Birgit Meyer argues in her insightful study of these churches (1999, 170). A second strand involves the desire to live a middle-class life as represented by colonial and postcolonial government-built housing: a detached bungalow surrounded by a garden and enclosed by a fence or wall. Finally, educated parents are concerned with the intergenerational transmission of cultural capital: they seek to have their children grow up in a disciplined and "civilized" way, which they feel they can best provide.

This version of the nuclear family differs from conventional Western ideals in that they are willing to bring the children of less fortunate relatives or nonrelatives into their households to be helping hands, give them familiarity with educated ways of behaving or the city, and send them to school, thus enlarging their households, but they are not happy to foster their own children out (Ardayfio-Schandorf and Amissah 1996). A woman in her late forties said that her mother, the wife of a policeman, brought her siblings' children to live with them, but did not send her children to live elsewhere. Analyzing the 1971 supplement to the 1970 census, Uche Isiugo-Abanihe (1983) found that women educated through secondary school were less likely to foster-out their children than women with no education, some primary-school education, or some middle-school education; 8 percent of the children of mothers with a secondary-school education were fostered.

One woman who was taking care of her brother's son explained why educated people were less willing to foster-out their own children:

Though, sɛ kan no de, wode—wo nua bi wɔ ha, wose, kɔ ne nkyɛn, kɔ sukuu wɔ hɔ, kɔtena ne nkyɛn, ebia boa no adwuma yɛ. Na seisei no, sɛ abofra no ne ne papa—Mprempren asetena yi de, sɛ abofra no ne ne papa yɛ adwuma na ne maame yɛ adwuma a, wɔremma wɔn ba no bɛkɔ baabi. Wɔpɛ sɛ wɔn ankasa ara bɛ-train wɔn ba, sɛ wote ase? Seisei de, education enti, ɔmma ne ba no nkɔ baabi, efisɛ ɔkɔ baabi a, ebia, onipa baako bɛyɛ no, ɔno ɔrenyɛ ne ba saa.

Although, in the past, if your sibling was alive, you would say to your child, "Go live with him, go to school there, maybe help in his work." But nowadays, if the child's father—the way things are now, if the child's father and mother work, they don't want their child to go live elsewhere. They want to train the child themselves, you see? Nowadays, because of education, one doesn't let one's child go live elsewhere, because maybe if he goes there, the way that person would treat the child is not the way the parent would do so.

As she suggests, educated and salaried people would rather raise their own children, because they would like to socialize their children into a middle-class lifestyle. They are worried that a foster parent may treat the child like a servant, not giving him or her enough to eat, thus making the child into a thief by stealing food or encouraging bad company through seeking food from other people. Or the foster parent may beat the child too harshly. Her point compares both the past (*kan no*) and the present (*nnansa yi*) and the uneducated and the educated simultaneously, as if they were one and the same. While more people are more highly educated today than in the past, there were highly educated people in the past who held the view she describes, and there are younger, less educated people today who have also embraced it.

Among those with whom I discussed this issue, some people in Akro-pong held very strong views that a child's biological parents are the best caregivers. They were all younger than fifty, but people from previous generations also alluded to this perspective. For instance, a seventy-year-old woman from Akropong, describing why she lived with her parents during her childhood, said that her father, a farmer, did not want his children to live with anyone else because he thought they would be maltreated. A fifty-two-year-old woman from Akropong whose father was also a farmer gave a similar reason.

> *se na ɔmpɛ se neba bɛkɔ akɔtena obi nkyɛn, woba, wode woba kɔtena obi nkyɛn a, sɛ abɔfra no obi wɔ hɔ ɔbɛyɛ no papa, obi wɔ hɔ nso a ɔnwhwɛ abɔfra no yie. Enti ɔno bɛhwɛ n'ade.*
> He said he didn't want his child to live with someone else, because some treated the child well but some did not. So he would look after his own.

More commonly, informants talked about this unease with their children rather than about their own childhoods. Three women raising their children during the 1960s and 1970s described their or their husband's concerns about having someone else raise their children. A woman raising her children in the 1960s said she wouldn't want her children to live with someone else because she was concerned that they would not eat well there. Another woman married to a Presbyterian pastor said that an elder brother had maltreated the pastor during his childhood and so he refused to have his children live with someone else. A third, a teacher, said that she wanted her children to get good training, which she could better ensure in her own household.

The growing emphasis on raising one's own children means that the support of siblings and other relatives has become less important. Shirley, the wife of a secondary-school teacher I met in Akropong and raised in the regional capital of Koforidua, said:

> Oow sɛ wɔ mo nyinaa, obiara na ɔhwɛɛ ne ba, wɔ mo a obiara hwɛɛ ne ba koduu baabi. . . . Enti obiara pɛ sɛ ɔbɛhwɛ n'adeɛ, mhmm, ɛna wobetumi ahwɛ w'adeɛ yiye ama wadu n'anim, saa!
> They [my siblings] all look after their own children; they all look after their children to a certain level. . . . So everyone wants to look after their own, to look after their own well so they attain higher heights—that is it!

What is ironic about her statement is that the daughter of Shirley's sister had come to help her when Shirley had given birth to twins. Shirley's niece was able to go to secondary school at the institution where her husband taught. However, barring an unforeseen event, Shirley did not anticipate her own children going to live with her sister or other siblings. Although siblings may help one another in crisis, many people in urban areas increasingly expect to take care of their own children.

Although the ideals of raising one's own children extend beyond the educated, urban middle class to nonsalaried workers, those in the urban middle class are more likely to be able to live up to its ideals. Their poorer relatives, on the other hand, may have to rely on kin or nonkin to help provide their children with what they need. Thus the most common reason given for fosterage in Akropong today has to do with the relative financial strength or social stability of the foster parent in comparison to the parents.

Conclusion

Like other African kinship practices (Clark 1999), fosterage is a flexible practice. It allows people to shift the care of children when they need to, as their and others' life circumstances change. This has been particularly important for women, on whom the care of children has increasingly fallen (Ardayfio-Schandorf and Amissah 1996) and who are more dependent on their connections to others because of their poverty (Robertson 1984; see also Coe 2011b). Women who have migrated within Ghana and who work, have used fosterage to promote their productive and reproductive lives simultaneously. As a result, over the past fifty years the meaning of fosterage has changed. Although companionship, training, and schooling used to be the dominant reasons for fosterage, at least in Akuapem, two forms seem to be dominant today. One is grandmother fostering, in which older women support their daughters' work and migration by taking care of young grandchildren, in part to enable their own well-being through their daughters' remittances and visits. The second is associated with social and economic inequality, in which children are fostered out of a parent's need—their poverty, as my informants eloquently explained—to someone who needs the child's labor. Since the 1990s, young women from Akropong have been domestic servants to distant kin and nonkin in large metropolitan areas.

Fostering-in, whether of domestic servants or dependent kin, and not fostering-out one's own children are signs of class status. First promulgated by Christians, building on older ideologies in which rich and powerful people had large followings bolstered by slaves and pawns, this ideology became dominant in the educated and urban middle class before spreading to less educated, nonsalaried workers in Akuapem. The latter are not always able to live up to the ideals of raising their own children, partly because they are most in need of the flexibility across their life courses that fosterage offers.

The materiality of care described in the last chapter and the distribution of child raising described in this one are practices and ideas in the repertoires of Ghanaians, on which they can draw when they migrate internationally. As we have seen, some of these practices were shaped by patterns of migration within Ghana, such as the cocoa migrations of the early twentieth century and the labor migrations of young women beginning in the 1960s. This history makes clear that these practices do not disappear but rather shift and change form, with some new meanings emphasized and others downplayed. As Ghanaians migrate abroad, as we shall see in subsequent chapters, this repertoire of child raising opens up possibilities that facilitate their labor migration but also makes some options painful. In using their repertoire in the world, they further change it. The next four chapters will detail the impact of American immigration laws, international adoption conventions, and social and economic conditions in the United States that have meant that Ghanaians abroad depend on fostering-out their children even when they, as former middle-class, urban residents in Ghana, would rather look after their own.

THREE

International Migration and Fosterage
How US Immigration Law Separates Families

When Ghanaians migrate abroad, they draw on their repertoires, which include kinship practices such as care expressed through material exchanges and distributed parenting. Ghanaian migration to the United States has largely been a phenomenon of the urban middle class, those who would rather not foster-*out* their own children but are willing to foster-*in* others' children. Yet many of them are neither able to raise their own children, nor are they able to foster their younger siblings or nieces and nephews. This and the next two chapters explore the main reasons why.

One reason is US immigration law, which leads to the separation of spouses from each other and parents from their children, not only for Ghanaians but for other immigrants also. What makes this paradoxical is that US immigration law and policy seem oriented to support family reunification. After all, two-thirds of legal immigration to the United States occurs under the auspices of family reunification rather than for the purposes of employment or asylum. Furthermore, the US government has supported family reunification since 1921. If, like many East Asian and Arabian Gulf countries, the United States had mainly guestworkers, who had two- or three-year visas conditional on their employment but could not bring along their dependents (Constable 2007; Gamburd 2000), one would expect long-term separations between migrants and their families. Why would separated families also be common among migrants to countries like the United States whose immigration policies favor family reunification in contrast to other routes of legal entry?

An Urban Middle-Class Migration

Going abroad to the United Kingdom, France, or the United States for an education has long been a pathway to elite status in West Africa (and in other African countries, as in the example of President Barack Obama's father). In the decades prior to and after independence, those who were educated abroad for a few years often returned with high status and to a government position, primarily because they had been educated abroad. In Ghana, the United Kingdom, as the colonial seat of power, has historically been the prestigious place to go, although the first president of Ghana, Kwame Nkrumah, went to Lincoln University and the University of Pennsylvania in the United States (1935–45). Working to support himself through school in the Chester shipyard, in a soap factory, and as a dishwasher and waiter on a ship, he appropriately titled the chapter of his autobiography (1957) describing his experiences in the United States "Hard Times." He, more than most students abroad, returned to the Gold Coast in glory, to participate prominently in the movement leading to Ghanaian independence.

Going "abroad" dominated adolescents' and young adults' dreams about their lives in the late 1990s and early 2000s. One day in 2002, I walked into an elementary-school classroom in Akropong to find a drawing of an army helicopter with the Ghanaian flag on the chalkboard. Drawn in pastel chalk colors by students during the break, amid sums and work from regular lessons, its caption read "Ghana Airways to America." The helicopter representing Ghana Airways has the Black Star from the center of the Ghanaian flag displayed prominently; both the Black Star and the Ghanaian flag are common pieces of iconography in students' drawings.

"America" and "London" function symbolically as key sites of "abroad," or *Aburokyiri* (Van Hear 2002). In children's eyes, "abroad" is considered to be high in the hierarchy of place, more like a city than a village, with greater opportunities, status, wealth, and physical infrastructure, as I have discussed in greater depth elsewhere (Coe 2012a). In their drawings, children in Akropong found it easier to represent the physical infrastructure than their expectation that they would be able to work and get rich abroad. They drew life abroad as full of beautiful plants and flowers, technology such as cars and airplanes, high-rise buildings, and schools with many resources. For instance, a sixteen-year-old girl drew and labeled a ship shaped like a fishing canoe in the colors of the Ghanaian flag, an airplane with similar helicopter features to the airplane in "Ghana Airways to America," a public water spigot, and large buses traveling down the road in her "Picture of

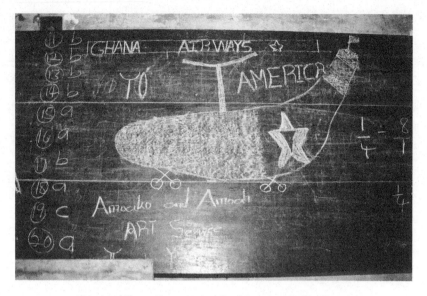

Figure 6. "Ghana Airways to America," drawn on the blackboard
by students in a primary school in Akropong. Photo by author.

London," copying a photograph that her uncle, an international migrant,
had taken there.

Although education loomed large in the initial international migration of Ghanaians, later and larger migrations were prompted primarily by
economic reasons. Economic considerations for migration began to dominate with the economically stagnant and politically unstable period of the
1970s and 1980s, which caused teachers and other professionals to migrate
to Libya and Nigeria, both booming with oil wealth (Twum-Baah, Nabila,
and Aryee 1995). International migration to the West increased substan-
tially after the World Bank and the International Monetary Fund instituted
structural adjustment programs in Ghana in the 1980s and as Ghana began to experience economic growth in the 1990s. Structural adjustment
programs particularly hurt the urban middle class, many of whom earned
government salaries. As in other countries in Latin America and Southeast
Asia (Parreñas 2004; Sassen 1998), such structural adjustment programs
instituted as conditions for future loans were aimed at helping Ghana repay its existing debts to international banks by reducing government ex-
penditure for social services and creating an attractive environment for
private investment in revenue-generating enterprises, particularly related to
export industries.

Figure 7. A girl's "Picture of London," with buses, a public water spigot, an airplane, and a large ship shaped like a canoe and in the colors of the Ghanaian flag.

Ghanaians not only began going abroad in greater numbers in the 1990s but also began traveling farther afield, including to Dubai, Israel, Jamaica, Japan, and South Africa. Almost one million Ghanaians were estimated to be living outside their country in 2005, representing about 5 percent of the population of twenty-two million people. Most of them went to other West African countries that are part of the Economic Community of West African States (ECOWAS), which makes travel between these countries easier, similar to the European Union (Benneh 2004; International Organization for Migration 2009). The United States and the United Kingdom each receive 5 to 7 percent of Ghana's emigrants, with migrants usually using an initial migration to another country in Africa such as Togo, Nigeria, Botswana, or Gabon to enable a migration to a more developed country (International Organization for Migration 2009).

Many of the Ghanaians I knew in the United States mentioned economic concerns as the reasons for their migration, although a few left because of their political allegiances in the 1980s and early 1990s. Many had had high-status and stable employment in Ghana: they worked in a bank, a port, a hotel, or government offices; they were teachers and nurses, secretaries and electricians, customs officials and social security administrators. However, their pay was not enough to support their families, a definition that primarily included their children and their parents, but that could also extend to their siblings and siblings' children. A woman who now works as a live-in certified nursing assistant in the United States was formerly an employee of the water and sewage department in Ghana. Despite her stable, government job, she complained that the pay was terrible, so she could not feed her three children three times a day, as she would like to, or make her pay last until the end of the month. Another migrant, a former research assistant at a major university in Ghana, talked to me about the cost of school fees for his children. Before he emigrated, he supplemented his income by teaching French part-time. He remarked, "If you see the pay given to workers, it's something very scanty. So it is very hard for an average man to care for, say, two or three kids at school. It's very difficult." A former secretary at a bank talked about how the little money she sent back home was a major contribution, whereas when she was working in Ghana, even though members of her family—such as her brothers and sisters—were working, what they could contribute to their mother as a group was not sufficient.

> Even today, I'm going to send my Mummy money. If I send $100, it is [so much in cedis] and she is already full. You see? So the time I was [in] Ghana, you know everybody is working, in the family, everybody, but the little we contribute, we all combine, still it doesn't reach [it is not enough]. You are here, you are blessed. You are blessed that when you get the strength to work and you send [money] home, your family too will be blessed.

Although migrants may have difficult lives abroad, of struggle and loneliness, long hours of work, and poor housing conditions, particularly if they do not have appropriate papers, once they are established, after a year or so, they are relatively wealthy in comparison to family members back in Ghana because of the exchange rate between the dollar and the Ghanaian cedi and the differences in the cost of living. Thus even if migrants can save the equivalent of $100 a month to send home to their families, this is generally far more than someone in Ghana could. Ghanaian international migrants are exceptional in their remittance behavior, with one survey finding that they send on average $380 and do so regularly thirteen times a year (Orozco et al. 2005), far more than those within Ghana remit (Mazzucato, van den Boom, and Nsowah-Nuamah 2005).

Of the thirty immigrant parents I interviewed who talked about their place of residence before their migration, nineteen (63 percent) lived in a major metropolitan area in Ghana (Accra-Tema, Kumasi, or Sekondi-Takoradi) prior to migrating to the United States. Seven of the total (20 percent) had completed university, a smaller proportion than the 31 percent of the Ghanaian-born surveyed in the American Community Survey (2006–8), which is given annually by the US Census Bureau to a subsection of the US population. Given that about 20 percent of workers in Ghana are salaried (International Labour Organization 2006) and only 9 percent of Ghanaians completed tertiary education in 2009, which now includes teacher training and technical vocational education as well as university (UNESCO 2010), migrants to the United States represent a highly educated group. Many migrants I met were already the ones on whom the rest of their families depended before they migrated abroad, and they helped their siblings, parents, nieces, and nephews regularly and in times of crisis. Those who migrated were therefore by no means the most desperate or the poorest; in fact, they seemed to mainly be members of the urban middle class. They are thus similar to other immigrants to America, who mainly come from middle-income countries (such as Mexico, India, China, and the Philippines) and are not the poorest strata in those countries (Georges 1990).[1] It is primarily those living in urban areas in southern Ghana who can raise the capital and have the connections to migrate (Adeku 1995).

Furthermore, it is members of that class who have dreams of a Ghanaian middle-class life—including a particular vision of their family life—that they have not been able to sustain on their salaries in Ghana, but which they hope to create through their remittances from abroad. For example, one secondary-school student mentioned that one of the positive aspects of her father's migration to the United Kingdom was that it allowed him to build his own house. "Before he was going, we were living in a compound house with different people [nonrelatives and other renters]. But now, when he went, like, we built our own house." When I asked what this change meant for her, she elaborated, "Like, in our own house, like we are not living with any other people apart from my family."

US immigration law has further contributed to the emigration of the urban middle class in Ghana. African immigration to the United States has increased since the 1990s, in part because of the passage of two immigration laws. The Immigration Act of 1965 did away with long-standing quotas that discriminated against citizens from countries not in Western Europe. However, even more significant was the Immigration Act of 1990, which established a green card lottery for nationals of countries with historically low rates of immigration to the United States, known as "the

Table 3. Ghanaians obtaining legal permanent resident status by broad class of admission, 2010

Total	Immediate relatives of US citizens	Diversity lottery	Family-sponsored preferences	Employment-based preferences	Refugees and asylees	Other
7,429	4,393 (59%)	2,086 (28%)	527 (7%)	264 (3.6%)	135 (1.8%)	24 (0.3%)

Source: Office of Immigration Statistics 2011, Table 10, p. 28.

diversity lottery." Every year, fifty thousand permanent resident visas (or green cards) are made available through this lottery to foreign nationals who have completed the equivalent of high school or several years of work in a skilled craft. Although these diversity immigrants, as they are known, account for a small share of legal permanent admissions to the United States (4.8 percent of green cards in 2010), African nationals received 41 percent of diversity lottery visas in 2010. Twenty-eight percent of Ghanaians who received legal permanent resident status in 2010 obtained it through the diversity lottery (see table 3).

The educational and work requirements, as well as the processing fees, help to screen out those who do not belong to the urban middle class. The table also shows that, as is true for two-thirds of all permanent residents, the most common route by which Ghanaians receive a green card is through a family member who already has permission to live and work in the United States as a citizen or permanent resident.[2] Sixty-six percent of the 7,429 Ghanaians in 2010 who received green cards obtained them through some form of family reunification. Most (59 percent) were "the immediate relatives"—the spouse or unmarried children under the age of twenty-one—of American citizens, probably of Ghanaian origin. "Immediate relatives" are automatically eligible to immigrate upon approval of their application. An additional, much smaller, number (or 7 percent) received a green card through the broader category of "family-sponsored preferences," as the spouse or unmarried children of permanent residents, as well as the more distant relatives of citizens. In all cases, the sponsor must demonstrate his capacity to support his relatives financially above the poverty level and provide proof of their relationship.[3]

US immigration law is based on the assumption that immigration is a one-time, permanent step that leads naturally to citizenship. For this reason, for Ghanaians as well as other immigrants, family reunification looms large as a pathway to legal residence and work, particularly for workers who fall outside the very narrow categories by which one can obtain a work-based temporary visa, which would better suit their reasons for migrating.

To illustrate how a system oriented around family reunification can keep children and parents apart in practice, I want to share the experience of Afua. When I talked to her in 2005, Afua was a twenty-five-year-old woman attending community college and working as a nanny in the suburbs of a major city in the midwestern United States.

Family Separation through Family Reunification: Afua's Story

Afua's father had been the first of her family to emigrate from Ghana to the United States, in 1993. He had left Ghana when his contracting company was being stymied by the government because he belonged to a rival political party. The government had seized some of his equipment, and he feared for his own safety. He came to the United States on a visa for religious personnel,[4] through his involvement with an evangelical fellowship in Ghana that now has branches in the United States.

Afua told me, "See my dad left, and left us with our mom, and we were with her for a period of two years, so we were more attached to her." Afua was the eldest of five children. Two years after her father left, in 1995, her mother won the opportunity to apply for a green card through the diversity lottery, run by the American Embassy in Ghana. Winners of the diversity lottery do not automatically receive green cards. Rather, they are given the opportunity to apply for green cards for themselves, their spouse, and unmarried children under the age of twenty-one years (their "immediate relatives"). The lottery winner and his or her immediate relatives have to be healthy, vaccinated, and free of a criminal record; not be considered a security risk; and have a sponsor who can guarantee that the new immigrants will not require government assistance such as food stamps (US Citizenship and Immigration Services 2010a). The immediate relatives had to be listed on the applicant's initial diversity lottery application, but in some cases, Ghanaians mistakenly do not list them because they feel that having many people on the application will damage their chances. In Afua's case, she, her three brothers, and one sister were all listed on their mother's application.

Applicants also have to pay an application fee, set currently at $330 per person.[5] While many Americans would find such a sum daunting, it is even more so for Ghanaians, whose average *yearly* earnings in the late 1990s were equivalent to $575 (Kingdon and Söderbom 2008).[6] As Afua's mother worked for a regional department of education, her salary was likely higher than that of the average Ghanaian, perhaps as much as the equivalent of $942, the average annual salary of Ghanaian public servants. The cost of applying for six green cards was simply too expensive for a religious worker in the United States and a midlevel government bureaucrat in Ghana. Afua explained, "They *couldn't* bring all five of us [children] because of financial problems."

The reason the fees are so high is that the US Citizenship and Immigration Service, which handles applications for permanent residency and citizenship, is funded primarily by the revenue generated by application fees. As of May 2012, the current fees associated with getting a green card for a single relative outside of the diversity lottery add up to $1,405 (US Citizenship and Immigration Services 2012a).[7] Such official fees are usually only the tip of the iceberg, as applicants also spend money on brokers, lawyers, transportation, and the necessary documents. For example, Mary, a permanent resident in the United States, whose story I detail further below, had sponsored her three children living in Ghana. A home health aide, she estimated she had spent $15,000 on their applications, including lawyers' fees; the fees for her children's DNA testing at a special, trusted facility in Ghana and all their vaccination shots; and the application fees for their green cards.

Because of the expense involved, sponsors sometimes file for only one person at a time. Once the sponsored person receives permanent residency status and is working abroad, he or she begins the process of applying for others. For instance, one boy in a private school in Kumasi told me that his father was bringing over his family one by one.

> Ade koro nti a mewɔ ha ne sɛ, me papa aka akyerɛ me sɛ papers ho yɛ den nti waba abɛfa me maame kɔ. Nnansa yi ara na ɔbɛfaa me maame nti ɔse sɛ me maame ba a, na wɔn aka wɔn sika abom nti mentwɛn sɛ mewie sukuu a na waba abɛfa me kɔ.

> The reason I am here is that my father has told me that getting the proper documents is hard, so he was only able to take my mother with him. He has just taken my mother abroad. Once she is abroad, they will be able to combine their earnings. So I should wait [to join them] until after I finish school and they will take me with them.

The cost of the application fees is one reason that children remain behind in Ghana years after their parents have migrated. Because distributed parenting is in the repertoire of many Ghanaian migrants, they turn to it as a creative strategy for coping with the costs and legal hurdles of emigration, even if they would rather take their children with them.

Afua's mother did not want to foster-out her children. However, given that she did not have the money to take all her children at once, she tried to design the transition so that it would be minimally disruptive. Afua's mother decided to take the two youngest children, aged five and eight, with her, leaving behind the three eldest—Afua, then age fifteen, and two younger brothers, ages thirteen and eleven, in the care of her younger sister.

As we saw in the last chapter, a more well-established and older sister with a spouse and children often brought a younger sister into her household to help out and to enable the younger sister's upward mobility. Afua's younger aunt had stayed with the family previously in such a situation. This scenario was therefore an option available in the repertoire of Afua's mother, but the problem was that Afua's mother would be away. Another option was sending her children to live with her sister, but this was not attractive because her sister lived and worked in a village.

Afua's mother proposed a creative variation on the first strategy in her repertoire. She brought her sister to live with her children in her house in Kumasi; because Afua's mother left with her youngest children, her younger sister became the everyday head of the household. Because I did not have an opportunity to speak to Afua's mother, I do not know her reasons for choosing this step, but other parents have made similar decisions and in explaining them to me highlighted the importance of their children staying in an urban area, where there were better educational facilities and minimal disruption to their daily lives.

> Afua: We didn't go to live with our aunt; she actually moved.
> Cati: To stay with you?
> Afua: Yes. Because we had a big house and everything. My mom, my parents were actually paying for her rent and everything; she wasn't spending her money on anything.
> Cati: And they were sending money back to pay for you and of course that was paying for her food and other things?
> Afua: She never had to use anything, her money, on us—anything. [My mother] asked the question, "Who do you want [to live with you when I go]?" And looking at her family, this particular aunt was the youngest. And before, we used to be very close to her. She had actually stayed with us before, when my parents were here. And we were very connected to her in so many ways. She was a teacher; she would teach us stuff. We actually liked her. So that was the first name that came.

As Afua's recollection makes clear, Afua's mother did several things to make the process as positive as possible. She consulted with her children about whom they would like to take care of them. She chose a sibling who was a teacher, fresh out of teacher-training college, who would be able to raise her children in the way Afua's mother expected. Faced with taking some of her children but not all, she fostered-out her older children; as national surveys show, older children are more likely to be fostered than younger ones. And finally, the aunt was a young woman, without a family of her own, who was mobile and flexible in her place of residence. Through her connections at the education office, Afua's mother was able to get her younger sister transferred from her station in a remote village to a school in Kumasi so that she could simultaneously work and take care of her niece and nephews. Based on my discussions with other newly minted teachers, the sister's move to the city would be seen as in her own best interests, because she would be able to have greater creature comforts that might be unavailable in the village (running water and electricity being key), and because she might be able to further her education through the numerous educational facilities available in the metropolis.

Afua's mother also thought that her sister's stay would be temporary, lasting only a few months. Afua explained:

> The Embassy told them that within a period of six months, they could bring out the three of us, that is, the older ones, they could bring us here [to the United States] if they are able to get their resources together in a period of six months. . . . So they left, you know, thinking that, you know, within— 'cause my mom told us that they were going to try and within two, three months, we would join her. Because we actually went to the interview [at the American Embassy] with her. So we were thinking it was going to be very easy.

Afua's mother hoped that after a few months of employment in the United States, she would be able to raise the money to bring over her older children. Afua reported that they all thought, "We're not going to be separated after all; we're going to be together." However, that was not to be.

Afua continued her story:

> So after three months, you know, they were ready to get us here, but we were told by the Embassy that things had changed, their policies and everything had changed, so they couldn't bring us anymore. So, yeah, they got a law-

yer and they tried and tried and tried, but I guess, you know, it just wasn't possible.

In their frustration and confusion about the process, many immigrants turn to expensive immigration lawyers and brokers, many of whom provide useful advice. Some, however, are fraudulent, taking immigrants' money without filing anything or derailing legitimate cases with false claims (Coutin 2000; Nazario 2006). In Afua's case, to her knowledge as an adolescent at the time, the lawyer was not fraudulent, but their attempts were not successful.

As a result of winning the diversity lottery, Afua's mother had received a green card and was a permanent resident. Unable to bring over her three older children through her initial visa application in the diversity lottery program, Afua's mother, as a permanent resident, could apply for "family-sponsorship" visas for her children. Permanent residents can sponsor their spouse and unmarried sons and daughters; adult citizens can sponsor, in addition, their parents, siblings, and married children.[8] However, a person eligible to immigrate to the United States through family sponsorship must wait until a green card becomes available, because there is a quota of green cards given out each year. Furthermore, a preference system governs the order in which these green cards become available, in which certain categories of relatives—such as the adult[9] unmarried sons and daughters of citizens—take precedence over the spouses and children of permanent residents or the siblings of citizens. There are quotas for each category of relatives, and no one country can receive more than 7 percent of the total number of green cards given out.

Because there are more qualified applicants than there are green cards available, there was a backlog of relatives waiting for a green card under family sponsorship until recently. In March 2010, the Consular Section of the Department of State was processing family sponsorship applications that had been filed between four and twenty-two years previously (US Department of State 2010a). Those with the shortest wait were the minor children and spouses of permanent residents; Afua and her siblings fit this category. For this category, applications that had been received in April 2006 were being processed in March 2010, as were the applications of adult, unmarried children received in February 2002. Also in March 2010, the applications of unmarried and married adult sons and daughters of citizens that had been received in 2004 were being processed, as were those of the brothers and sisters of citizens filed in 2000. People from the countries that have the most applications—China, India, Mexico, and the Philippines—

have the longest wait, because of the 7 percent country restriction, with the longest wait time experienced by the brothers and sisters of citizens from the Philippines, over twenty years. It then takes an additional period of time for the application to be reviewed and approved, or denied. By April 2012, the US Citizenship and Immigration Services had drastically reduced wait times, such that it was only five or so months behind on its applications (US Citizenship and Immigration Services 2012b), but the longer wait times were more characteristic of the period when Afua's parents were applying for her and her brothers.

Because of the backlog for family sponsorship visas, one way that permanent residents can speed up the processing of immediate relatives is by becoming American citizens. Afua said, "So, my mom, her only hope was to be a citizen and then file all together again for all of us."

I responded, "Wow. But that took several years? That took five years?"

Afua said, "It took over five years." A permanent resident can only apply for citizenship after five years of continuous residence in the United States, and the processing of the application takes an additional period, currently around five months after that, although it took longer in the past when Afua's mother applied (US Citizenship and Immigration Services 2012b).[10] Afua observed, "So, you know, when she also left, thinking that, oh, we're going to see her in like two months or whatever and, you know, it was years and years and years."

During this time Afua and her two brothers continued to live with their maternal aunt, who got married and had a child of her own. However, there were tensions between Afua's aunt's husband, who acted like the head of the household, and Afua's children. Afua said:

> When she [her aunt Constance] moved, before her husband moved in, things were okay. When he moved [in], he was like, she always listened to him. He was authoritative: "You guys should listen to whatever I say. You should do this, you shouldn't do that. I should choose the friends you go out with." It was like, "Who are you?" You don't just come and take over like that. It was, really! There were times we wouldn't listen to him. For [Constance], she had to choose between her husband and her sister's children.

To take the husband's viewpoint, he may have seen it as part of his role to discipline the children as the male adult and head of household. However, because Afua's children had not moved into another household as fostered children and they saw the household as dependent on their mother's remittances, they treated their mother as the head of the household and their aunt's husband as a usurper. As tensions increased, Afua's aunt, Afua, and her brothers all grew more distant from one another, causing Afua to affirm middle-class notions of family, in which parents are the best source of affection and training for children.

> Living with my aunt is not like living with your parents, you know. I would say that it really had much effect on my brothers. . . . They lacked that parental love. Before, my mom really loved us. That was almost the only thing she could do, like, call us and talk. Almost every Sunday, she would call. We've been so attached to her than to my dad [who had left earlier]. . . . My aunt wasn't so, so nice to us. We didn't really get all the *love* from her. It was more like each one for himself. You do whatever you have to do to survive. That was really hard.

While an application for citizenship is pending, the applicant cannot leave and reenter the United States without special permission, called, ironically, "advance parole." Furthermore, applicants tend to delay returning home as they scrimp and save, preparing for the expenses of the application and for their relatives' arrival. They calculate long-term savings against frequent visits. For example, a woman who has lived in the United States for ten years without authorization[11] had been joined by her husband who had received permanent residency status through his brother a year and a half ago. He had looked after their three children back in Ghana during her absence, but they had decided it would be better for him to join her in the United States so that they could both earn money and because the separation was hurting their marriage. She told me that her husband could go visit their three children back in Ghana, as she could not, because he was a permanent resident, but they have decided it is not worth it. They would rather remit the money they would use up on a visit to those in Ghana. Her three children in Ghana, on the other hand, long to see their parents and their new baby brother, born after their parents reunited.

Airfare to Ghana is expensive (about $1,500 round trip from the New York City area, depending on the season). To travel to Ghana, migrants have to take time off from work, resulting in a loss of income as many do not work in employment that offers paid vacations, and they are expected to contribute money to many friends and family members when they return to Ghana. One survey found that most Ghanaians in the United States spent between one and three thousand dollars on a visit to Ghana (Orozco et al. 2005). Bringing a child or spouse for a short visit or school holidays to the United States might also be possible, but it can be difficult to obtain a visitor's visa for them, because authorities at the American embassy fear that visitors will overstay their visas, the most common way for Ghanaians to live and work in the United States without authorization. Therefore, family members do not see one another for many years during the waiting period. Only after Afua's mother became a citizen, in 2002, did she visit her children, for a month, once in the seven years between her departure and the arrival of her children in the United States. In part, she returned to Ghana because she was concerned about Afua's application.

By then Afua was twenty-two years old. Afua said, "Eventually, by then, I had finished secondary school and started college," studying computer science at a private university in Accra. Because she was over the age of twenty-one, she was considered an adult in the eyes of US immigration law. She was therefore no longer considered an immediate relative of a citizen, eligible for immediate receipt of a green card as her younger, still minor, brothers were. Instead, as the adult, unmarried child of a citizen, she fell under the family sponsorship program once more, although she had first priority as a relative of a citizen, higher than she did as the child of a permanent resident. In Afua's words, "Because, then [when my mother left], I was fifteen. When I turned eighteen, um, I mean, it kept changing because, you know, she [my mother] would start something and then, they would say, because of her age, she can't come." However, her application under the family sponsorship program was approved relatively quickly. "You know, God being so good, finally everything went through. I went to the Embassy and do all this, go for all these shots, do a HIV test[12] and all these things." Fortunately, she and her mother looked alike, so the pictures of her mother were sufficient to prove their relationship when she visited the American embassy, and she did not have to do a DNA test, which would have required additional time and expense. "So then, you know, when everything went through, I just forgot everything [leaving her studies] and I came here [to the United States]."

In the midst of such happiness at being reunited with her mother, father, and younger siblings, tragedy struck. Afua's mother died two months after Afua arrived in the United States. Her two younger brothers got approval through their application as the immediate relatives of a US citizen to come only after their mother's death, without seeing their mother for seven years except for the one month when she had visited them in Ghana. Afua said, "What I was holding onto, eventually we would come over here, be a family again, and everything would be fine. That was what

I was hoping for, we'd all come together again, be what we have always been. This thing would just be a period and it will be over with. It never really happened."

The mother's death tore the family apart. Grieving, Afua's father went back to Ghana with the youngest child, now old enough to attend secondary school, and later remarried there. The four oldest children remained in the United States, living in a suburban house the father had bought before he left and trying to combine college with part- or full-time work. Afua decided not to return with her father to Ghana because she hopes to apply for medical school one day and thinks, probably correctly, that her chances for medical study are better in the United States than in Ghana. She is concerned about her middle brothers, whom she thinks ought to be attending community college but are working instead. She thinks they are not dedicated to furthering their education because they grew up without sufficient love and attention during their mother's absence; in her words, they lacked "parental control."

From Afua's story of coming to the United States, we have a sense of how financial constraint, the categories of persons, and administrative backlogs combine to keep Ghanaian parents and children separated for many years. Immigration laws define family members in specific ways, as "immediate relatives" or more distant ones, and as adults or children. Relations need to be proven biologically and genetically, through the use of DNA testing or photographs that show facial resemblance, and through documents such as marriage and birth certificates. That biological criteria such as a DNA test are viewed as more verifiable than social relations has a long history in social policy in the United States (Duster 1990). Although some of these characteristics are fixed in the identity or body of a person, others change over the period of time it takes to apply for someone: minor children become adults and are therefore no longer considered immediate relatives.

To deal with these hurdles, Ghanaians turn to their kin to help distribute the care of their children, but in ways that represent adaptations of their existing repertoire. In some cases, these creative enactments work out well, as I discuss further in chapter 7: some children highlight the "parental love" they receive from a grandmother or married-in uncle. In others, when they do not, the children left behind focus on how only parents can provide the affection and training a child growing up needs. In this case, the separation was extremely painful because a key member—Afua's mother—became sick and died just as the family was almost reunited. Legal pathways to citizenship and green cards for family reunification did finally allow this family to live together in accordance with their middle-class ideals of family, as it did for other Ghanaian families I knew, but more slowly than the course of a mother's disease and the rate of her children's development. When they were finally able to "come together" as "a family," to use Afua's words, they no longer wanted to, because of the degree of emotional pain caused by the separation and its tragic aftermath.

Documentation of Relationships: Mary's Story

People's eligibility for various kinds of legal status is dependent on their personal characteristics or history—their relationships, nationality, education, and experience of persecution—but to be accepted as deserving of belonging to a particular category of persons, they must prove that characteristic through documentation and a paper trail. As Susan Bibler Coutin, an anthropologist working on Salvadoran immigration (2000), has noted,

> Forms must be submitted by particular deadlines, documents must be translated into English, fingerprint checks must be obtained, the proper number of copies of all documentation must be submitted, documentation packets must be numbered and paginated according to local rules [that may be unfamiliar to applicants]. (53; see also Hagan 1994)

A life must be made legible, and legible in ways that are comprehensible to immigration authorities. Even when a person's application is otherwise viable, and they are eligible to become a permanent resident or citizen, a request for particular documents can derail an application.

For instance, Mary has been a permanent resident of the United States for fifteen years, mainly working as a home health aide for the elderly and disabled. She was once married to an American citizen with whom she had a son, also an American citizen, who in 2009, at the age of eight years, was being raised in Ghana. She and her husband divorced when she learned that he was an alcoholic and was using up all her money, even after they separated, because he could garnish her wages. Their separation and divorce may have resulted in the failure of an application for her three older children from a previous marriage with a Ghanaian now living in Botswana. Her older children, in their late teens and early twenties, were living with Mary's mother and stepfather in a house Mary had built on the outskirts of Accra. More recently, like Afua's mother, Mary applied for citizenship as a way of bringing over her older children.

At her citizenship interview, Mary was asked for documents she did not have: a title to the house she had in Ghana and receipts for the past five years for the money she had remitted home to care for her children, with affidavits and photos from the people who had received and spent the money for the children's care. This request was quite unusual, surprising Mary and her lawyer, as they had not heard of such a request in other, similar situations. It was unclear to her what these documents had to do with her application for citizenship. She did not have the receipts for the money she had remitted, and she had sent much of the money home through different family members and friends, so she worried that she would be unable to provide the requested documentation and the affidavits. As for the title to the house, Mary was told by her contacts in Ghana that she would need to pay $1,000 to get a deed for the house. Such official documents, relatively easy and cheap to obtain in the United States, require personal connections, multiple visits, and bribes to key officials in Ghana. For example, although birth certificates are now given automatically when births take place in formal health facilities, only 51 percent of births were registered prior to 2006, for those parents who took the initiative to do so (Mba et al. 2009).

Because Mary did not have that sum of money, and she wanted to use her existing savings to finance her children's higher education, she was considering giving up her application for citizenship. But I spoke to her at a low moment, shortly after her citizenship interview, because she later got the title to her house through her friendship with a local chief and pulled together what affidavits and receipts she could. At her return interview, she was granted citizenship, to her great delight, and began the process of applying for her children, an effort in which she was successful eighteen months later. Another woman, married to a permanent resident who was applying for citizenship, was asked to provide three years of tax receipts on a business she had previously owned in Togo, which borders Ghana. As Coutin (2000) has noted, papers and documents become as important as a person's life history in determining eligibility for a particular status.

The emphasis on documents within immigration services comes from several sources. At the basic level, having to provide documents and pass physical tests to prove personal information is critical to the audit cultures that permeate institutions and bureaucracies in Western societies, above and beyond the realm of finance and accounting from which auditing first emerged (Power 1997; Shore and Wright 2000; Strathern 2000). Documentation puts the onus for verification on the applicants, rather than the auditor, in terms of the time and cost of doing investigative or surveillance work. Audit cultures are premised on mistrust and generate hierarchical relationships between the verifier and the audited. The mistrust and hierarchy implicit in such arrangements are further fueled, in the case of immigration bureaucracies, by the characterization of immigrants as criminals—and hence probable liars and cheats—within public discourse and by immigration officials (Dow 2004; Heyman 1995; Welch and Schuster 2005). Thus immigrants' word is fundamentally in doubt from the start and requires overwhelming documentation to be taken as truthful. Finally, immigration officials may feel under political pressure to make it difficult for immigrants to become a citizen, undermining the relatively easy legal process of a permanent resident becoming a citizen by making documentation into an administrative roadblock.

Generated at particular historical moments, immigration laws since the nineteenth century have been full of compromises to reconcile contradictory pressures—which Kitty Calavita defines as "on the one hand the economic utility of immigrants as cheap labor and on the other by the political and fiscal costs of nurturing a surplus labor supply" (Calavita 1992, 179). Laws and policies are often not fully rational or coherent, but are "contingent interconnections amongst diverse elements each of which has its own history," "full of parts that come from elsewhere, strange couplings, chance relations, cogs and levers that aren't connected, that don't work, and yet somehow produce judgements, prisoners, sanctions, and much more" (Rose 1999, 276; see also De Genova 2002, 424–25). The desire for documentation and the associated costs for family sponsorship applications are signs of incoherence: despite a law on paper intended to bring family members together, bureaucratic practice may keep them apart.

Fostered Children and the Definition of Family: Rosamund's Story

Laws governing family reunification follow mainstream American ideals of the family in which the nuclear family composed of a couple and their minor children is seen as the premier site of love and intimacy (Zelizer 2005). It is on the basis of these ideals that guidelines are generated on who is included and who is excluded from living and working in the United States. Those with closer kinship ties are assumed to be more emotionally connected and should therefore be allowed to live together, while those with more extended kinship ties are assumed to be more emotionally distant and should be able to handle living apart. As minor children age into adults, they are expected to form their own families and grow more emotionally independent from their parents. As a result, the legally married spouses and biological children under the age of twenty-one ("immediate relatives") of citizens and permanent residents are given priority over those citizens' and permanent residents' brothers and sisters, parents, and married and unmarried adult children. Cousins, aunts, uncles, nieces, nephews, common-law spouses, and even more extended family are not considered close enough as family to be eligible to be united with the citizen or permanent resident. An implicit and cultural sense of what is normal and natural for family relationships as well as political pressures to limit the total number of immigrants play a part in the law's determination of who can join a legal migrant and who cannot. The universal imposition of this conception on families from all over the world is a sign of US power, as Kamari Clarke (2009) has argued in relation to human rights laws that "universalize the structure and meaning of the human condition" (232).

It is important to note that such definitions of family do not reflect the reality of many Americans who are not immigrants. For instance, biological parents are not the sole or even primary caregivers of all children in the United States. Grandmothers, aunts, and uncles are significant caregivers for children in some communities, particularly when parents are young adults or in crisis (Hansen 2005). About 8 percent of all children were living with a grandparent in 2005, a number that has increased since the 1990s (Casper and Bryson 1998; US Census Bureau 2008). A stepparent can be more involved in a child's life, because they are living together, than a biological parent is.[13] Although immigration law does not give priority to children older than twenty-one years to join their parents in the United States, because they are assumed to be well on their way to establishing independent households and their own families as adults, more and more adult children of Americans are not financially independent by the age of twenty-one (Wadler 2009).[14] In the area of marriage, immigrant couples are held to higher standards of intimacy and emotional closeness than nonimmigrant couples. American couples often get married for a mix of emotional and practical reasons—such as economic stability, health insurance or other benefits, or the legal protection of their children—whereas a citizen marrying a noncitizen is asked to prove the level of their emotional closeness in contradistinction to practical concerns (Constable 2003; Fleischer 2008). More and more couples in the United States are cohabiting for longer periods of time and having children without getting legally married.[15] US immigration laws are based on a myth or fiction of family life rather than the ways that Americans actually live together and care for one another, but one the US immigration agencies (US Citizenship and Immigration Services and consulates abroad) have considerable power to enforce over those who come under their jurisdiction.

Not surprisingly, given the focus on "immediate relatives" established formally and legally or through blood, American immigration laws do not recognize fosterage relationships as significant. A Ghanaian who is a permanent resident or citizen can file for her biological children, but not for other children who are residing with her, even if they have lived with her since their birth and are more emotionally attached to her than to their own parents. Thus migration tends to disrupt the relations between adults and the foster children they were caring for. For instance, Rosamund, a twelve-year-old girl I met in Akropong, believed that her father and mother were in Britain with her two older siblings. In fact, the family secret—known to all but Rosamund, although she must have suspected—was that the person she thought was her father was in fact her uncle, her biological mother's older brother. Rosamund's mother's marriage and work as a trader were not very stable, and so the brother, then in Ghana, agreed to help his sister out by raising her child as his own. Rosamund's mother had given Rosamund to the brother at her birth, even naming Rosamund after the brother's wife. But when Rosamund's "father" migrated to the United Kingdom ten years ago, he did not bring Rosamund along with his two biological children.

After the emigration of her "father," Rosamund lived with her maternal grandmother, a thin and cheerful woman in her eighties, to help her around the house during the week. On the weekends, the grandmother was visited by one or more of her nine living children, including Rosamund's biological mother, who lived in Accra, a few hours away. They came to cook for their mother, do her laundry, give her money, take her to the local medical clinic, and handle whatever bureaucratic problems arose, such as with her utility bills. Rosamund's "father" sends Rosamund toys and gifts, making her feel continued affection for him. He and his wife have truly taken Rosamund as their last-born child, explained the grandmother to me.

Three years later, I learned that Rosamund had gone to live with her biological mother in Accra, because she had not done well in primary school in Akropong. By sending her to a private school in Accra, funded by her remittances from her "father," the family—a well-educated family in Akropong with close ties to the Presbyterian Church—hoped she would do better in school. This story illustrates the flexibility and pragmatism of child fosterage: Rosamund's place of residence was decided on the basis of her needs and those of her family members, including her parents' and caregivers' financial stability and physical well-being. Needs shift—children need more help in school, elderly caregivers grow frail and sick, foster parents travel abroad, parents divorce, a single parent works from early in the morning to late at night in the market—and Rosamund moved from one home to another, but not to the home of those abroad.

American immigration laws do not allow nieces and nephews like Rosamund easy entry into the United States, preventing fosterage from occurring when needs of children and their family members change. From the American legal perspective, one problem with fosterage is that the arrangement is made informally and without documents. Another difficulty is that family reunification is based on biological notions of kinship in which blood trumps shared living arrangements or emotional connection; the documentation of a DNA test confirming shared genetic material is the final arbiter of kinship ties, rather than the more fuzzy signs of emotional closeness, shared experience, or coresidence (Carsten 1997; Schneider 1968). Finally, family reunification is based on a model of the nuclear family, rather than a more expansive sense of the kinds of bonds and ties that people experience as rich and deep. Because most children, like Rosamund, circulate to relatives' households, if a permanent resident or citizen could file for more extended relatives, such as a niece or nephew, then a child and her caregiver would not have to separate. If Rosamund's biological uncle had been able to file for his younger sister's daughter, then Rosamund could live with the man she took to be her father and who took her, by others' accounts, to be his daughter.

One might think that Ghanaian immigrants might try to formally adopt the nieces and nephews they had been raising informally. US procedures on international adoption follow the Hague Adoption Convention, an international agreement that establishes safeguards to protect the best interests of adopted children and prevent their abduction or sale across borders (Bergquist 2009; The Hague Conference on Private International Law 2007). Children adopted from Ghana—not a signatory to The Hague Convention—must be orphans, in which both parents are deceased or the sole remaining parent is "unable to care for the child and has, in writing, irrevocably released the child for emigration and adoption." If the child is not an orphan, then the prospective parent must have lived with the adopted child for two years prior to requesting a visa for that child, a provision under which Rosamund's aunt and uncle could have potentially adopted her. Furthermore, the child cannot be "abandoned, relinquished, or released to a specific prospective adoptive parent for adoption." In other words, the biological parent cannot designate the adopting parent, but must have an orphanage or adoption agency seek out and screen prospective adoptive parents.[16] Finally, the child being adopted must be under the age of sixteen. While the laws on domestic adoption in many states within the United States allow relatives to adopt, the procedure on international adoption assumes that the prospective adopting parent is a foreigner working through a recognized agency or organization in the United States, rather than adopting a child who is a relative. The formal parental relinquishing of rights to the adoptive parent, the inability of the parent to designate the caregiver, and the adoption of only orphans or abandoned children make American international adoption law incompatible with Ghanaian practices of fosterage within families. Although meant to protect children from international trafficking and exploitation, such adoption laws can go against children's best interests, which may require the kind of flexibility and pragmatism at which Ghanaian families excel, as Akua's story shows.[17]

Translating Fosterage into Adoption: Akua's Story

Akua was a forty-nine-year-old woman from Akropong working as a university administrator in the United States. Unusually for a Ghanaian, she was unmarried and childless. Her high level of education, professional occupation, and childlessness meant, from a Ghanaian perspective, that she was a prime candidate to help care for her siblings' children. She had worked for over a decade in the United Kingdom before winning the American diversity lottery nine years before I met her, after which she came to the United States as a permanent resident. I had visited Akua's weak and ailing mother in Akropong just a few days before the mother's death in July 2005, and in the months after, Akua and I met on several occasions in the United States to commiserate together.

Saddened by her mother's death, Akua was also concerned about her younger brother's two adolescent sons who had been living with her mother since they were very young. Age thirteen and fifteen at the time of her death, they had come to live with their grandmother when they were two and four years old. Although Akua's brother was a teacher in a nearby town in Akuapem, the family had agreed he was not fit to take care of his children because of his erratic nature, alcoholism, and divorce. The boys' mother was abroad in the United Kingdom, and her marriage with the boys' father had ended. Akua had been paying her nephews' school fees for many years, with the implication that she was responsible, to some extent, for their general welfare. Although Akua had long wanted to bring them over to live with her in the United States, she had only begun the process of formally adopting them eight months before, when her mother began seriously ailing, because she had been worried about her brother's feelings about being separated from his children. Because of her long experience in the United Kingdom and the United States, and her education and social status that gave her a proficiency in dealing with bureaucratic systems, she tried to translate Ghanaian concepts of fosterage to the American legal and social practice of adoption.

Before her mother's death, she had already gone through the process of getting approval to adopt from her state's social services, including having a home study done by a social worker, and she had applied for a visa for her nephews on the basis of her adoption. However, when she returned to the United States from her mother's funeral in Ghana, she found a letter from immigration services saying that her application to adopt was denied, because her brother had written a letter formally giving up his relationship with his sons, as a living parent is required to do to enable his children to be adopted. According to her, the immigration authorities said that the letter was a sign that the father was still attached to the boys, because he cared about putting them in the hands of a good person. Her brother's designation of Akua as the adoptive parent was another problem, according to her lawyer. The boys had two living parents—one abroad and one in Ghana—but Akua did not mention this as a factor, although it may have been one. Akua was upset because she felt that US immigration laws were inconsistent: although she won the lottery, which implied that she was allowed to live in the United States, she could not bring over the rest of her family. "It doesn't make sense," she said. Her efforts fell into a legal space of incommensurability, to draw on the useful term Susan Bibler Coutin (2003) has devised, or a bureaucratic Catch-22.

With close siblings and beloved nieces and nephews in the United Kingdom, California, and Ghana, Akua examined and considered her options, again enacting her repertoire creatively. Should she give up her secure and professional job at an American university on the East Coast to return to an uncertain life in Ghana? What would she do in Ghana to support herself? Maybe she could start a private school, as her brother in Ghana was urging her to do; she was certainly passionate about education and highly educated herself. Maybe she would have a better chance of bringing over her nephews if she applied for their adoption in Britain? Feeling she had exhausted the legal possibilities of adoption in the United States, she ended up selling her house and moving to Britain, finding employment at a university where she was one of only a few nonwhites. However, three years later, she had still been unsuccessful in bringing the boys over to live with her, for the same reasons that she had trouble with the US immigration service. When she tried to adopt her nephews, the British embassy in Ghana asked why she was not living with them. She wrote in response that United

States immigration laws had not allowed them to live together! When I last talked to her on the phone in 2008, she was still thinking about whether she should return to Ghana for their sake.

In the meantime, as she pursued the legal possibilities of adoption, the nephews grew up. In 2008, the oldest nephew was nineteen, finished with high school, and his younger brother, age fifteen, was in boarding second- ary school, as is typical in Ghana. They have bounced around in Ghana, staying first with a paternal uncle (Akua's brother) and then their mater- nal grandmother. A family friend told me that they have not done well in school and have a reputation for misbehavior. While not necessarily caused by Akua's unsuccessful efforts with immigration officials in Britain and the United States, their troubles are one of the reasons why Akua has been so persistent in pursuing their adoption.

I did not meet any other Ghanaian who had tried to adopt a niece or nephew, but many grappled with the lack of legal recognition granted fos- terage, as I discuss further in chapter 6. I take Akua's case as illustrating sev- eral tensions between assumptions embedded in US adoption procedures and Ghanaian practices of fosterage. Firstly, as conceived by The Hague Convention and by US law, international adoption is centered in Western cultural notions of the family. These notions privilege the parent-child re- lationship. However, adoption affects a wider array of relationships than the dyadic one of parent and child, even in the United States, entailing relationships with siblings, grandparents, neighbors, and school friends. The way that people are enmeshed in a web of dense kin relationships, not simply dyadic relationships, is more acknowledged in Ghana. Akua is pursuing the adoption of her nephews not simply for their sake but also (at least initially) to help her mother, and (still and yet) her brother and her other siblings.

Secondly, in US law, based on Western notions of the family, rights are established exclusively and permanently: one parent-child relationship has to be severed to establish another. Either the child has to be an orphan (with both parents dead) or the sole remaining parent has to give up all claims and obligations to the child. In Ghana, by contrast, as described in chapter 2, care is understood as partial and piecemeal, with each giving what they can, and with many people participating in care. The care does create obligations, in feelings of love and in reciprocal relations, but they are not exclusive and can overlap. One can also love and care for many people, just as one can be loved and cared for by many.

Finally, adoption is a highly legalistic and bureaucratic procedure, which is a culturally understood method of ensuring fairness and ethical behavior in the United States. In contrast, Ghanaian patterns of fosterage highlight flexibility and pragmatism to ensure that a safety net is assured at different stages of people's life course (and while not so in this case, flexibility can come at the risk of exploitation). As a result, Akua views American bureaucratic procedures as lacking in transparency and fairness. Akua, despite being a highly educated person who engages in cultural brokerage in numerous ways in her daily life, is unable, because of these obstacles, to translate fosterage to its American equivalent—the formal path of adoption.

International adoption seems to be designed for Americans adopting a stranger's child, a child from abroad, not for the purposes of caring for children within one's family, despite a history in the United States of European immigrants using international adoption as a back door strategy to bring over their relatives in the 1940s and 1950s (Balcom 2012). Nor did immigration policies allow a permanent resident to bring over her sibling's children through family reunification pathways: it was too distant a relation in American eyes. As a result, immigrants fall into a legal space where caring for their siblings' children—other than through remittances—becomes an impossibility. Akua attempted to translate West African understandings of fosterage into American ideas about adoption, but the cultural practice did not fit these categories, dropping into a zone of nonrecognition in which her actions and desires became inconsequential.

Conclusion

Given migrants' status in Ghana prior to migration, and their higher status as a result of going abroad, they expect to raise their own children as well as possibly their siblings and their siblings' children, as some did before they migrated. The growing focus on the nuclear family in Ghana means that many Ghanaians abroad, particularly those who are well educated and previously middle-class residents of urban areas in Ghana, feel that parents are the best people to raise and train their own children. Eunice, a teacher raising her three children in the United States, was adamant on this point: "The ideal is that if you are here, the child must be here with you." Afua's and Mary's stories illustrate some of the main reasons why Ghanaian parents and children live apart from one another when they would rather be together—a combination of fees, delays, and documentation hurdles. These mean that the law undermines its intent, in that a law designed to bring parents and children together separates them for many years, including formative years when children are growing up.

Transnational migrants manage the contradictions other countries' laws and policies generate through their repertoires of family life. Under these circumstances, urban middle-class parents, who would rather raise their own children and foster-*in* the children of others, find themselves foster-ing-*out* their children to their relatives. Some engage in creative adaptations of the fosterage practices they know because of their goals for their children and ambivalence about fosterage. Rather than sending their children to live with a relative, who would be in a position of authority over the child in a less-than-desirable locale, or bringing a dependent relative to live with them and remaining in the household as its head (or spouse of the head of household), as would more normally occur, some invite a relative to live in their own house with their children while they go abroad. In some cases, as in Afua's, conflicts result over who has authority in the household. Some migrant parents prefer to hire a nonrelative as an employee to care for their children, to avoid these problems with kin and make the lines of authority clearer, as I discuss further in chapter 6.

Urban, middle-class people would also like to foster-in their nieces and nephews, as they would do if they were in Ghana, particularly when their siblings or parents are unable to, as the stories of Rosamund and Akua show. However, because of the narrow definitions of family in American immigration law, relations between aunts and uncles, on the one hand, and their younger siblings or nieces and nephews, on the other, are not rec-ognized as being as salient as they are in Ghana. Foster parents abroad—like Akua and Rosamund's uncle—can send remittances that can give their wards access to private schools or higher education in Ghana, but they cannot give them the cachet of an education abroad, American social net-works, or work experience that might come from living in their households abroad. Akua was unable to translating fosterage to its American equiva-lent—adoption. These obstacles to fosterage mean that some of the flexi-bility and pragmatism inherent in the practices in migrants' repertoires and that create a safety net for many Ghanaians—both young and old—cannot be mobilized. Some of the creative enactments of the repertoires of Ghana-ian migrants do not work out, thwarted by narrow and formal definitions of family and bureaucratic methods of proving those relationships.

Despite their social class position within their families and their desires for their children and the children in their families, international migrants are more likely to send their own children to live with other people than to raise other people's children. International migration has thus reinvigo-rated fosterage among the middle class at a time when fosterage is being critiqued and is regarded as a second-best option, a safety net for people in crisis, when what is considered perfect for a child—the care of a mother and father—cannot be obtained.

This chapter has highlighted legal challenges to parents and children living together. However, the book began by introducing Irene, whose children were born in the United States and are therefore US citizens. Irene's separation from her children is not caused by the contradictions of US immigration laws. The next chapter examines the reasons Ghanaian immigrant parents like Irene find raising their children in the United States difficult. These reasons illustrate what other commentators of American family life have noted: that there is a lack of support for working families—immigrant and nonimmigrant alike.

FOUR

Work and Child Care in the United States

In her weekly column in a major Ghanaian newspaper, a pediatrician working in a hospital in Kumasi criticized women from abroad, like Irene, who sent their babies back to Ghana in what she called "the posted baby phenomenon" (Plange Rhule 2005). This was the only mention in the press that I encountered. To explain why women would "post" their babies to Ghana, Janet, a Ghanaian mother struggling to raise her infant and sixteen-month-old toddler in the United States, told me that women "give birth here and take their kids to Ghana because they cannot cope with raising a family and working at the same time. It's a very difficult combination."[1]

When Ghanaian mothers come to the United States, they experience the same pressures of combining work and motherhood that working mothers in the United States do. In coping with these pressures, they have a slightly different repertoire than most American women, for not only do they have experience with fostering from their own childhoods or as working mothers in Ghana, but they also have some awareness of the strategies by which American mothers balance these pressures. Numerous studies have documented how women in the United States cope. Some professional women in the United States make difficult and emotionally fraught decisions to give up work or children (Moe and Shandy 2010). Some households with children distribute parenting by using day care services or hiring nannies on the informal labor market (Brown 2011). Some households "outsource" other kinds of domestic work: prepared meals from take-out restaurants or grocery stores can replace cooking; companies or individuals specializing in housecleaning and lawn care can provide those services (Ehrenreich and Hochschild 2002; Folbre 2001, 2008). Some rely on nearby kin for help raising their children.

Ghanaian mothers are ambivalent about the practices that Americans use not because they are unfamiliar with them, but because there are structural and material reasons why such options are unattractive. I have encountered Ghanaian women who have stopped working for several years, like Janet, and professional women who did not have children, like Akua in the last chapter. However, being a mother is important to one's family and sense of self, and many need to work abroad because their families rely on their remittances. One of the reasons Janet was able to stop working for a few years after the birth of her first child was because her family in Ghana and Nigeria was relatively wealthy and did not depend on her for help. More attractive than leaving the workforce or not having children, then, are ways of distributing parenting through day care and kin support. However, these methods are less in Ghanaian immigrants' reach than they are for most Americans, for legal and economic reasons. As a result, despite their trepidations about doing so, many turn to fostering-out their children, particularly their babies, due to a lack of kin support and to economic precariousness in the United States.

Such a decision is not necessarily easy for parents to make, but, in general, members of the Ghanaian immigrant community support fostering-out because they are aware of the constraints that lead to these decisions. For example, one morning, in the basement of a Ghanaian church in the United States, a young woman compared pay and employment prospects in two major East Coast cities with two older women, as her toddler ran around the large round tables set up for an event later in the day.[2] The young mother complained about having to follow her husband to a city where wages were lower and job opportunities scarcer, and she shared, somewhat tentatively, that she would soon send her son to live with her sister in Ghana for a few years so that she could work more easily. The older woman listening to her reassured her that her plan was a good one and it would work out in the end.

Work in the United States

Ghanaian immigrants are more educated than native-born Americans, on average, but they tend to earn less than Americans with comparable levels of education. In these aspects, they are similar to other African immigrants (Capps, McCabe, and Fix 2011). According to three years of data (2006–8) pooled from the annual American Community Survey conducted by the US Census Bureau, 91 percent of those born in Ghana residing in the United States had a high school diploma or higher (in comparison to 84.5 percent among the total population in the United States), 31 percent had a bachelor's degree or higher (in comparison to 27.3 percent of the total population), and 14 percent had a professional or doctoral degree (in comparison to 10.1 percent of the total population). Analysis of this data shows that the median individual income among Ghanaians was $25,629 (lower than the median individual income of $39,740 for Americans overall), while median family income for Ghanaian households was $53,394 (in comparison to a median family income of $63,211 among all US households), despite their higher educational levels.

This disparity speaks to the difficulty Ghanaian immigrants have in transferring their credentials and skills when they migrate, and the lower-status and lower-paying work they find in the United States as a result. Like other African immigrants (Dodoo 1997; Kent 2007), Ghanaians are generally overqualified for the jobs they have in the United States.[3] Those who have been educated in the United States are more successful in obtaining professional employment that matched their educational credentials. The parents I interviewed who had been educated in the United States had occupations of social worker, accountant, civil servant, radiologist, and teacher. Some skilled professionals from Ghana manage to transfer their skills: some teachers, nurses, and doctors take the examinations and courses to be recertified in the United States. Those parents I interviewed varied in the degree to which their prior experience and training in Ghana enabled them to secure decent employment and earnings in the United States. Those working in skilled "blue-collar" jobs tended to experience continuity in their occupations: two men who had been electricians in Ghana worked as electricians in the United States, and a man who had been an automobile mechanic in Ghana also worked as a mechanic in the United States. On the other hand, of the six who had been teachers in Ghana, two went through the certification process to become teachers in the United States, one was a student, and the remaining three were working as mental health worker, home health aide, and babysitter. One woman who had worked as an accountant in a bank in Ghana (the equivalent of a certified public accountant) also worked for a bank in the United States, but felt she was overqualified for her current job. The two informants who reported they lacked legal status worked in the least stable and most poorly remunerated jobs.

The most common occupations in which Ghanaian immigrants were engaged, according to the American Community Survey (2006–8), were office and administrative support (12 percent of Ghanaian immigrants), health care professions (11 percent), health care support (11 percent), retail and sales (10 percent), and transport and moving (8 percent).[4] The most prevalent single occupational category at the detailed level was "nursing, psychiatric, and home health aide," for a full 8 percent of Ghanaian immigrants. Median wages for all US workers in this occupation in 2008 were $11.46 an hour (Bureau of Labor Statistics 2010a), with an annual median income of $24,010 in May 2010 (Bureau of Labor Statistics 2010b). Half of home-care workers are so poor they need to depend on food stamps or other public assistance, and they only recently became eligible for overtime pay (Greenhouse 2007; Martin 2009). My sample reflects the prevalence of health care employment among Ghanaians seen nationally, but my interviewees were less well educated than Ghanaian immigrants in the United States as a whole. As noted in the introduction, fourteen of forty-six interviewed parents whose US employment characteristics were obtained, worked in the health care field (30 percent): four as a nurse's aide, three as a home health aide, and the remaining seven in other occupations within the health care field. Many of those working in health care had not done such work in Ghana. They reported entering the health care field because of the availability of jobs and the low barriers to entry. Because extensive and costly retraining was unnecessary, they could begin remitting to their families quickly.

Women in Ghana are used to working, as described in chapter 2, but the pressure on women to work increases when they migrate, because of the expectations placed on emigrants to remit. Relatives' needs back home keep many migrants in the United States awake at night worrying. One woman in the United States imagined her parents and siblings starving back in Ghana without her remittances. "I have a lot of people over there; all their eyes are on me," she said. This pressure is reflected in the relatively high rates of employment among Ghanaian immigrants, men and women alike, higher than the US average (Hernandez 2012). Women often find that their employment opportunities are broader in the United States than in Ghana, and that some female-dominated occupational niches like nursing allow them to earn more than their husbands do. As with other immigrants, this shift gives women increased leverage in household decisions (Arthur 2008; Babou 2008; Hondagneu-Sotelo 1994). Because work is rewarding on multiple levels, Ghanaian women are encouraged to use the opportunity of being in the United States to focus on making money.[5] Work is a frequent topic in women's informal discussions, and many prayer requests in the Ghanaian church I regularly attended concerned employment: finding and keeping jobs, obtaining promotions, and managing conflicts with coworkers.

What allows Ghanaian mothers to work in Ghana, as described in chapter 2, is a combination of limited occupational choice and practices of distributed care. In contrast, in the United States, immigrants have difficulty drawing on their repertoire of distributed parenting because of restrictions on visas for relatives who are willing to provide support, financial difficulties in supporting other adults in the United States, and the need for relatives, including fathers, who are already in the United States to work as much as possible to pay the bills and remit back home. Institutional options that distribute care of young children more broadly—namely, day care—are a solution to these dilemmas only for Ghanaian parents who are middle-class professionals in the United States.

Family Support to New Mothers: Akosua, Ama, and Rita

Akosua, living in Philadelphia, talked about the support her mother provided when she gave birth to her first child in Ghana. In Ghana, she worked as a secretary in a bank, her husband had recently gone abroad, and she was living in a house belonging to her husband's family. She recounted what happened after the birth of her first child:

> My family is there; everybody is there, taking care of me. You know, in Africa, my sister [referring to me, Cati], everybody wants to come and see you when you have your first child. . . . My Mummy was with me, for about three weeks. I started work back [I went back to work]. The house is big and it is so quiet. So after some time, my mother says, "I have to go to my own house too." [After that, in the morning,] I take my daughter there [to my mother's house]. So after I am finished working, then I bring [take] a taxi and I took my daughter home. In the morning, I bring her back to my Mom. In the afternoon, they bring her to the office to breast-feed. *She laughs.*

These and other practices of distributing parenting make infant care manageable (if complicated), even for women with employment in the formal sector.

However, when Ghanaians have small children in the United States, their ways of balancing work and family life by bringing their own mothers and younger siblings to stay with them are less successful. Bringing their relatives over on a green card would take several years, as noted in chapter 3. Their relatives could apply for a short-term visitor's visa, which would allow them to stay for several months, but these are difficult to get because of the suspicions of the US embassy in Ghana that visitors will overstay their visas. One woman reported to me with great frustration that when she was denied a visitor's visa for her mother after the birth of her child, she was told that the reason given for the visit—to help with child care—was a form of work and thus prohibited to those on a visitor's visa, even when done without pay for a relative.

Although legal reasons block some parents from bringing over relatives to help with child care, other immigrant parents are challenged financially. An immigrant can only sponsor a relative if she can document sufficient income to support another household member. Some have difficulty proving they can support another adult, as well as their children, on their salaries. Akosua, on food stamps, was told she did not have the income to support an additional person in her household when she tried to bring her mother over to help with her second child.

In Ghana, I met a fifty-three-year-old grandmother who had recently moved from London, where she had lived for four years with her daughter and son-in-law to take care of her grandchildren, ages five and almost two. Her son-in-law was pursuing his PhD, supported by her daughter who worked with the disabled. Because they were having trouble making ends meet and the daughter wanted to pursue her own education as well, they asked the grandmother to return to Ghana with the two children, where the parents could support them more easily with their remittances because of the lower cost of living. The grandmother planned to live with her sister, a secondary-school teacher, along with her sister's family and adolescent househelp, so that she would have help and company raising her young grandchildren. The grandmother was a bit disoriented and downcast to be back in Ghana, having enjoyed her stay in London immensely.

Some migrant parents succeed in bringing over relatives. Ama, a nurse with now grown children, reported how she made it through the period when her children were young. She was really going crazy with her twins, she said, and she invited her mother over for a year. Her mother had a green card and therefore could easily travel to the United States. However, her mother did not want to stay more than six months because, as Ama explained, in Ghana elderly women can go visiting their friends, whereas in the United States her mother felt cooped up in the house without a social life and access to transportation and with only the television for company, because other household members were busy with work and school. Like Akosua's mother who got bored when she was alone in a big, empty house during the day and returned to her own residence, Ama's mother also returned to her own home, although hers was much farther away, in Ghana, so that she could not continue to support her daughter, as Akosua's mother was able to do with Akosua's first child. As a result, when Ama's mother returned to Ghana, Ama's twins, then twenty months old, went with her, staying in Ghana for a few years with their grandmother. When Ama felt she could rely on her oldest son, then in his teens, for babysitting, she brought the twins back to live with her in the United States. Ama's story reveals the significance of another woman's full-time support to a mother of young children, but also migrants' flexibility in the face of changing circumstances, as people's needs and capabilities shift.

In the absence of support from unemployed or underemployed relatives in Ghana, women rely on family support in the United States from relatives who are as busy as they are. Rita managed the birth of her first baby by living with her husband's sister: Rita took the graveyard shift as a certified nursing assistant and her sister-in-law the day shift. After she gave birth to her second child a year later, Rita considered taking the children back to Ghana, because this arrangement was more difficult to sustain with two children and she wanted to go back to school to become a nurse.[6] Some women reported that they similarly coordinated their schedules with their husbands, or with their older children, as Ama did. However, female relatives, husbands, and older children alike are constrained by work and their own continued schooling, so that they cannot provide as much assistance as new mothers need and as much as under- and unemployed relatives in Ghana are willing and able to provide. Rita reported on her phone conversations with her mother in Ghana: "I call, I am all the time crying: 'Mummy, it's too much for me to raise the kids and take care of them.'" Her mother, in turn, asks her to bring the children to Ghana, so that she can look after them and Rita can concentrate on her education.

Akosua contrasted the family support she received when she gave birth in Ghana to the way that she became solely responsible for child care and domestic work in the United States. After the birth of her first child, a daughter, in Ghana, she and her daughter joined her husband in the United States, where she had another child, a son. Three days after their son's birth, her husband was able to take a two-week vacation, but then had to go back to work as a nurse full time, on an evening shift (3–11 p.m.). All the domestic work then fell on Akosua. Even though she had relatives in the United States, she said:

> Nobody is there for you, because everybody is working, the bills are piling [up], the bills you are piling [up], you have to pay this, you have to pay that. If you call out [from work] for one or two days, you lack something.

In the absence of helpful relatives, some of the household labor fell on Akosua's husband when she was recovering from her son's birth.[7] But even

122 / Chapter Four

Akosua's husband and other relatives who lived in the United States were not able to help much, because they had to work many hours to pay the ever-accumulating bills. The lack of grandparent support for child care is typical among pioneer immigrants (Yoshikawa 2011), the situation of many African immigrants.

Ghanaian parents reported that fathers participate in household chores and child care more than they would in Ghana, but like American men, their share of the housework and child care is nowhere near half (Moe and Shandy 2010). Some couples reported that tensions over the balance of housework and paid work brought new disagreements into their married life, as they had to coordinate child care or as men had to begin to help with cooking or at least heating already prepared meals. Many women worried that household disagreements made divorce more likely abroad (see also Manuh 1998), although marriages are unstable in Ghana also. Disagreements over domestic duties are not necessarily the cause of divorce in either Ghana or the United States. Rather, accomplishing key domestic tasks well are a coded communication through which women show their affection or anger toward their husbands, and therefore are important symbols of the strength and well-being of the marriage (Clark 2001).[8] As a result of the symbolic significance of household chores in conjugal relationships, a woman's difficulty doing them (or not doing them well) can be interpreted by others as a sign of her lack of commitment to the marriage.

Because they are unable to enact the strategies of balancing work and family they would use in Ghana, Ghanaian mothers in the United States are faced with a similar set of dilemmas that other mothers, immigrant and nonimmigrant, in the United States face: asking fathers and other relations to do more, cutting back on work, and/or relying on day care. The next section discusses why distributing child care through day care does not meet Ghanaian immigrant mothers' needs.

A Deeper Look at the Day Care Option

Day care is an institutional and formal way of distributing parenting more widely; it is a more temporary and market-based form of fostering, which can be provided or subsidized by the state. There is a high turnover of stranger caregivers, for whom child care is exchanged for money, rather than through long-term and reciprocal relationships. Although child care centers vary in their quality, as a whole they have been associated with improvements in children's cognitive abilities, such as motor and language skills, in early childhood. However, like other immigrant parents

(Bohr and Tse 2009), Ghanaian parents find it an imperfect substitute for the practices of distributed parenting they would prefer to use, primarily because of day care's cost, exacerbated by concerns about low quality of care, inflexibility for nonstandard work schedules (particularly important in health care work), and lack of care when children are sick, thus preventing parents from working. Senegalese parents in New York City mentioned similar concerns as the reasons why they sent their infants and toddlers back to Senegal for grandparents to raise (Kane 2011).

Cost is the most critical factor, suggesting that Ghanaian immigrants, who use day care at relatively high rates compared to other immigrants (Hernandez 2012), would be even more likely to use day care if they had greater access to child care subsidies or low-cost daycare. The Children's Defense Fund (2010) reported that in 2008, the annual cost of day care was similar to the annual in-state tuition at public four-year colleges. The Ghanaians who used day care for their young children (and thus were raising their children in the United States) tended to have more middle-class employment and thus could afford what was one of the largest items in their monthly budget. The class-based dimension of immigrant day care use supports the findings of another study, conducted in four European countries, that showed that professional immigrant families are more likely to use formal and institutional day care than immigrants with more modest incomes (Wall and São José 2004). The costs multiply because of the number of children Ghanaians want and have; day care costs are also higher for infants. A couple—both teachers—with three children, five to nine years old, told me that their children go to the YMCA for an hour before school and two hours after school. They feel that they pay a lot of money, enough to rent an additional two-bedroom apartment in their northern New Jersey neighborhood, for the three hours daily. Another couple—he with a PhD in public health and working for a state agency, she with the Ghanaian equivalent of a CPA and working for a bank while going to school part-time—with three small children in full-time day care, complained that day care costs more than the mortgage on their townhouse in Maryland, even though the day care was subsidized through the mother's school. Working-class Ghanaians cannot afford formal day care. Rita, working as a certified nursing aide, complained she was asked to pay "$800 per *person*, $1,600 for the two" children per month. She felt that all she could afford for child care in her monthly budget was $250 or $300. Given that the average salary of a nurse's aide is $24,010, $1,600 might indeed use up all or most of her posttax monthly income.

Ghanaian parents also expressed worry about the quality of care of day care providers. This concern is well founded. Karine Moe and Dianna Shandy (2010) report on a study on day care centers, conducted in the mid-1990s, that found that on average, they were rated about halfway between "minimal" and "good" (75). For Irene, working as a home health aide, her concerns about day care were a major factor in her decision to take her baby back to Ghana:

> As much as it is hard, but at times it is the best way because you know they are with family. . . . But supposing you had the kid here, then you have to worry what is going on and at times you may see them in a state you don't like [i.e., you may not like how they are taken care of].

Irene also felt that if her children were in day care while she worked, she would never see them except when she was exhausted, and she therefore might as well foster them in Ghana. Finally, she argued, if a child was in day care and became sick, the child would have to stay home or be taken to the emergency room, making the mother not only miss a day of work but also run the risk of losing her job if the child became sick too frequently. Irene mentioned "the emergency room" rather than a "doctor" because of her lack of health insurance, a common occurrence among low-income workers, including home health aides, in the United States. That she speaks of the emergency room also suggests that programs to expand health coverage for low-income children do not always reach immigrants. Twice as many immigrant children (16 percent) are uninsured as native-born children (8 percent) (Hernandez and Cervantes 2011).

If a child is in Ghana, Irene told me, a mother can work double shifts or in a live-in arrangement (as she does) and make more money. She can be sure that her child gets the best medical treatment in Ghana her remittances can buy. For healthy children, this strategy tends to work well, although some parents with children with more severe medical problems bring them to the United States temporarily for specialized therapy or surgery. On the other hand, a mother of a son with autism returned with him to Ghana because she could get better and cheaper all-day care for him there than in the United States.

Ironically, Ghanaians in Ghana have greater access to government-funded preschool for three- and four-year-olds than Ghanaians in the United States do. In 2008–9, only 25 percent of four-year-olds and 4 percent of three-year-olds were in state-funded prekindergarten programs in the United States, in comparison to 35 percent and 18 percent, respectively, in government-funded programs in Ghana in 2002–3 (Children's

Defense Fund 2010; UNESCO 2006). Since then, much effort has gone into expanding preprimary education in Ghana: in 2009, the World Bank estimated that 70 percent of four- and five-year-olds were enrolled in pre-school.[9] Because the United States puts less emphasis on access to pre-school, fewer children go. Children of immigrants, in particular, have low rates of prekindergarten enrollment due to socioeconomic barriers, lack of awareness about the availability of early childhood education, and con-fusion about eligibility rules (Cervantes 2011). Low-cost opportunities for early childhood education, such as Head Start, should be expanded, as the Obama administration has done in its recent budgets (Office of Manage-ment and Budget 2010). Still, more could be done, particularly in terms of immigrants' access to Head Start and public child care subsidies that are available to low-income families. Ghanaians tend to live in states that are not among the worst in providing resources and access to early childhood education, yet still clearly face significant barriers to accessing high-quality, low-cost preschool and day care.[10]

Under these circumstances, wanting to work but lacking assistance for child care, many mothers—particularly those in time-intensive, low-wage occupations—foster their infants out for several years with grandmothers or other trusted relatives in Ghana. They may bring their children back to the United States when they are ready for school and require a few hours of after-school care, or as adolescents. In other words, they rely on family net-works as they would in Ghana, except that they foster-out their children, sending them to live with family in Ghana, rather than adding relatives to their household, perhaps through fostering-in a helper.

Conclusion

When Ghanaians come to the United States and start or add to their fami-lies, they draw on multiple practices in their repertoire to balance work and child care, as American parents do. However, because their goals and con-straints differ from those of American parents, who experience less pressure to simultaneously have children and work, who might have more support from family members close by, and who have greater access to government support, Ghanaians turn to a different set of strategies than American par-ents do. That some Ghanaian mothers foster their infants and toddlers with relatives back in Ghana is not a sign of a rigid cultural tradition, but rather of a flexible repertoire adjusting to new challenges and constraints expe-rienced in the United States. What seems most salient to Ghanaian par-ents are immigration laws that make it difficult to bring over relatives, the lack of affordable day care in relation to their wages, and the constraints of their time-intensive but relatively low-paying occupations that do not allow flexible schedules or provide health insurance. By drawing on their repertoire of child fosterage, they manage the contradictions posed by the American economy's need for low-wage workers and a lack of support for those workers' child care needs.

Most low-income American parents rely on unpaid family child care, but Ghanaian immigrants have difficulty doing so. Current US immigration law makes it difficult for Ghanaian immigrants in the United States—especially those with lower incomes or without substantial assets—to bring over their parents on temporary visas or to petition for permanent visas, either of which would allow grandmothers or other relatives to come to the United States to help raise young children. Furthermore, their wages, and the mismatch between their credentials and their employment, make it difficult for them to afford long hours of day care.

That Ghanaian immigrant parents foster their infants and toddlers back in Ghana is a signal that the United States has weak societal and institutional supports for raising young children—supports that some other countries like Ghana provide to a greater extent. Those supports are likely to become even weaker as federal and state governments curb costs and shed even more of the social services they currently provide. In the process, the costs of training and raising children are being devolved from one of the world's strongest economies to those that are poorer, even though some of those children, like Irene's children, are US citizens and will constitute some of its future workforce, when immigrant parents bring them back to the United States in their adolescence or young adulthood.

This chapter has detailed the reasons why Ghanaians send their babies and young children born in the United States back to Ghana to be fostered; the next chapter looks at the situation of adolescents who are sent back. Some of the teenagers were born in the United States; others were born in Ghana and joined their parents in the United States earlier in their childhoods. In general, the reasons they were sent back does not entail immigration constraints or parents' work, as parents view older children as able to be on their own and even to contribute to household management, including providing child care to younger siblings during parents' working hours. Rather, adolescents are sent to Ghana because of a lack of wider social supports for raising young people to be responsible and respectful in the United States, which leads Ghanaian immigrant parents to see the United States as a difficult place to raise children and Ghana as the solution to their problems.

FIVE

Borderwork

A Repertoire Made Conscious

I met Emmanuel in an elite boys' boarding school in Kumasi, the second-largest city in Ghana. Age eighteen, he stood out from the other boys because of his height and his American accent. Born in the United States, his parents had sent him to Ghana a year before. Quite unhappy, he told me that he felt uncomfortable in Ghana because some people did not always understand his American English. He said he had trouble not gesturing with his left hand, which is disrespectful in Ghana. He was struggling with his schoolwork, even though he had been a senior in his American high school and had been put into the equivalent of tenth grade in Ghana. His mother, with whom I spoke a few months later, when I returned to the United States, told me that she and his father sent Emmanuel back to Ghana because "he was misbehaving and not listening," particularly in school. She said they would bring him back to the United States when he had finished secondary school and was ready for college, in three years' time. When I visited Emmanuel's mother and father a month later, in the suburbs of an East Coast city, his father had just returned from a short trip to Ghana and said he was surprised that his son had changed so much in the past year. For example, over the school vacation, Emmanuel washed his father's car every day without being told. Whereas when Emmanuel was in the United States, the father said, you would call him from his bedroom and he wouldn't even respond.

There are similar children in Ghanaian boarding secondary schools, sent back because their parents thought their children were going astray in some way or "wayward," in Ghanaian parlance. Although they are fewer than the number of children left behind or sent to Ghana by migrant parents for legal or economic reasons, they are prominent in the discourse of the Ghanaian immigrant community, as a lesson to parents and children alike. Like Emmanuel's father, Ghanaian parents share success stories of how a stint in Ghana, with its more difficult living conditions, competitive school environment, and standards of conduct, helped their children become responsible and respectful.[1] Sending adolescents who seem to be going off track to the home country is a strategy discussed not only by Ghanaians but also more generally among immigrant parents.[2] This strategy is supported by a conscious opposition between the homeland and the United States, in which life in the United States is the cause of a child's waywardness and life in the homeland the solution to a child's learning to be an appropriately socialized person.

Ghanaian immigrants codified and essentialized their dynamic cultural repertoire through language highlighting national differences as if they were essential features of groups of people, an "American" way and a "Ghanaian" way. For example, when I asked Kwasi and his wife, Doris, what they hoped for their eldest daughter, then a toddler, Doris responded by contrasting her hopes with what she saw as a typical American adolescence:

> Every parent wish their kids don't go wayward from what they expect them to be. So I hope that she will be respectful, I hope that she will listen to what we tell her—advice—and I hope that she will not go follow [her] friends, instead of being closer to [her] family members. 'Cause I hope she will grow up to be serious with her studies, her God, that she will be serious with her lifestyle, you know, not going the American way, having boyfriends, having babies without mar[riage]—I don't want that to happen to her.

For Doris and other parents I met within the Ghanaian immigrant community, "American" meant a set of practices associated with being "wayward," or children's misbehavior and disrespect, while "Ghanaian" meant being respectful to adults, obedient to direction, hard working, studious, and Christian. In Ghana anyone in the community can reprimand or punish a child, at least in the parents' memories and childhood experiences. In Ghana life is hard: children do household chores and have less access to TV and the Internet. Children are safe from crime. They feel fortunate to go to school and so treat their teachers with respect and approach their studies with diligence. In America, by contrast, children have too much "freedom"; are closer to their peers than to family; and are lured out of the home by "the street," a potent symbol of adolescent waywardness in Ghana also.

In making these oppositions, Ghanaian immigrants ignore the variation within Ghanaian and American parenting practices. Although some Ghanaians are able to return home frequently (Orozco et al. 2005), many lack the economic means to visit often. For those who do not return, Ghana can become frozen in time, in which adults remember a Ghana of their childhood and adolescence. By ignoring differences *among* Ghanaians and Americans, Doris and other Ghanaian immigrants occasionally made cultural boundaries into borders, to use Frederick Erickson's terms from his research on schools. Erickson (1987) writes, "Cultural boundaries can be thought of as behavioral evidence of culturally different standards of appropriateness"—for instance, in Emmanuel's case, how children should respond to adult requests (345). As boundaries, such cultural differences are neutral, without special value placed on one way of doing things over another. However, people can begin to treat cultural differences—boundaries—as cultural borders, in which they not only see the cultural differences as hard and fast but also use them as the basis of moral evaluations, political rights, and social affiliation, as teachers do about their students. As Ghanaian immigrants examined their parenting repertoires, they tended to organize parenting differences into rigid and oppositional categories defined by national borders.

I argue that the reason they do so is that immigrant parents' experiences of transposing their parenting repertoires in the United States make other aspects of their repertoires more available to consciousness. The act of transposing their repertoires to a new situation may result in frustrations as they struggle to figure out successful strategies. This process can cause unease, as parents seek to understand, name, and define what is going on that feels inchoate and uncertain. In other words, although the oppositions exist to be elaborated upon, people can do their own ideological work to understand and organize their experience, which they sense as incomprehensible or frustrating, as Raymond Williams (1982) discerned. To provide an example of frustration and unintelligibility: Kwasi, who was raising his two children in the United States, complained to me that parents can "shape" their children in Ghana but they seem to have much less effect on their children's characters in the United States, for reasons that were unfathomable to him. As William Sewell (2005) has noted, the explicit organization of experience tends to take the form of hierarchies, comparisons, and dichotomies.

In my previous work (Coe 2005), I observed teachers and cultural officers defining "culture" in particular ways, but in the Ghanaian immigrant community there is not evidence that institutions are disseminating a set of contrasts around Ghana/America. In the Ghanaian church I attended regularly for two and a half years, there was not a strong ideology around parenting from the church leadership, unlike a church described in a study of

Caribbean immigrants in New York, in which pastors cajoled "parents into accepting some aspects of the 'Americanization' of their teens, while basically upholding the overall values of the parents, which stressed hard work, stability, education, and striving for upward mobility" (Waters 1999, 202). Although Ann Swidler (2001) argues that institutions—as enduring, self-perpetuating systems—are key in creating similar responses by constraining people's action and providing a basic set of experiences that people share, in my view what makes institutions like churches and community organizations so useful to the reshuffling of repertoires is that they bring people together to share their inchoate understandings of what they are going through and allow them to hear others' initial formulations and explanations of what is going on. What I observed in the Ghanaian church was older and newer immigrants talking about their parenting experiences with one another and developing a way of talking that named and delineated certain aspects of their experiences. When Ghanaian immigrant churches and community events bring Ghanaian immigrants together, or when they talk to friends and relatives on the phone, they discuss their initial observations, puzzled thoughts, and hard-won understandings like these, as they, like Kwasi, shared them with me in our conversations in their continued attempts to figure out what was going on and what they should do.

Fostering was not a practice consciously marked as "Ghanaian" in the set of contrasts between "Ghana" and "America," perhaps because immigrants as former middle-class, urban residents of Ghana treated fostering with ambivalence. Instead, fostering of immigrant children in Ghanaian boarding schools was a commonsensical response to a child's going wayward, because of the cultural borderwork that emphasized differences between "America" and "Ghana."

Although most children of Ghanaian immigrants who are being raised in Ghana are there for legal or economic reasons, as detailed in the last two chapters, a few, like Emmanuel, are there for their education and socialization. Those in this latter category are more likely to be US citizens and be the children of long-term, established immigrants with authorization to live and work in the United States. However, the issues that persuade parents to send their children to Ghana are widely discussed by parents in the Ghanaian immigrant community, among those raising their children in the United States, those raising their children in Ghana, or those, like Emmanuel's father, with children in both places.

Losing Your Children in America

In thinking about raising their children to be "good," Ghanaian parents focus on inculcating particular values within the child and strengthening the child's character. These attributes, while significant in Ghana, are emphasized even more strongly in the context of the United States, because they are perceived as being under threat *and* as crucial for taking advantage of the opportunities and resources available in the United States. Parents worried about "losing your child" or all their hard work coming to "nothing," phrases that came up over and over again in my discussions with parents. When I asked a father whose four children—aged thirteen to twenty-three—were living in Ghana what he meant by losing children in America, Kofi replied,

> Lose the child, like, the training you give to your child may be lost. If you say, "Don't do it," they might talk back. The kids here talk back to you. Back home, [as a child] you have to listen, you have to listen to what you are told to do. Because the parents know what is right for you to do, that's why he's telling you to do that. When you bring your child here and you don't take full control over him or her, that's what I mean by losing your child. Once character is lost, so is everything else.

The sadness of the phrase "losing one's child" is that there seems to be little hope of changing the values and character of a child, although Ghanaian parents' actual experience may be quite different, such that they find their children raised in the United States do begin engaging in proper behavior as they age. For example, a visiting minister to the church talked about her "porcupine children," including a son who refused to be hugged when he was a teenager, but who is now in the choir in church and wants to be an usher. His increased participation in church is symbolic of being of good character. "God can turn the spikes," she told the audience, suggesting another model—a religious one—for changing a child's behavior. However, a more dominant discourse was that of "losing one's child" in the United States. "Losing one's child" had many meanings, from losing one's child to the prison system to having one's child taken away by the foster care system for parental abuse, but its most common usage was to the moral character of the child being lost, as Kofi suggests.

Yao, living with his wife and physically disabled youngest child in the United States while two older daughters stayed in Ghana with their grandmother, told me that what he saw as he met other Ghanaians across the United States was that "people are losing their children. Parents are really, really breaking down emotionally, and some parents have adopted the system of returning their children back home these days because they have *no* option." Although he appreciated the system of education in the United States, Yao, college educated in Ghana, told me that he would prefer to raise his children in Ghana because:

> I know that I—or we—can easily lose the children to anything else and once we lose them, the tendency to focus on education would even be killed. . . . They could have the best resources, education-wise, that my wife and I never got, but it wouldn't matter because if the value system is not there to hold them, they would not even look at this, *a book on the table which he taps.*

Given that education was so important to success in his own life, and to that of other urban, middle-class Ghanaians, he felt that it was also necessary for his own children's futures. But he felt that children's ability to take advantage of education was due not to increased opportunities, more available in the United States than in Ghana, but to his children's values and character, which might be destroyed in the United States.

One reason disrespect and disobedience toward elders was taken so seriously is because such behavior was viewed as leading to more serious lapses in responsibility and loss of connection to one's family. It signaled not only that a child, out of a lack of discipline, would be unsuccessful as an adult, but also that the child would not want to reciprocate in future for the care given by his or her parents, out of a lack of gratitude or obligation. Furthermore, some parents were worried about their children becoming involved in more serious misbehavior and getting a criminal record in the United States, issues that arise for parents in Ghana but that create more anxiety for those in the United States. Ghanaians are often wary of the police and the law because of the threat of deportation that hangs over immigrant communities (Foxen 2007; Levitt 2001). Eunice, a teacher raising her three children—ages five to nine—in the United States with considerable concern and anxiety, said, "Some [parents] send them [their children] home with the fear that they will be killed or be in prison, or that they will get in trouble with the law." Because parents worked many hours, their children often did not have parental supervision at home. Although parents expected their children to be studying or doing chores in the afternoons, young people might use unsupervised afternoons and evenings to be out in the streets with friends or invite friends home. Ama, a nurse with five children, thought that her eldest son when he was a teenager would be able to look after the younger ones after school. As a result, when she finished nursing school, she took the evening shift of 3:00–11:00 at work so that in the morning, when her children were at school, she could cook and clean. In fact, she learned her oldest son went roaming out into the streets until ten o'clock at night, and occasionally she would be called to the police station on his behalf.

Like other immigrant parents (Le Espiritu 2009; Thorne et al. 2003), Ghanaian parents were particularly worried about girls in their adolescence. Eunice's husband, Robert, also a teacher, told me the story of a man in New York who found his daughter with boys in the father's bedroom. "He packaged her like sardines [back to Ghana]," he said, laughing. "Every day she's calling [him] and wants to come back." The concern with girls is not only that they might get pregnant, but also that a daughter's pregnancy in the United States might increase her independence and separation from her family.[3] Margaret, a nurse who has been in the United States for six years, told me, "I think I know of two, I know of two—not too many— girls who they, because of peer pressure, they were very disobedient, they got pregnant, moved away from home, and things like that." Teenage pregnancy happens in Ghana too, but family members shower the new baby with love and teach the young mother how to care for the infant. Margaret said about Ghana, "And even *if* they [the daughters] get pregnant, they don't move away from home. They stay home, because there is no support system out there that is going to support you. Your parents will still have to take care of you." In the United States, in contrast, a young adult's pregnancy mobilizes public funds that enable her to establish her own household, rather than relying on her parents for support.

Ghana was felt to be a better place than the United States to raise children who remained connected to their parents. In adults' eyes, children's disrespect for their parents in the United States was affected by their peers at school and knowing that they had rights, and of parents— rather than a larger network—being solely responsible for the child's training. Thus much more depended on a parent's individual approach in the United States, whereas in Ghana, family members, neighbors, and schools would fill any deficiency or time gap in a parent's child-raising. Janet said:

> In Ghana, the bulk of the work [of child-raising] doesn't fall on you. Their kids grow up knowing [how to behave] because they learn in school. Your kids can't play outside [in the United States]. This is a very private lifestyle here, very individualistic.

Thus parents felt more responsible for their children's character training than they would in Ghana, where they felt that they could rely on others, including relatives, schools, churches, and peers. The reliance on them as parents—what we might call an undistributed view of parenting—heightened their anxiety about their children's futures.

One of the key reasons Ghanaian parents cited among the difficulties of raising children in the United States was that one was restrained from physically punishing one's child. This issue was mentioned in every interview among parents I conducted and was generally among the first things people said when I asked about raising children in the United States. This complaint is a common one among immigrant parents in the United States (Guarnizo 1997; Holtzman 2000; Levitt 2001; Portes and Rumbaut 2001; Waters and Sykes 2009). Akosua reported:

> I said [to my eldest daughter when she had just arrived from Ghana], "That cane [the lack of it in the United States], that doesn't mean that in this place you have to misbehave. This place, it is their culture that they don't beat kids. But Africa, because we want you to know more, that is why we use cane." . . . Everything, you have to do it *right*. If you don't do it right, the cane will give you the thing [motivation] to do. But this place [the United States], because there is no cane, people will behave anything [any which way].

Like other immigrant parents, Ghanaian parents said their children were well aware of their rights and would not hesitate to contact the police if they were being physically punished or even sharply scolded. Several Ghanaian parents talked about America as the land of freedom. Adwoa said, "Here [in the United States], children are free, but it is not good. We are used to disciplining them, but you can't do that here, because it is called 'abuse' and you can call the police." Yemeni, Mexican, and Central American immigrant parents say similar things: "This dangerous kind of freedom, which they associate with American culture and especially with American teens, is the freedom to 'do whatever you want,' to claim independence from family and parental authority, and to engage in age-graded activities like going out with friends, dating, and participating in commercialized youth culture" (Thorne et al. 2003, 256).[4] Ghanaian parents said quite explicitly that the reason they held back from punishing their children in the United States was because they were afraid of getting arrested by the police for child abuse and having their children taken away from them to be put into the foster care system.[5] One unauthorized couple with an infant in the United States and an older daughter in Ghana joked that their baby—since she was being raised in the United States—might one day call the police on them and get them deported. As a result of fears about the police, members of the Ghanaian church I attended who had been in the United States longer told more recent arrivals that all they could do to raise their kids in the United States was talk to their children and pray for them.

Although physical punishment is threatened and used in Ghana, it is in coordination with more subtle means, like peer pressure and shaming, that are not available in the United States because of different standards of behavior within the larger society.[6] A teenager sent to a Ghanaian secondary school for stealing and gang activity in the United Kingdom told a journalist for the *Sunday Times*, "What gets you respect over there [in the United Kingdom] is a disgrace over here [in Ghana]" (McConnell 2007). In the absence of other, subtler motivating forces, parents felt a greater need to threaten and to physically punish their children in the United States, even as American laws and institutions made that practice more difficult.

Ghanaians varied in their awareness of the subtleties in Americans' conceptions of physical punishment, such as the differentiation between "spanking" and "abuse." Parental corporal punishment is not prohibited by law in the United States, except where it results in injury. Luis Eduardo Guarnizo (1997) comments that Dominican immigrant parents' "knowledge of the law was usually the often grossly altered version presented by their children" (40). At the same time, parents idealized Ghana's harshness, remembering their own childhoods, and were not necessarily aware of how child-rearing and disciplinary norms have since changed in contemporary Ghana, including new regulations banning corporal punishment in schools.[7] As Ghanaians try to make sense of their experiences as parents in the United States, the lack of corporal punishment in the United States becomes salient as an explanation for young people's misbehavior. That social institutions such as the police, social workers, and schools do not back up parental authority makes parents even more vigilant about their children's behavior and wary of "American" parenting.

Hardship and Ease: Comparing Schools in Ghana and the United States

Another major difference between America and Ghana in parents' evaluations concerned schooling. Parents considered schooling in Ghana to be a greater struggle than schooling in the United States. In Ghanaian parents' and adolescents' eyes, what made school easier in the United States were grades dependent on homework, quizzes, and tests rather than a terminal exam based on years of study; resources like computers and textbooks; helpful and hard-working teachers; and easy access to high school and college for those who can afford it. In Ghana, to be accepted to secondary school and university, students had to pass make-or-break examinations requiring regurgitations of large amounts of memorized material learned over many years. Because there are not enough available seats in secondary schools and universities, a student has to do well on the exam to even continue at the next level. Furthermore, a student's score on these exams determines the prestige and quality of the school he or she will attend as well as the program or major he or she will pursue, and so they are highly competitive. Although the number of positions has improved in recent years with the expansion of educational institutions, passing the exam still does not guarantee a position at the next level. Many students retake portions of the examination six months later to try to improve their total score, so that they can proceed to the next level of schooling. Although the best students are educated to high standards, such a system does not do well by its weaker students, who do not continue their education and repeat the same grade many times.

Kwasi regularly taught the youth group at his Ghanaian church in the United States, although he was often frustrated by the young people's responses to his discussion topics.[8] One day, he talked to the teenagers about how "fortunate" (his word) they were to be in the United States and that they should make the most of the opportunities they had here. In Ghana, he told them, you have to be the best to continue, but here education is easy. In his secondary school, he was afraid of the teacher and could not raise his left hand to answer a question or he would be slapped. Here, teachers ask you about your problems and give you lots of help if you do not understand. So you should try your best in school. One teenage girl who came regularly to church with her mother and had been raised in the United States from birth commented in response that even if she didn't do her homework, she still passed the class. At the same time as she confirmed his view that school in the United States was easy, she also raised the question of how much she learned in her American school.

Thus although the ease of school in the United States might seem to be a positive feature, parents and young people alike felt that the struggle of schooling in Ghana inculcated a sense of discipline and fortitude that translated into school success wherever the students might go thereafter, similar to the way that hardship is valued in children's education in other parts of West Africa (Bledsoe 1990; Bledsoe and Sow 2011). Grace, a student in a prestigious girls' secondary school in Ghana, said that her father sent her back to Ghana from Canada because "he wanted me to come here to learn how to study. He says, there [in Canada] they don't know how to study, and here [in Ghana] they know how to study and learn more. If I finish school here [in Ghana] and go to university there [in Canada], it will be for my own benefit." Yaa, at the same school, who had not been outside the country but whose mother was abroad, said that in Ghana one had to "struggle" in one's schooling, so one becomes disciplined and "excels" wherever one goes. Afua, introduced in chapter 3, whose mother had died shortly after she joined her in the United States, said she was glad her younger sister followed her father back to Ghana after her mother's death and was going to secondary school there:

> Things are too free over here [in the United States]. Kids have too much freedom, too much rights. It [being in Ghana] makes you strong, in a way. That is my opinion. It makes you strong because—you [Cati] know how secondary schools in Ghana are. You don't get what you want all the time. . . . It makes you strong, in a way that you can handle every situation you find yourself in.

Hardship might even be considered a goal of schooling in Ghana. In the repertoires of Ghanaian parents and adolescents, the hardships of Ghanaian education were highly valued for creating disciplined, motivated, and respectful young people. In contrast, the ease of American schools generated not only many opportunities but also students who were not used to working hard. If young people were persistent and diligent, they could do well in school, but if they were not, their school would not make them so.

Young people I met who had recently made the transition from Ghanaian to American schools affirmed the ease of American schooling in relation to Ghanaian schooling. Young people who came from Ghana to the United States had encountered English in their schools, the media, and sometimes as their home language,[9] but they, like other newly arrived African children (Shabaya 2006), often struggled with the English they heard in the United States, spoken with an American, rather than a Ghanaian, accent. Some adolescents recently arrived from Ghana discussed with me how they had trouble with the ways Americans—particularly their peers— spoke English, but only a few were put into English as a Second Language (ESL) classes because most catch on to the different pronunciation of English in a few months. They generally reported to me that on the whole, school in the United States is easier. They told me they had already covered the subject matter in earlier grades, except for American history, which was completely new to them. They commented that because there are multiple tests, they have many chances to pass the class.

The North American–educated students I met in elite Ghanaian schools were struggling academically; Emmanuel and Grace, for instance, sent back to Ghana, were having difficulty mastering the skill of rote memorization. Ama described arranging for tutoring for her daughter when she sent her back to Ghana, because she felt that her daughter would need to catch up with her Ghanaian counterparts, particularly in mathematics and geography.

There are a few exceptions to this general trend. Janet described to me the experience of a cousin who brought her two children, aged four and five, from Ghana to the United States. Raised in "the typical Ghanaian way" by her cousin's illiterate mother, said Janet, the children were later put into remedial classes in their elementary school in the United States.

These impressions of students and parents in which Ghanaian education rated higher than American education surprised me. Large-scale achievement tests indicate that in general Ghanaian education is not more effective in terms of students' academic learning: for example, the eighth-grade Ghanaian students sampled in the 2007 Trends in International Math and Science study (TIMSS) did much worse than their American counterparts (Gonzales et al. 2009). Teacher absenteeism and student grade repetition are common in schools in Ghana. However, Ghanaian parents and adolescents value not only *what* students learn but also *how* they learn in Ghanaian schools, with rote memorization, respect for or even fear of teachers, and strict discipline seen as leading to hard-working students, again, under the aegis of "hardship." Parents in the United States, similarly, will value a school for characteristics other than the quality of its academic instruction or academic test scores, such as its perceived safety or racial and class composition of its student population (Holme 2002). Furthermore, in Ghana as well as in the United States, there is educational inequality, with great differences in the quality of education between schools *within* each of the two countries, so that when Ghanaians compare schools in Ghana and the United States, they are comparing the better schools in Ghana with worse schools in the United States.

Part of what fuels Ghanaian parents' and students' impressions is that immigrant parents can afford a higher quality of education in Ghana than they can in the United States. For instance, through their remittances, migrant parents can usually afford private schools and private tutoring for their children in Ghana. In the United States, by contrast, most Ghanaians can only afford to send their children to the neighborhood public school, a quality of education that is determined by where they can afford to live. Margaret, who was raising her teenage daughter in a middle-class African-American neighborhood in a large city, commented, "Most Ghanaians that I know [in the United States], their kids go to the area schools, but when they reach the teenage ages, some of them really go astray because of the influence of their friends." Going to the neighborhood school, in her mind, put children at risk of peer pressure toward wayward behavior.

I was able to spend some time in a school with a growing African student population, including some Ghanaians, in an inner-ring suburb of an East Coast city. African-American working- and middle-class families were moving from the city to this suburb. The principal told me that the students talked about how they liked the school in comparison to what they had experienced in the nearby city. With the influx of black students, white residents of the town became less willing to send their children to the school. One teacher who also served as the coach of the school soccer team, composed of many African youngsters, commented that "the white flight" from the school made it less "diverse" in its population (his words are in quotes). The school was 90 percent Black, even though the surrounding community was 70 percent white, according to the 2000 census. The principal told me that because the students are "like inner-city kids but without the dangers," the school is popular as a placement for student teachers from various local universities. His comment indicates how the pathologization of the poor is extended to working-class and lower-middle-class kids and how Blackness becomes equated with the underclass (Wilcox 1982). Like this school, the neighborhood public schools that Ghanaian children attend tend to be more Black and poor than their surrounding communities, because more of the middle-class and white families in the neighborhood send their children to private schools, including Catholic schools, precisely to escape the stigma of going to school with Black kids who are perceived as "inner-city kids."

Like other residents of the town, Ghanaian parents might want their children to attend a private school or be less surrounded by "inner-city kids." Of course, as Blacks in the United States, others might consider their children to be "inner-city kids." However, on their wages, and with the need to send remittances to their relatives in Ghana, many Ghanaians are not able to afford private education or residence in a locality with high property values that can support high-quality and well-funded public schools. If a child struggles in school in the United States, the parents cannot afford tutoring as they can in Ghana; several parents commented on the high cost of private tutoring in the United States in their conversations with me.

Irene's two school-age children in Ghana, on the other hand, attend a private school and receive tutoring from a math teacher who lives rent-free in the house she built in Ghana. Joanna, a young woman who had recently joined her father in the United States, said she was surprised she had to attend a public university in the United States, because in Ghana she had been educated, from kindergarten to the end of secondary school, in a private school of which she was very fond. But in the United States, she rationalized, what matters is the degree, not whether it is from an Ivy League university. Although Joanna's assessment that the education credential matters more than the institutional reputation is correct, attending a high-quality or selective college in the United States and the United Kingdom does seem to have some effect on future earnings, controlling for the field of study and other factors (Black, Smith, and Daniel 2005; Georgetown University Center on Education and the Workforce 2010; Smetherham 2006; Strathdee 2009; Zhang 2005).

Migrant parents also recall attending boarding school with nostalgia and want their children to have that experience. Many secondary schools in Ghana are boarding schools. Migrants who attended such schools reminisce fondly about their time there, even when or because they experienced hardship. One mother said her boarding school helped her manage her time well and learn to do things on her own. One father who rose high in political circles in Ghana told me he had harsh teachers whose behavior bordered on "abuse" (his word); yet he also had teachers who made him want to learn and he made wonderful friends there. Two of his three children are currently being educated in an elite boarding school in Ghana, while the youngest lives with him and his wife in the United States. Boarding schools in Ghana are places where strong and enduring bonds are forged between young people, sometimes due to the shared abuse, and those connections have proved useful for their alumni's careers or marriage prospects.[10] Some parents explore sending their children to boarding school or military academy in the United States, but often find it too expensive. With salaries earned in the United States, however, they can afford boarding school tuition in Ghana. As in the Dominican Republic (Guarnizo 1997), boarding schools also reduce the burden that an adolescent might place on a foster parent back in Ghana.

Parents' evaluations of schools in Ghana and the United States make sending their children back to Ghana for an education attractive, at least for elementary, middle, and high school. But once a child is ready for college, the calculation shifts and the United States becomes more attractive. Although higher education is certainly important in Ghana in providing access to stable, high-paying, and high-status jobs, Ghanaian immigrant parents' view of the importance of higher education increases as a result of their work experience in the United States, as is true for other immigrant parents (Zhou 2009). Educational credentials, even only a high-school diploma, are important in the United States for even the most low-status and low-paying jobs. For example, Kwaku was quite well educated in Ghana: he had been a social worker with the equivalent of an associate's degree. When he came to the United States, he went on to obtain a bachelor of arts degree and a master of social work degree. He told me, "If you don't go to school and don't get an education, you won't be able to live a good life at all." Akosua, who went to commercial school in Ghana to train as a secretary and worked in a bank, shared this sentiment. Unemployed at the time of our interview, she told me, "Because in this country [the United States], if you don't have a good education, to get a good job is hard." Her own qualifications, she lamented, do not count for much in the United States. That their Ghanaian-acquired credentials are not valued in the United States drives parents to push their children to obtain an American college degree. Furthermore, access to higher education is easier in the United States than in Ghana, a matter of financial, rather than academic, ability.

As a result of these considerations, even parents who have raised their children in Ghana anticipate bringing them to the United States in their late adolescence, as Emmanuel's parents plan to do.[11] Some young people attend an American high school for a year or two, taking the Scholastic Aptitude Test (SAT) in their junior or senior year in preparation for college. Others complete secondary school in Ghana, when they can then apply straight to an American college after passing the Test of English as a Foreign Language (TOEFL) and the SAT through the American embassy in Ghana. Well-discussed oppositions between schools in Ghana and the United States influence parents' decision making about sending their children to Ghana to be educated and the timing of their return to the United States.

Gossip and Maintaining a Reputation

One of the reasons why Ghanaian parenting in the United States is so fraught with tension is that the child's character reflects on the parent's character. Kwasi told me, "If the child becomes a problem in future, people will look at you as a bad parent; you couldn't bring up your child in a good way. So it is your responsibility. You didn't do your duties well. So you will pass through all possible means to straighten out your kid before he gets out of hand." While true in Ghana also, the gossip about young people seemed more prominent in the United States. During activities where Ghanaians gather—such as funerals, weddings, birthday parties, church events, traditional festivals, and associational meetings—children and young people being raised in the United States tag along with their parents, participating in the Ghanaian immigrant community. Children's behavior at these events is discussed and evaluated, affecting their parents' reputation among their coethnics in the United States. For instance, at a youth barbeque at the Ghanaian church, when teenage girls at a nearby picnic table were talking loudly, the mother of an infant turned to the other women at her table to remark, "This is why one should send children back to Ghana."[12] Similarly, Jonathan, whose wife and children were living in Ghana, told me a story about his friend, Isaac, and Isaac's son. Isaac and his sixteen-year-old son had come to Jonathan's house to drop off some items, with Isaac doing all the unloading and his son just standing there, not helping. Jonathan had called Isaac later to say that the way of life in the United States made his son like that. Jonathan reported that Isaac is so embarrassed by the way his son acts that Isaac will not let anyone come over to his house; he keeps his son out of public view. Like the woman at the church picnic, Jonathan recommended to Isaac that the son should be sent back to Ghana. The children of both of these critics were in Ghana, for different reasons, and they were highly skeptical about successful outcomes for children raised in the United States.

Gossip about children and parenting was criticized in a Bible study class during one church service, illustrating its prevalence and significance. The woman reporting for the English-language group advised the reunited congregation that rather than saying, "Look at her son," an implied criticism of another person's child, everyone in the church was responsible for raising the children in the church.

Ghanaians also compare notes about parenting with other Ghanaians at work and social gatherings and through telephone conversations. They learn about what happened to the children of friends, as well as the friends of friends, as in the sardine-packing story of the father and daughter in New York City. What could be dismissed as mean-spirited gossip functions as lessons through which parents reflect on and rationalize their own parenting choices, sifting through information that will help them make the fraught decisions about how to best raise their children. Stories serve as an indirect warning to children and parents alike. In other words, gossip generates a feedback loop, arising out of Ghanaians' consciousness of their repertoire, but also fueling their anxiety about their children and their parenting strategies.

Ghanaians' Experiences of America

How do Ghanaians in the United States come to consider and name certain practices as "American"? After all, there are many different kinds of Americans, Americans raise their children in different ways, and young people take many different pathways to adulthood, influenced by their gender, social class, and neighborhood, for example (Lareau 2003). Although Ghanaians know something about America before they arrive—through the stories of already-migrant friends and family members and through the mass media (Grewal 2005)—in general, the "America" they use as contrast to "Ghana" when thinking about their children and parenting comes from their experiences in America rather than preimmigration expectations.

Work

Some of Ghanaians' views about American children come from their work experiences. Alex Stepick and his colleagues (2003) note that "for adult newcomers, Americanization occurs primarily in the workplace" (32). Workplaces vary in their organization, management, clientele, and employees, mainly by industry. As a result, what "America" means varies by employment sector. As noted in chapter 4, many Ghanaians work in social services, as mental health counselors, social workers, and home health aides. Because of the nature of their work, they see American families and individuals when they are struggling and the institutionalization of such struggles.

That Ghanaians learn about American life through their work was driven home to me by Theresa, a young woman who returned to church one Sunday after a long absence because her work schedule now allowed it. After church, she caught up on news with the other women, including telling them about her current and previous jobs as a mental health nurse with children in a facility. Impressing the other women with the horrific aspects of her work, Theresa shared with them how the children were locked in their rooms and wore plastic handcuffs, like they were in jail. She said that even six-year-olds were doing terrible things to one another. There were rapes, for instance, even though the boys and girls slept in different places. The other women, curious, asked if the kids would marry, a sign of whether they would become social adults. Theresa said no, but rather they would live their whole lives in these kinds of facilities. Returning to surer ground, she said that they were on all kinds of medication, which she named. Theresa summarized, *"Aborɔfo nkwadaa yɛ bɔne pa!"* [American children are very wicked!]^{13} Her demonization of children in such facilities is not unusual: Andy West (1999) analyzes media representations of children "in care" in the United Kingdom that portray them as "victims, burglars, and prostitutes" (265).

Theresa was not the only church member to work in places where the angry, confused, and deviant behavior of Americans was regularly on display. For example, one leader of the church youth group drew on her experiences as a counselor in a drug addiction clinic to advise the youth group members. Furthermore, during a sermon on Father's Day, a visiting minister shared the story of a boy who wanted to follow his father into prison, a boy he had met during his day job as a social worker. With work making up many of their hours in the United States, Ghanaians' work experiences colored their sense of American children and family life. Like other commentators, they attributed these problems to American ways of parenting rather than to the lack of support that many American families face (Coontz 2000).

Ghanaians also learn about America through conversations with their coworkers who share their family lives and problems in the workplace. Particularly in the health care field, Ghanaian women tend to work with African-American and immigrant women and learn of their coworkers' home lives through conversations on their breaks or when working together. Irene, for instance, was living with an elderly woman in hospice care. Because of Irene's twenty-four-hour workday, an African-American woman relieved her for two hours each day. One day, Irene reported to me, her coworker was talking on her cell phone to her eleven-year-old son who was in trouble at school. Drawing on her repertoire, Irene decided to give her coworker some advice about raising her son. She had previously learned that her coworker was a single mother who took her son to the movies and bought him consumer goods all the time. Concerned that the boy would get spoiled, becoming a terror as he grew older, Irene recommended to her coworker that when the son misbehaved, she should punish him by not taking him to the movies or buying him shoes. However, Irene later learned that her advice backfired: when her coworker followed her advice, the boy completely trashed his room. Interestingly enough, the lesson Irene learned from this incident was that she should no longer give her coworker advice. Interactions with coworkers provide opportunities for intercultural exchanges about parenting styles, creating possibilities for Americans and Ghanaians alike to expand their repertoires. However, such interactions can also be interpreted through the lens of cultural borders, making Irene more wary about trying to cross what she sees as a cultural divide again.

Media

Ghanaians also learn about "America" from the news and talk-show media, as Americans do. The media, in its search for exciting and interesting stories, often portrays America as more dangerous than it really is and focuses on dramatic events that happen within and to American families, rather than the ordinary routines of life. Crime is a staple news story, and crimes involving violence are more likely to be reported than their incidence would otherwise suggest, creating a public impression of lawlessness (Muncie 1999; Warr 2009; Williams and Dickinson 1993). Ghanaians learn about violent personal crime in their neighborhoods through personal experiences as well as the media. Joanna, a young woman who had just joined her father in the United States from Ghana and lived in an inner-ring, middle-class African-American suburb of an East Coast city, commented on the differences between her expectations and the reality of the United States, both shaped by the media:

> Like when you are back home [in Ghana], you watch TV and you see America, and all you see is Hollywood and stuff and you really don't see anything like about the ghetto and everything. *She laughs.* You know. You really don't see anything about that. And you come [to the United States] and you are living so close to some of these areas, and you hear, there is a shooting here, there is a kidnapping here. And there is a murder here, and there is fire here, and you are like, "Wow, this is not the America I heard about."

Several parents told me about sending their children back to Ghana in part because of fears of crime in their neighborhood. A newspaper story reported on the fatal stabbing of a fifteen-year-old Ghanaian boy by two other adolescent boys in the Bronx, reportedly because of a resisted mugging. His aunt apparently responded to the news of the arrest and the perpetrators' ages with the dispirited comment, "I'm not surprised at whatever happens in this country" (Fahim and Sweeney 2006). These kinds of incidents do not come up overwhelmingly in my conversations with Ghanaian interviewees, but crime as an indicator of American bad behavior is clearly of concern to some.

Neighborhoods

Finally, many Ghanaians learn about American life from their neighbors. "Not having the critical mass of population to form their own ethnic

Table 4. Top ten metropolitan areas for Ghanaian immigrants, 2006–8

Metro area	Number	Frequency (%)
Total in Top 10	1467	63
New York–Northeastern New Jersey	462	20
Washington, DC/MD/VA	398	17
Atlanta, GA	120	5
Newark, NJ	111	5
Chicago–Gary–Lake Charles, IL	91	4
Philadelphia, PA/NJ	67	3
Columbus, OH	61	3
Baltimore, MD	56	2
Worcester, MA	54	2
Middlesex-Somerset-Hunterdon, NJ	47	2

Note: Those born in Ghana, identifying as Black ($N = 2,331$).
Source: American Community Survey, 2006–8.

enclave and self-sufficient communities, Ghanaian immigrants tend to disperse in a mixture of urban and suburban localities where they blend in with immigrant and non-immigrant alike," reports John Arthur (2008, 195). Some of their learning in this regard is based more on observation than dialogue and conversation, given that many Ghanaians live as strangers among their neighbors, as many Americans do. The desire for work plus the desire for cheap housing so that wages can be saved and remitted to relatives mean that they tend to live in or near cities. New York City is a common first destination for Ghanaian immigrants. Ghanaians in New York tend to cluster in the South Bronx and Harlem, historically poor- to working-class African-American neighborhoods (Shani 2010), although Harlem in particular has gentrified rapidly over the past fifteen years. Some then move out to live in the New Jersey, Philadelphia, or the New York suburbs, or even to North Carolina, where they say that life is less "busy," or filled with the hustle and bustle of making a living.[14] The metropolitan areas of Washington, DC, Chicago, Atlanta, and Columbus are other places where many Ghanaians live and work (see table 4).

I have visited over fifty Ghanaians' homes on the East Coast—from the northern Virginia suburbs of Washington, DC, at the southern end, to Worcester, Massachusetts, at the northern end. Two-thirds of those I visited have been in New Jersey and the metropolitan area of Philadelphia and its suburbs. Outside of New York City, the majority of those whose houses I visited lived in small houses in working-class or middle-class neighborhoods in older, inner-ring suburbs. Some live in white working-class neighborhoods, particularly around Philadelphia. One gets a sense that the people in their neighborhoods, like my Ghanaian informants, are working hard to keep their heads above water and make ends meet.

Drawing on American Community Survey data from 2006 to 2008 collected annually by the US Census Bureau, Ghanaians tend to live in neighborhoods where there are an above-average number of immigrants (foreign-born) and of other Africans, but usually not in overwhelming numbers. The average census tract of the residences of forty-three interviewees whose addresses I obtained had the following characteristics: a relatively high 20 percent foreign-born population, of whom 19 percent were African born; a relatively diverse racial/ethnic composition of 40 percent white, 44 percent Black, and 15 percent Latino; a median household income (1999) of $47,833 (near the national average); a poverty rate of 12 percent (also near the national average); a four-year college completion rate of 25 percent; and a high-school completion rate of 85 percent.

However, there was also great variation in the characteristics of the neighborhoods in which respondents lived. Twelve households lived in census tracts where poverty rates were 18 percent, above the national average; seventeen households lived in census tracts with about average rates of poverty; and thirteen households lived in census tracts with low rates of poverty (less than 5 percent). Fifteen lived in areas where whites were the largest group (three in the Midwest, one in the Northeast); ten lived in census tracts in highly segregated Black neighborhoods, where Blacks were over 80 percent of the residents, with varying levels of income; eight lived in majority Black neighborhoods, three of which were Black, middle-class areas in terms of income and education; six lived in segregated white neighborhoods; and three, all in New York City, lived in majority Latino neighborhoods, with high foreign-born populations and an average high poverty rate, working-poor income, and low educational level. Overall, then, Ghanaians interviewed as part of the US portion of my study tended to live disproportionately with other immigrants, African-Americans, and other Africans, in neighborhoods with lower-middle-class household income and average education levels among its resident adults. One teenage girl living in Worcester, Massachusetts, who had recently joined her father in the United States, expressed surprise at her school and new friends: she had expected to meet whites in the United States, but instead found herself in a diverse school of Central American, South Asian, and African immigrants. In most of the interviews, it was to African-Americans and first- and second-generation Latinos—their neighbors and work colleagues—with whom Ghanaians compared themselves, and in particular, their ways of parenting.

I heard a great deal about Latino and African-American neighbors from Ghanaians who used these observations as the source of contrast and comparison. For instance, more than one mother told me admiringly that the children of her Latino neighbors spoke "their language," which many Ghanaian youngsters lose growing up in the United States. Those interviewees who lived in the poorest neighborhoods (in Newark, West Philadelphia, and the South Bronx) were most critical of African-Americans, with the primary criticism concerning their perceptions of them as workers, not surprising given Ghanaians' focus on work in their own migrations.

Ghanaian migrants' stereotypes of what "American" and "Ghanaian" mean are formed through Ghanaians' experiences of living and working in the United States and indicate how Ghanaian parents' repertoires have been modified and reorganized according to these categories. As Yen Le Espiritu (1999) noted, "Group identities necessarily form through interaction with other groups—through complicated experiences of conflict and cooperation—and in structural contexts of power" (511). The understanding that "these people are different in this way" is formed through interaction, observation, and communication with those others at work and home (Garc'a Canclini 1995; Malkki 1995; Rosaldo 2003). As a result, although conscious identities explicitly signal differences between groups, we might also say that they imply connections and similarities between groups, to the extent that they are formed through living and working together in the same society.

Christianity and Being American

The leaders of the church youth group wanted the young people to be good Christians. At times the opposition between American and Ghanaian ways were used to drive home the lesson of how Christians ought to act, ways that were dependent on the repertoire of the adult leaders, born and raised in Ghana, and exposed through their work, friends, and neighborhoods to "America." To be more specific, American ways, particular those coded as marking an African-American underclass, were signaled as being not Christian. African-American identity serves as a potent marker for Africans because it is in the United States that they encounter their racialization as Blacks in ways they did not experience or anticipate in Africa (Hintzen and Rahier 2003). Being Black in America, in the words of Tejumola Olaniyan, a Nigerian academic who lives and works in the United States, "puts one in a certain unfavorable relationship to opportunities offered by the system, because it is white-controlled and racist" (2003, 57). However, like other immigrants, Africans tend to see the United States as more open to hard work, drive, and talent than other oppressed minorities like African-Americans, who have a long historical memory of oppression, more accumulated everyday experiences of racism, and a better understanding of how the structural legacies of slavery and segregation are present today (Ogbu 1978; Olaniyan 2003). Africans' migration is premised on American promises of a better life, "the American Dream"; as a result, psychically, it might be hard to acknowledge the constraints on opportunities by "this prison called my skin" (Táíwò 2003). Consequently, one strategy for upward mobility in a racially charged environment has been distancing oneself from African-Americans and highlighting one's foreignness, as has been well documented in Caribbean communities (Waters 1999). This strategy has often been accompanied by adopting standard hegemonic narratives of African-Americans in the United States about their lack of work ethic and immoral family life. Youth leaders learned to position "bad" African-Americans against "good" (Christian) Africans in youth group discussions through their experiences of living and working in the United States.

During one lesson, after talking about music lyrics, Kwasi's coleader demonstrated a particular kind of greeting as a behavior in which the young people should not engage—he walked up, swaying in an exaggerated way from side to side, to greet one of the young men in the group, touching fist to fist, and said, "What's up, man?" The leader enjoyed this example so much that he and the other young man repeated this action a few times. In the context of the overall discussion, the leader was defining this as un-Christian behavior. Although there is nothing morally wrong with this particular kind of greeting from my perspective, the handshake was symbolic of a "ghetto style" that youth group leaders warned young people through multiple means against. The example shows that the opposition between bad "American" and good/Christian "Ghanaian" requires some knowledge and awareness of "American" practices, even the ability to reenact or "copy" a particular kind of greeting, even if only to criticize it. Lessons in the youth group encouraged Ghanaian young people to distinguish themselves from underclass and working-class African-Americans, although such direct language was muted in the public discourse of the church.

In a private interview, Kwasi was more candid about wanting to insulate his daughter from a particular style of speech he associated with African-Americans. He told me he was pleased with his daughter's preschool. Because the student population was almost all white, he thought his daughter "can copy that aspect of life, like the way she speaks," without picking up a way of speaking he associated with African-Americans. "The accent will be accepted, yeah, accepted." Acting "white" or at least separating oneself from African-Americans was seen as a route to his daughter's being accepted and upwardly mobile, in a employment market in which she would be viewed by the master status of being Black (Anderson 1990). Becoming white has been significant in the history of Europeans immigrants' inclusion in the United States (Roediger 2005).

The adult lessons were not always successful, as some of the young people in the church, particularly those born and raised in the United States, identified as African-American more than "African" or Ghanaian. Teasing from schoolmates about their Ghanaian-accented English encouraged them to pick up an American accent as part of other modifications they were making in their repertoires.

Christianity and moral behavior can be presented as a Ghanaian attribute, or as a shared religion under which differences between Ghanaians and (African) Americans dissolve. Neighbors and work provide not only opportunities for a tightening of cultural borders but also for recognition that cultural differences may not be so deep and wide after all. I will illustrate this point through an observation of an "outdooring" ceremony for Janet's eldest son, in which the baby was given a name and received community blessings.

Mainly, members of Janet's church attended the gathering, but a few of her neighbors also came: an African-American couple with their toddler and an Asian-American young man. Janet lived in a working-class inner-ring suburb of a major East Coast city, where many people worked at the nearby airport or in the industrial zone that bordered it. After the ceremony, while we were still gathered together in a circle of chairs in Janet's finished basement, the guests were invited to give parenting advice to the happy parents. These speeches revealed the individuals' habitual repertoires—their sense of who was empowered to speak in such a gathering, their knowledge of what was appropriate to say in such a gathering and how to say it, and what their own expectations and hopes for the family were.

After a brief pause, a respected Ghanaian elder from Janet's church who had raised her daughter and grandchildren in the United States said that because they were in America, they should have "patience" with their children. Even if you felt like yelling at your children because of the stresses of life, she said, you should be patient. Children in the United States are not like those in Ghana and so they should be treated differently. In the silence that followed her statement, the husband in the African-American couple added hesitantly that he would also like to say something, and, on being given the floor, said that children should respect their mother and father.

After a longer pause, another woman from Janet's church was persuaded by others to speak, and she said she would do so, if she could use Twi. Encouraged to continue, she said that the only thing you could do as a parent was pray. The children might summon the police if you beat them, so you should just pray.

The content and mode of the guests' advice are their repertoires in action. The Ghanaians emphasized the differences between American and Ghanaian ways of parenting, encouraging the new parents, in a general way, to change their parenting repertoire to accommodate to "America," by being more patient and relying on God. As a result of their experiences in the United States and their discussions with other parents in the Ghanaian immigrant community, they had a heightened consciousness of their repertoire and what specifically needed to be modified. In doing so, they relied on distinctions between "Ghana" and "America" to give their advice.

The advice of the African-American neighbor may have surprised them, although no one commented to that effect, at least in my hearing. His advice was an example of ways in which repertoires may overlap, in this case, through Christianity. He did not emphasize national differences between Ghana and the United States. The content of his statement was very much in line with the emphasis many Ghanaian parents place on children's respect of and obedience to their elders. It echoed the biblical sixth commandment, which was emphasized again and again in Janet's church. No doubt, his compatibility was one reason he and his wife had been invited to the celebration. Regardless, although the Ghanaians emphasized national borders in thinking about children, due to the ways their experiences of living and working in America made them reflect on their repertoires, the neighbor's public statement showed those borders might be bridged (in this case, by a shared religious idiom).

Conclusion

Although parents in Ghana are also careful about their children's character and training, their anxieties about parenting increase in the United States. To paraphrase Kwasi, while they knew how to parent in Ghana, their competence feels fragile and hard-won in the United States. At the same time, the stakes rise: their reputations are monitored, gossip within the Ghanaian immigrant community evaluates their parenting, and their children might not take advantage of the increased opportunities and resources available in the United States. They feel alone as parents, as Janet said, without the support of other institutions and relatives. Furthermore, some of their repertoire that might bolster their authority, such as physical punishment, cannot be enacted without the risk of state sanction and power.

In this state of unease, parents become self-conscious about their repertoire. Through their networks and community organizations, they share their nascent understandings of and confusion about their experiences, building a coherent picture with one another through the opposition of "Ghanaian" and "American." Respect, perseverance through hardship, obedience, discipline, and Christianity—precisely the character traits they hope to inculcate in their children—get labeled as Ghanaian, in contrast to the freedom and wayward behavior associated with America. A nostalgic image of Ghana is generated alongside a dystopian view of families in the United States, a country where anything can happen, in the negative sense, to paraphrase the woman whose nephew was fatally stabbed.

To the extent that a way of organizing experiences helps address some people's frustrations and unease, it becomes more widely shared within the Ghanaian community. This way of speaking was particularly common in the Ghanaian church I attended, not because of the coordinated efforts of the church leadership, but because the church brought people together in ways that they could communicate their understandings with one another, during discussions in and around the service, at social occasions sponsored by the church, and in the youth group, where church leaders actively tried to influence the next generation.

Like other studies (e.g., Kibria 1993; Small 1997), this research raises serious questions about the dominant trope of assimilation or Americanization in studies of immigrant families. Articulating a pedagogical opposition between America and one's homeland seems common among immigrants to the United States, suggesting that national identification is heightened by the context of reception (Malkki 1995). Therefore, contrasting America and Ghana might be considered part of becoming American, and "America" itself the product of immigrant or transnational practices (Grewal 2005). However, rather than positing that what is happening to Ghanaian parents is Americanization or a re-Ghanaianization, this chapter suggests a more nuanced approach in which people self-consciously revise and reshuffle their repertoire in response to new conditions and new ideas. Immigrants are adding to their repertoire in self-conscious ways, not replacing it, as the concept of Americanization suggests. For example, the ability to critique a particular style of handshake in a church youth group is dependent on the ability to enact it over and over again, even with pleasure. Furthermore, coming to the United States can prompt a revival of a "traditional" parenting strategy, otherwise dismissed by the urban middle class in Ghana as a second-best option. Scholars should not take their infor-mants' oppositions as their own social analysis. As this chapter has shown, in place of the concept of Americanization, what is happening is a more complex process in which immigrants are adding to, rather than replac-ing, their repertoire. They are representing some aspects of their repertoire self-consciously as "Ghanaian," in opposition to "American," while other aspects, including practices of distributing parenthood and the materiality of care, remain commonsensical and assumed.

Parents turn to fostering their children in Ghana not because fostering becomes self-consciously a symbol of Ghanaian identity. Rather, their con-scious opposition between Ghanaian and American parenting makes send-ing their children to Ghana an obvious solution to a child's misbehavior or poor grades, for parents and their parents' peers. Out of frustration, parents revive an aspect of their repertoire they would not otherwise have used. The number of children sent to Ghana from the United States is much less than the number left behind by a migrant parent. However, the discourse that fuels sending a child back is widespread within the Ghanaian immi-grant community, affecting those who raise their children in the United States as well as those who leave them behind. Fostering is, therefore, to some extent, a product of migrants' encounters with the United States, as I have detailed in the last few chapters, particularly migrants' work and neighborhood experiences, restrictive immigration laws, and lack of public and social support for new immigrant workers in the lowest-paid sectors of the American economy. The next two chapters examine the effects of these practices on those in Ghana, chapter 6 focusing on migrant parents' rela-tionships with caregivers and chapter 7 on the emotional responses of the children of migrants to separation from their parents.

SIX

The Dilemmas of Fostering the
Children of Transnational Migrants

In chapter 2, I described two patterns in fosterage practices in Akropong, one more emergent than the other. In the older pattern, dating from the 1970s at least, grandmothers foster their grandchildren to support their working daughters. In the newer pattern, fostering-out one's children is viewed as being caused by hardship, and thus not something middle-class, urban residents would prefer to do. Partly as a result of the first pattern, fosterage is in the habitual repertoire of transnational migrants: they can turn to it as a solution when confronted with immigration laws, working conditions, or concerns for their children's character development. At the same time, because of the second pattern, tensions arise when those more favored (transnational migrants) foster-out their children with poorer relations in Ghana. The changes in the flow of children through households create new expectations regarding flows of gratitude and resources. As a result, some migrants find themselves turning to more commercial and impersonal arrangements for their children's care, like boarding schools or hired help, where the obligations seem more straightforward and less emotionally complicated. This shift to commercial arrangements is occurring in other areas of Ghanaian family life, including in domestic service and eldercare, fueled by the greater access to cash among international migrants and other members of the middle class and changing expectations about reciprocities between kin, a topic I hope to explore further in future research.

Transnational migrants are considered wealthy because of their work abroad, yet they turn to relatives, poorer by virtue of living in Ghana, to raise their children rather than fostering those poorer relatives' children as they might were they in Ghana. They might have financially helped out the parents of the children they fostered. The class dimensions of fosterage are thus reversed: middle-class, urban residents, rather than doing a favor for their poorer kin by fostering their children, are now in the position of asking those relatives to foster their own. Parents abroad feel indebted and obligated to their relatives in Ghana, an uncomfortable situation to be in.

Because of this reversal in class relations and obligations, remittances become more prominent within fosterage relations, with the biological parent sending money to the foster parent to help care for the child. Remittances serve a complex function within this delicately managed relationship. Remittances are not payment to relatives for their care, but rather serve as a sign of appreciation and gratitude, a gift rather than a contract. When the relationship goes awry, remittances can be the focal complaint. Typically, migrants feel they are sacrificing and working hard to send remittances home, while those in Ghana feel the remittances are insufficient. Remittances become central to the evaluation of these intricate relationships, as we will see through comments by foster parents in this chapter and by children in chapter 7.

The pattern is similar to that of grandmother fosterage, in which an older woman helped her daughter, a female urban migrant, balance work and child care, and in appreciation, was assured of receiving the financial, social, and physical support that would normally be her due, but which was not always regularly forthcoming from her children. Indeed, many transnational migrants turn to their mothers to help them raise their children. However, grandmother fosterage is considered problematic for older children because of concerns about a grandmother's lack of education or inability to discipline. These concerns have a class dimension, particularly in Akuapem, where discipline is associated with Presbyterian schooling. In other words, these concerns are focused on creating a particular kind of repertoire in the child that is seen as cultural capital in Ghana, to become an educated and middle-class person.

Furthermore, those abroad would like to raise their children in an urban, middle-class environment with access to high-quality schools, as the parents would want to do if they were in Ghana, and which their wages abroad enable. Poorer relatives and grandmothers living in less urban areas are therefore not favored as foster parents. Instead, parents seek out foster parents like themselves: middle-aged, formally employed, educated, urban residents. These kinds of adults are less dependent on their remittances and have less free time than those not fully employed. Because of the complications with fosterage, and the tensions and strains that can result with loved ones, some transnational parents expand their repertoires to seek new solutions, such as relying on nonrelatives or hired help to care for their children.

Reversals in Fosterage

Kelda was a middle-aged woman I met in Akropong through a friend. The mother of three children, she had a tiny shop where she sold candy and groceries; given its small size and inventory, the business did not seem to be prosperous. She described her own childhood, when she had gone to live with her aunt, her father's sister, when she was four or five years old, because her aunt had only one child. She told me that her aunt "is my mother," signaling that she had more affection for her aunt than for her biological mother. Perhaps influenced by this positive experience, she later gave a daughter to her aunt to raise and a son to her younger sister, because her sister liked him and had no children. When Kelda's sister and her sister's husband went to the United States ten years ago, they wanted to take Kelda's son with them, but like Rosamund's father described in chapter 3, they could not. The sister continues to pay the school fees for Kelda's children's and calls them often, to the extent that Kelda calls her biological children "my sister's children." Kelda's brother also went to the United States, obtaining a green card through the diversity lottery, and he took his wife and youngest child with him. He left behind his oldest child who was over the age of sixteen and did not have a birth certificate, two factors that, as described in chapter 3, made it difficult for the child to accompany his parents. This nephew is now living with Kelda and her three children. Because of her siblings' international migrations, the children of her family—including her own—have been redistributed to Kelda. She had given two of her three children to be fostered by others, but on her sister's international migration, one returned to Kelda, although her sister continues to support him and his siblings through her remittances. Furthermore, Kelda has become the recipient of her brother's oldest child, despite her difficulty making ends meet. International migration has therefore made poorer relatives, typically fostering-out parents, into fostering-in parents dependent on parents' remittances.

I encountered two families in which a man with young children had died and in which one of the man's siblings had migrated abroad. The death of a parent of young children is a crisis situation in which siblings are supposed to step in and offer to take in one or more children to assist the widow or widower. However, siblings who are international migrants cannot make such an offer, despite being in the best financial position, theoretically, to help out. In one case, a brother of the deceased had traveled to the United Kingdom and was remitting money regularly to the children's mother. Three of the four children stayed with their mother in Kumasi, while the fourth, David, stayed with his father's sister and her husband, a Presbyterian minister, in Akuapem. David and his uncle saw the uncle abroad as fulfilling his responsibilities, although the uncle David lived with sometimes had to use his own money for David's expenses, such as when the money remitted was not sufficient or did not arrive in time (to pay school fees, for example). David, age sixteen, said about his relationship with his uncle abroad: "It seems he is doing what is expected of him to do because, *enti, yɛn ntɛm ye* [so our relationship is good]."

However, Rexford, another uncle in a similar situation—a migrant in the United States when his brother Stephen died—was viewed as having absconded from his responsibilities. After Stephen's passing, his five children went to live with another brother and his wife, Cynthia. But when that brother, Cynthia's husband, later died, Cynthia sent the children—her husband's nieces and nephews—to live with their mother in another town in Ghana. But then the mother too became sick and died, and her relatives brought the children back to Cynthia, saying that there was no one in the mother's family who could look after them. Cynthia appealed to Rexford, the last brother of her husband's siblings still alive, the uncle who had migrated to the United States:

> But ɔno nso, mekyerɛw no se, anka ɔmmɛhwɛ wɔn nso. Ɛnna ɔno nso se, seisei n'adwuma asɛe. Ɛnyɛ adwuma na ne yere nso wɔ hɔ nti, menkɔ so na owie a, na sɛ ɔba back a, na ɔba bɛhwɛ wɔn so. Yɛnte ne nka bio.
> I wrote to him, saying he should look after them. But he said that he was out of work and he was married [that is, he had his own family responsibilities] so I should continue [looking after the children], but if he returns to Ghana, then he will look after them. We haven't heard from him since.

Because Cynthia feels that the orphaned children—not her relatives—were dumped on her, she feels bitter at both her husband's relatives and the relatives of the mother of the children for not taking care of them. But because she was worried that the children's future would be ruined by their relatives' neglect, she took some responsibility for them, giving two of the three youngest children to her elder sister and letting the eldest two children, in their early twenties, make their own way in the world. Now recently retired and suffering from the effects of a minor stroke, she is eager to no longer have even the responsibility of the youngest, age fifteen.

When I talked to Rexford by phone on my return to the United States, he said that he sent money to help his nieces and nephews with their educations, but could not bring them to the United States because of "the DNA," which allowed him to bring over only his biological children. "I am the only provider," he said, as all his siblings have now died, a fact that upsets him greatly. "That weighs very heavily on me," he said. If he had been in Ghana, he told me,

> at least they would have somebody to go to. Wherever I am, they would be there with me. Because my brothers' children and my sisters' children are just like my own children, so they would have been there with me. But as things stand now, some of them are with [Cynthia] and some of them are with my cousin, and so they are scattered all over the place.

Because he migrated to the United States over twenty years ago and only visited Ghana once since, for his mother's funeral, he does not know his nieces or nephews well. However, his affection for his siblings spills over to their children, fueling his sense of obligation for their care.

As Rexford suggests, remittances do not fully substitute for living with a child. Someone who is living with a child is likely to spend more of his or her money than someone sending remittances, for living with a child allows the caregiver to see the child's needs and take care of the child's living expenses as they arise. One can see that the child's shoes are getting worn, or that the child's hair is getting long. Remittances may pay for the major expenses, such as the child's schooling or medical bills, but the day-to-day expenses of meals and pocket money may well be borne by the person with whom the child is living. One study found that remittances comprise, on average, only 9 percent of household income in Ghanaian households that receive remittances (Mazzucato, van den Boom, and Nsowah-Nuamah 2005). It would be hard for a foster parent to quantify the expenses of an additional child, for they are either subsumed into household expenses (as in meals) or small, daily sums of money (like pocket money for snacks at school). Remittances, on the other hand, make the flow of money from the parent or migrant relative to the foster parent explicit. Because of the costs of sending money, large amounts are sent at a single point in time. They are signed for at the post office or money transfer center. Remittance money is therefore highly visible in the relationship between foster parent and migrant parent.

Remittances also played a role in parents' concerns that foster parents would not discipline the children properly. Rather than "correcting" their children, foster parents would "pamper" them, which would "spoil" the child's character. One reason they felt that foster parents might not correct and discipline a child well is because if a child complained about his or her treatment, the parent might move the child to another foster parent and the original foster parent would lose the remittances. Kwabena reported there are "problems when people raise" your children. They might "pamper the child because of remittances." Ama thought that only 20 percent of her friends would raise her child properly. Because they would want the money, she thought, they would spoil and pamper the child. She felt that only her mother or sister cared enough about her to discipline her child as she would like. Although migrants told me they were worried that foster parents were motivated by money, foster parents told me about their resentment that they had to supplement the remittances sent, as is the case among other caregivers of children of migrants (Dreby 2010; Moran-Taylor 2008).

International migration shifts the burden of day-to-day care to poorer relatives "back home," and may also shift some of its costs. Some foster parents appreciate the remittances, which give them greater access to cash, but others find them less significant to their own well-being. Remittances substitute for migrants' fostering children in to support struggling or deceased siblings and therefore become more significant in fosterage relationships, for all involved. At times, migrants' exclusion from the network of potential foster parents threatens children with abandonment, as in the case of Rexford and his nieces and nephews. In general, however, the fact that international migrants leave their children with kin in Ghana rather than taking their kin's children with them abroad does not bother those I talked to in Akropong. In Kelda's case, as in others, remittances were considered an adequate, even welcome, substitute for migrants' inability to foster the children of their needy relatives or relatives in crisis. Complaints about international migrants ducking their family care responsibilities were directed at those migrants who did not remit and were not heard from again, not toward those who remitted and called but could not foster the children of poorer relatives. And although those in Ghana can also avoid these family responsibilities, or can substitute funds for the daily labor of caring, people seem more upset when those abroad do not send remittances because they are seen as being in a better position to provide help.

Grandmother Fostering

The trend of grandmothers raising children to support working, migrant mothers is compatible with transnational migration and has become more significant as a result. Grandmothers, as I have already described, have helped their daughters combine work and reproduction by fostering their daughters' children. Grandmothers fostering the children of their daughters and sons abroad find clear continuities in fosterage patterns and very few changes introduced by migration abroad. One grandmother living in Akropong was taking care of an infant granddaughter whose mother and father were living in the United Kingdom. Living in a multigenerational compound house with many other women, including another daughter with a baby, she found her grandchild a joy rather than a burden.[1] The courtyard was often lively with conversation over communal work, whether making food, cooking, or washing baby clothes. Further easing her burden, she took the baby to day care every morning. She commented that all her children were providing for her, both those abroad and those in Ghana:

> Wɔn nyinaa bɔ mmɔden, wɔn a wɔwɔ Aburokyiri no, wɔmena, wɔn a wɔwɔ ha
> nso wɔmena, enti ne nyinaa ɛyɛ the same.
> They all do well: those abroad remit money, those here in Ghana also remit,
> and so they are all the same.

The only difference she saw was that those in Ghana gave her money every week or every other week when they visited her, while those abroad remitted monthly. Her son and his wife were nurses abroad, and so they had the financial resources and documents to travel back and forth to visit their children every three months or so, an unusual situation.

Grandmothers are available to take care of children—they have the time as their work is marginal and does not pay well—and they may drop what they are doing to help a migrant relative. In addition, grandmothers want their children to succeed, and they are mindful of their need for financial support as they age. However, other factors militate against leaving children with grandmothers and poor relatives in villages and hometowns. Grandmothers are both the ones to whom Ghanaian parents most easily turn as caregivers and the most suspect as pamperers, similar to the representation of grandmothers in Mexican transnational families (Dreby 2010). Winifred, an immigrant in the United States, whose mother was raising her daughters in Ghana, said, "One other thing too is if we were there, we would spank them more, like we would discipline them more than their grandmothers would discipline them. Because usually the grandmothers are happy having their grandchildren around, so there are certain things they will overlook." Irene complained that her parents do not discipline her son who was living with them, although she felt that they raised her

Figure 8. A grandmother taking her two granddaughters to preschool
one misty morning. Photo by author.

generation well. Joanna, a young woman raised in Ghana and now attending a state university in the United States, reflected on her own future as a mother and on whether she would send her child back to Ghana to be raised. She said, "My mom [back in Ghana] will probably spoil him or her, but I hope, you know, my brothers or someone who is in a good position [will be able to take care of my child back home]. Grandparents are good but they just spoil kids." As noted in chapter 2, some schoolteachers in Akropong attribute grandmother fosterage to children's indiscipline and poor academic work.

Raising children either with poorer relatives or grandmothers is thus problematic for transnational parents abroad and for their relatives in Ghana. Furthermore, migrants abroad would like their children to go to good schools and live where there is electricity and running water. They would like their children to live with the accoutrements of a middle-class lifestyle. This means that given the opportunity migrants would rather their children live in urban areas rather than rural ones or in the town of Akropong. Although some grandmothers do live in cities, usually in an adult child's house, it is more common for them, as their economic opportunities decline, to retire to their hometowns where they can live in family housing, which is rent free. There, too, they can live with other relatives who can help with daily life and be a source of companionship.

The Preference for Middle-Aged and Middle-Class Foster Parents Living in Urban Areas

I first met the elderly Mr. and Mrs. Yirenkyi in Akropong in 2005 when they were taking care of their daughter's eleven-year-old son, Offei. Offei's father had just gone to work in the United States, and their daughter lived in a commercial town elsewhere in the Eastern Region. When I visited them three years later, however, Offei had gone to live with his father's sister in Accra, where he had previously spent school vacations and through whom his father had always funneled remittances. Mr. Yirenkyi, a genteel retired teacher who had been transferred many times during his career, listed the reasons for Offei's "small transfer," as he put it, feeling that it was, overall, a good thing for all involved. Mrs. Yirenkyi had had a stroke in the interval, unfortunately, and in helping her around the house, Offei had less opportunity to study. Offei's education in general had been suffering, and a private school in Accra was seen as a better option than the poorer-quality public and private schools of Akropong. The father's sister had a self-contained house in Accra in contrast to the family compound house in Akropong, where Mr. Yirenkyi felt that Offei might be influenced in the wrong direction by other residents. The house of Offei's aunt in Accra was located near the private school Offei attended, so Offei could easily attend tutorials termed "extra classes" that teachers organized after school. Furthermore, although Mr. Yirenkyi had a TV, he mentioned that in the aunt's house, Offei could watch educational programs on TV and play with cousins about his age. In Akropong, I met and heard of other children of migrants abroad who had moved to live with relatives or go to boarding school in Accra or its twin city of Tema. People considered the major cities, with their middle-class amenities and educational opportunities, more appropriate for the children of migrants. Fathers and the father's side of the family tended to take more interest in boys as they got older, and this may also have played a part in Offei's move from living with his maternal grandparents to staying with his paternal aunt.

Olivia, another resident of Akropong, had a similar experience: the children of her younger sister, Veronica, left her care. Olivia had moved to stay with Veronica's two children in Veronica's rented accommodation in Akropong while Veronica visited her husband in France, on what she said would be a one-month stay. Olivia had been working as a cook in her father's private school in the regional capital, Koforidua, but the school was not doing well, and so she was ready to help Veronica out when Veronica asked for her help. Instead of a short visit, however, when Veronica became pregnant in France, she decided to continue living there without authorization and has stayed there ever since. Three years later Olivia continues to live in Akropong, taking some responsibility for Veronica's daughter and son, aged fifteen and eighteen respectively, albeit with great reluctance. Olivia now makes a living selling prepared food by the side of the road in Akropong, rising early each day to cook or to travel to a regional market for cheaper ingredients. She sold the lease of the kiosk that Veronica used from her days as a seamstress in Akropong to help fund her nephew's education. She helped her niece gain admission to a boarding secondary school a year ago. Because Veronica had a baby and was not working, in part because she was in France without authorization, she did not send much in the way of remittances, requiring Olivia to draw on her own resources, including those Veronica left behind in her care. However, Olivia became less central to Veronica's children's care over time, as the young people went to stay with another aunt in Tema during their school vacations. Olivia explained that the children could take remedial and vacation classes in Tema, although there may be other reasons for the move, such as Olivia's annoyance with the children's laziness in helping her around the house or with Veronica for leaving her in this pickle. The children did, however, sometimes pass through Akropong on their way between Tema and their respective schools to greet Olivia and her children, so that I was able to briefly meet them.

Because migrants want their children to live a middle-class lifestyle in Ghana and have access to a good education, they do not want to leave their children with their poorer and elderly relatives in Akropong.[2] Relatives who can provide access to a middle-class lifestyle tended to be more middle-aged than elderly, more urban than rural, more educated than not, and more likely to be employed as a salaried worker than working in the informal sector. A middle-aged person is seen as being in a better position to discipline a child than a frail grandparent; migrants preferred siblings over grandparents even though grandparents were more available. In other words, the preferred foster parents of the children of migrants were similar, in terms of class position and age, to the parents or what they aspired to be before they went abroad. Parents sought replacements for themselves rather than using fosterage to expand a child's range of opportunities, patronage, and training.

Such preferred foster parents were, however, likely to feel that taking care of the children of migrants was a burden, because they themselves were stretched thin by their work and family responsibilities. I particularly heard the complaint about caring for children of migrant parents from foster parents who were women working in salaried positions, well educated, and living in cities. Some had to commute long distances across the city to get to their workplace using public transportation. Some were single mothers, separated from their spouses; others lived apart from their husbands in long-distance relationships, a relatively common occurrence among educated couples who are regularly transferred between different schools or district offices. Many talked to me about supplementing a migrant's remittances with their own salaries. Some required the help of other young people—children of poorer relatives or strangers—to manage their households, in part because the addition of children of migrants abroad to those households had increased the amount of labor required to run the household.

Charlotte is one example of this kind of caregiver. In her fifties, she worked as a secretary for a government office in a regional capital and was looking forward to retirement. She was taking care of two grandchildren, ages three and six, the children of her daughters. One daughter was in South Africa, living with Charlotte's husband, a migrant there; the other was in Holland, having previously found South Africa a difficult place to live.[3] Charlotte found it hard to get to work on time, because she had to bathe her grandchildren, make them breakfast, and take them to school and day care in the mornings. She rushed home from work quickly to feed them. The eldest grandchild was particularly fond of imported sweets and soda, so she worked hard to feed him more filling and cheap Ghanaian food, which he would take only when she fed him with her own hand.[4] She was helped in the household by three adolescents, two of whom were her husband's brother's children "from the village" (her words) and one a child of a sister whose father was poor. Charlotte was paying for the hairdressing apprenticeship of one of her nieces. These dependent relatives were at home when the grandchildren came home from school and day care, but the grandchildren often asked Charlotte to feed or bathe them. Without the grandchildren in the house, she said, she would be "very free," although other family obligations might very well take their place. For example, she discussed taking care of a beloved sister after she had a stroke prior to the arrival of her grandchildren.

Comfort was a single mother and the principal of a large junior-secondary school in Accra, a job with many responsibilities that kept her running between her school, her teachers' residences, and the central educational office. Several years after her sister, Cecilia, and her husband went to live in the United States, Comfort moved into Cecilia's house in an Accra suburb with her own three teenage children to take care of Cecilia's three children, a move that lengthened her commute to school and to the home of her elderly mother, whom she tried to visit regularly. Comfort also kept alive her social networks to help her nieces and nephew make progress in their troubled educational pathways. One Saturday, for instance, in addition to doing the household grocery shopping for the week at a low-cost market and visiting her mother, she deliberately attended a wedding where she expected to encounter one of her friends who teaches at a university. Cecilia's oldest son had been suspended from a private university on suspicion of stealing a cell phone, and Comfort hoped her friend could help him gain admittance to her university. Similarly, Cecilia's oldest daughter had been kicked out of a secondary school in Accra because of her poor academic performance, and Comfort asked a friend who was the principal of a secondary school in Kumasi to take her niece on probation. Helping Comfort manage her complicated household was a student of a poor family, from Comfort's school, whom Comfort was fostering because of her intellectual promise. This adolescent girl lived with Comfort, and Comfort paid her school fees.

Cecilia's oldest daughter, sixteen years old, was very aware of how she and her siblings made her aunt Comfort's life more complicated. In her headlong way of speaking, she talked about how Comfort had visited her often when she went to secondary school in Accra:

> Aunty has been visiting me, but every day, I think every day. If I need something, I will call her and she will come, even if she is doing something. She will stop and come. . . . It is like we are worrying her. It makes me feel bad. "I want something tomorrow." You call her back; you want another thing. You call her. She, too, she has children to look after. Maybe her children would call her to bring things and because of me, she wouldn't be able to go. And maybe her children too will feel she doesn't like them, that she is paying [too] much attention to us.

Comfort agreed that taking care of Cecilia's children was a burden on her, but for different reasons than the time burden Cecilia's daughter mentioned. Instead she focused on cost. She said that she spent more than twice the amount Cecilia remits every month on food, supplementing the remittances with her salary. Comfort wanted to make sure the children eat well as she feels that a lack of proper meals causes children to go buy prepared food and snacks, leading to loitering in the streets and acquiring bad company. In other words, she links the provision of substantial, abundant, and readily available food to discipline (as Afua also did, more obliquely, in chapter 3). Furthermore, in moving to Cecilia's house, her transportation costs to school and her mother's house have also increased. But when she made the move to her sister's house, she told me, she reasoned, "Here is my sister" whose children were not being looked after well by a woman hired to take care of them. "So I would sacrifice and do it myself," Comfort said. "Because if they come out well one day, it will be to my credit."

Both Cecilia and Comfort describe themselves as giving up a great deal to help each other; each feels the other is indebted to her. I describe Cecilia's perspective on remittances more in the next chapter. Comfort, as a teacher, is used to fostering children, particularly poor children, who can help her manage her busy life. But fostering her sister's children, children who demand special attention and are less useful around the household, feels quite different: it causes her to reflect on her obligations to her family and the honor that might accrue to her in future. In general, even when the children of international migrants have grown up a little and are able to contribute to housework, they tend to be treated as special, allowed to watch TV and play rather than contributing to the household chores. They are fed imported and more expensive food, like fruit juices, ice cream, and soda. This leads to parents abroad worrying about their children being spoiled, making the option of fostering them in Ghana produce anxiety and concern, while the foster parents resent the expense and burden of taking care of children who require special treatment.

Hired Help or Schools as Foster Parents

International migrants were also concerned about the burden on their relatives—for the sake of their own children and for the sake of their relationship with their sibling or mother. Anita, a mother who had raised her six children in the United States for the past seventeen years, explained that her mother had died and her sister had her own children; she felt it would be a burden to ask someone to look after her children, even if she sent money home. She thought about sending her children to boarding school in Ghana. Her American colleagues at her workplace in a public library thought she was considering boarding school to punish her children for their misbehavior, but Anita explained that she was instead intrigued by this option because of the greater sense of self-reliance and independence she had learned from going to boarding school. But she did not want to place a burden on a teacher to look after them and did not know any teacher personally whom she could ask to do such a special favor for her. Like Anita, some considered the possible conflicts that resulted from leaving a child with a relative too onerous and turned to other options—a domestic servant, a boarding school, or not sending their children to Ghana at all.

Comfort's sister, Cecilia, who had lived in the United States for eight years, explained why she hired a woman as a caregiver before asking her siblings for help: "Sometimes you don't want to turn to family, because they might do something to hurt you. If a stranger treats you badly, it doesn't hurt so much, because you expect it." She worried that conflict between siblings could ruin relationships in the next generation. During the five years she was away, her husband traveled to London for two years and was in Ghana for three years. Even when he lived in Ghana, he was away from the household a great deal because of his business travel. A hired woman lived in her house with her three children, but Comfort did not think she was taking good care of them. When the husband joined his wife in the United States, Comfort persuaded Cecilia to let her move into Cecilia's house with her own three children, and the situation for Cecilia's children in the two years since, by all accounts, has much improved.

Both Mary and Irene, in contrast, first tried to rely on relatives before turning to a nonrelative in frustration. Mary took her eight-year-old son out of the care of her sister after he repeated several grades at school. She felt that one of the reasons for his poor academic performance was that her sister did not have the time to supervise his homework after school. Mary's sister seemed ideal as a caregiver: she was a teacher and lived in a small city, a regional capital, where Mary's son was able to attend private school. However, Mary's sister also had her own three children, aged five to thirteen, and her husband was a teacher who worked in another town far away, so that he was only home on weekends. Mary brought her son to live in her mostly completed house on the outskirts of Accra and put him in the full-time care of an old friend, a kindergarten teacher, whose salary she paid in lieu of her friend going to work.[5] Enrolling him in a nearby private school, she hoped that her son's academic abilities would improve. A few years later, as described in chapter 2, she was successful in bringing all her children to the United States.

Similarly, when I first met Irene, in 2005, her three children, aged nine months to thirteen years, were living with her parents in a seven-bedroom house she had built in Kumasi. Her parents considered the house their own, her gift to them, whereas from her perspective, the house belonged to her and she let them live there. As tensions built between them, in 2007, she used the occasion of my visit to arrange to have her parents relocate to a house her younger sister, a migrant in Germany, had recently built in another suburb of Kumasi. Separating her parents from her house also entailed separating them from the care of her children. A woman she found through friends came to live with the two youngest children, while the eldest, a boy of fifteen, went to stay in the boarding facilities of the private school he attended. After it turned out that this situation was not working out, Irene was referred to another woman by a pastor in Ghana who had become her friend and whom she called regularly from the United States. Irene was reassured about the new situation when she called her house from the United States shortly after making these arrangements from afar. When the caregiver laughed on the phone, Irene learned that she and the children were outside, "enjoying" themselves (her word). Irene barely had a chance to talk to her children because they were having such a good time and she let them get back to their play. "It made my day," she told me in our phone conversation shortly after this incident.

Another approach parents take to avoid tensions with relatives is to rely on boarding schools for their older children, who then spend only school vacations with relatives or family friends. Boarding elementary schools have sprung up in the major cities in Ghana, like Kumasi and Accra, in part to cater to this need. Children of migrants are present in the most well regarded boarding secondary schools, but they are not popular among the principals or heads of dormitories with whom I discussed the children of transnational migrants. A teacher in one elite boys' high school in Kumasi considered them "troublesome." He explained this assessment by saying that some were sent back to Ghana from abroad for disciplinary concerns, with the expectation that Ghanaian schools would straighten out such children; others had been spoiled by their guardians in Ghana because of the remittances their parents sent. Another teacher who was head of a dormitory in an elite girls' high school in Takoradi told me the story of a girl who tried to commit suicide several times because she had twice been denied entry to Switzerland, where her parents and other siblings lived. Although an unusual and particularly sad situation, this girl exemplified, for this housemistress, the pain that many of the children of migrants abroad are in and the effort the school authorities take to deal with the range of problems such pain causes. In general, while school authorities are confident they can handle the difficulties associated with children of migrants abroad, they also feel that such students required extra effort and posed a special burden.

Conclusion

Fostering by schools and paid caregivers seems to be a growing alternative to using relatives as foster parents. It is a way parents can navigate between opposing forces that make raising children in Ghana both difficult and necessary. The conditions of life and immigration laws in the United States encourage parents to raise their children in Ghana at the same time as trends against fostering by middle-class parents in Ghana make such a situation unattractive. The remittances that migrants send to their relatives to help care for their children and the sense of obligation can be a source of conflict because of differences in expectations, leading to potentially long-term and multigenerational family fissures. Furthermore, parents desire to raise their children in a middle-class, urban environment, even though the relatives who are the most middle class are also those most burdened by fostering children, without the time to give them much attention and least in need of (and least grateful for) the remittances offered. Thus paying someone to provide care can feel much more straightforward, in terms of the obligations and expectations involved, without causing harm to more reciprocal relationships with kin. However, because these practices are emergent and different, as parents expand and extend their repertoires, it is not clear whether hiring paid caregivers or turning to boarding schools solves the dilemmas parents and foster parents have: parents may also face conflicts with paid caregivers and teachers over expectations and obligations.

Because of the flow of remittances, the children of international migrants are unlikely to be useful to a foster parent in maintaining a household, and certainly much less helpful than a child of a needy relative or stranger who feels obligated to assist with domestic duties in exchange for the support he or she receives. The labor of poorer adolescents helps urban, middle-class caregivers take care of the children of international migrants. Although the fostering of siblings' children or grandchildren would seem to fit into traditional models of fostering, the children of international migrants become a special case, a new category of children, in the minds of parents, caregivers, and children alike. So far, I have been describing the perspectives of the adults involved in fostering; I turn next to the young people's perspectives on these dilemmas.

SEVEN

Children's Expectations of Care

Love, Money, and Living Together

Contemporary forms of global capitalism encourage an internationally mobile labor force. In order for this economic system to run smoothly, one might expect that people's emotional expectations—their emotional repertoire—would have to be in sync with the demands of mobility. In other words, a globally mobile labor force would seem to require emotional expectations that enable parents and children to live apart but have sufficient feelings for one another that adult migrants would want to support both their parents and children back home, rather than abandoning them outright.[1]

Yet people's emotional lives do not always fit or adapt to a particular political and economic situation. A person's emotion is dependent on his or her interpretation of a situation, one that is culturally and socially shaped: anger, for example, is shaped by a sense of what is wrong and what is right. People may check with others to see whether they agree that a situation deservedly elicits anger. They also actively shape their emotions to make them appropriate to the situations in which they find themselves, what William Reddy (2001) calls an emotional regime—waitresses and other service personnel may choke down irritation to continue smiling at their customers; debt collectors may imagine deadbeats with expensive consumer items in order to elicit the anger necessary to humiliate and degrade the debtor (Hochschild 2003). However, people do not always adapt happily to new situations, even when there is considerable pressure to do so. There is a limit to how much an emotional regime can actually regulate emotions. Such emotional regulation, Arlie Russell Hochschild (2003) argues, results in an alienation from the self. Reddy (2001) describes how improper emotions can burst forth regardless of ideals of stoicism, eruptions from which new emotional regimes can come into being. Both authors place emotion outside discourse; they do not equate the two.

Global capitalism, as a diffuse and uncoordinated set of activities generated by multiple actors, is not necessarily accompanied by a clear repeated pattern of statements or ideology that reflect a new way of thinking about family life (Terray 1972). It does not seem to produce a coherent discourse that generates new emotional expectations, an emotional regime, unlike some significant historical moments like the French Revolution (Reddy 2001). Rather, migrants and their children affected by migration try to make sense of family separation by extending and revising their existing repertoires. As described in chapter 5, parents abroad organize their experiences and feelings by contrasting "America" with "Ghana." They feel a sense of risk and uncertainty, in which raising their children in the United States seems problematic, but so does raising their children in Ghana, where children can be pampered by a grandmother or through remittances. Parents do not express a lot of emotion about being separated from their children, but rather subsume those emotions into practical goals for and concerns about their children's character and academic development. As I have discussed in greater depth elsewhere (Coe 2008), the emotions they express are those of anxiety, a sense of responsibility, and risk. They often feel ambivalent about the choices they have made, feeling that each path has serious downsides.

Their children in Ghana, on the other hand, do express their emotions, and in far more certain and forceful ways than their parents do. In their conversations with me, young people were working to name and describe their emotions through recognizable cultural idioms. What is striking is how the same cultural idioms could be used to express a range of emotions, both contentment and discontent. Like Ann Swidler (2001), I consider this flexibility and fluidity in discourse due to the fact that the situation is "unsettled," so that the children are searching for idioms with which to express their emotions. Nothing coherent and stable has been developed, by them or by other institutional forms, although they are sharing these discourses with one another in their schools and friendship networks.

Those near the children of migrant parents—caregivers, relatives, teachers, peers, and the press—help shape children's interpretation of their parent's migration as they themselves transpose their repertoires to a migration context (Rae-Espinoza 2011). Furthermore, children's feelings may change over the years, so that as they grow up and consider migrating themselves, they may come to revise their understanding of their parents' choices (Dreby 2010; Foner 2009). Some of the discourses within children's repertoires, on which they draw to interpret their parent's actions, have considerable historical depth, like the materiality of care; others, like love, are of more recent origin. Because the criteria for what makes a good parent vary cross-culturally and cross-generationally, the extent to which parental transnational migration is in tension with those repertoires varies. Consequently, there is considerable variation in how parents and children around the world respond emotionally to being separated and in how much emotional pain they experience.

Three Young People's Responses

Here are three illustrative samples of the range of young people's responses to my questions about what it was like to have a parent abroad. Like other children "left behind" by migrant parents I talked to in Ghana, their expressions of their emotional responses to their situation and evaluation of their parent's and foster parent's actions revolved around three sets of issues: emotional intimacy (love), material support (money), and parents and children living together.

I met Mercy at a boarding secondary school in southern Ghana during an extended conversation with a group of secondary students who had a parent abroad. She was sixteen and lived with her mother in Accra. Talking about her father, who left for the United States when she was nine years old, she said, "When my dad was here, I was very close to my dad. I was always with my dad. Now since he's left, I've lost that kind of paternal love. So whenever my dad calls, when I call him and I talk to my dad on the phone, I fall sick—I don't know—because, like, I miss him." A year later, in a private interview, she told me again that she felt sick after her father left. He used a certain cologne and if she happened to smell it accidentally, she would again feel physically ill. But gradually she has become used to his absence. Mercy focused exclusively on the loss of "paternal love" when she discussed her father's migration.

Charles, age nineteen, reported similar feelings about his mother's migration to the United States three years ago. His father and mother had divorced, and she married a man who had already gone abroad.

> There was a vacuum when she left; I felt alone even though my sisters were there [here in Ghana]. I was feeling like I am half, or incomplete.

Having graduated from the same secondary school as Mercy, he was studying to make up portions of the secondary-school examination, since he had not done well enough to continue on to university. He attributed his disappointing academic results to his mother's migration.

> She had all the time for all of us, especially our studies. I was very good. There were things she used to do to help me, waking me up at dawn and sitting by me. . . . Since she left, everything turned upside down, especially my studies. I wasn't getting any help from anyone, so my academic performance in [secondary school] was good, though, but not what I expected.

Although his father lives in Ghana with a new girlfriend, Charles stays with his paternal great-uncle during school vacations. Charles felt he had a poor emotional connection with and received inadequate financial support from his great-uncle and father. He wished he had been sent to school with care packages and pocket money like the other students. Although Charles was able to joke with his fellow students when he did not receive visitors on visiting days at his school, he told me he felt sad about it when he was alone. He had also worried that the late payment of school fees would mean he would not be allowed to take the end-of-semester exams, which may have affected his academic performance. "These things really get me bothered," he said. Although he highlighted his emotional isolation in the wake of his mother's migration, the problems of material support in her absence—taken as a sign of lack of affection on the part of his paternal kin—also mattered a great deal to him. Both, he felt, damaged his dignity and contributed to his middling examination results, the concern foremost in his mind at the time we talked.

Unlike Mercy and Charles, Kwabena did not mind his mother's migration, because he felt materially supported by his mother and emotionally connected to his foster parent, his maternal aunt. Fifteen years old and about to enter secondary school, he had lived with his mother's older sister since he was sixteen months old so that his mother could study to be a seamstress in the capital, an hour or so away. After his mother finished her apprenticeship, she opened her own business in Accra. While his mother lived and worked in Accra, Kwabena remained with his aunt in the town of Akropong, and his mother visited on weekends. Kwabena's father lives in another house in town, but like Charles, Kwabena does not feel very close to him, perhaps because he does not help provide for him. After marrying a man who was already an international migrant, his mother left for the United Kingdom nine years ago and has had two more children there; she has been able to visit Ghana only once since. Kwabena said he was happy his mother was in the United Kingdom because,

Obetumi de nneɛma abrɛ yɛn ne ade. Ɛhɔnom asetena no ye kakra sɛn ehanom de no, enti sɛ onya biribi a na anka watumi de abrɛ yɛn.
She is able to bring me and my aunt things. Life there is better than life here, so if she gets some money, she can bring it to us.

He told me more specifically that his mother sent him clothes, shoes, and money, and that he was not at all unhappy that she was far away. He treats her remittances as a sign of affection and connection. Kwabena and his aunt seem relatively content with the situation and are attached to each other. In fact, the aunt wonders whether she can go to the United Kingdom with Kwabena when his mother sends for him, as his mother promises to do.

These three young people differ in the extent to which they use the idioms of "love" and "money" to express the effects of a parent's migration on their lives. These ways of thinking and speaking seem to coexist, each with its own history, rather than one replacing the other.[2] They also occasionally overlap in the ways that they are deployed in people's understanding of their situation (Cole 2009; Rebhun 1999). As Ann Swidler (2001) argues, people draw on a "hodgepodge of various understandings," in explaining why they do what they do, moving "among cultural logics with ease" or building "personal edifices out of bricks and mortar from polyglot cultural sources" (156, 147).

Without much self-consciousness, children left behind by migrant parents draw on all these discourses—those of love, living together, and material care—to describe, understand, and justify their response to the situation in which they find themselves, whether they were content or unhappy. These different idioms were representations of their feelings, a way of translating a complex and loosely connected mix of thoughts or a somatic response like crying or Mercy's "feeling sick" into words that are comprehensible to speaker and listener alike (Reddy 2001, 94).[3] Children's expressions of emotion regarding their parent's international migration depend on the available ways of speaking of family life, repertoires that are associated with particular social strata within Ghanaian society and that were thus variably accessible and familiar to them.

There was variation in whether these young people considered it appropriate to express negative emotions to a stranger. Although some were quite open with expressing their emotions to me, others were more reserved. In group discussions, one person's complaint sometimes gave others tacit permission to discuss their unhappiness. At other times, young people talked of the experience of "a friend," speaking indirectly of their own experiences. Negative emotions are dangerous and possibly disruptive to social relations; expressing unhappiness may result in interventions by adults who may make the situation worse or scold the child for being disrespectful. Younger children, children in a more precarious situation, and those who were less articulate were more reserved about their emotions in general. As a result, this chapter draws mainly on the expressions of those adolescents who were more confident and willing to express their feelings to me. They tended to discuss their feelings about their separation from a migrant parent through the idioms of "money," "love," and "living together."

"I Need Money": The Idiom of Material Care

The children of migrants used the idiom of material support to describe satisfaction with a parent's migration, because of the flow of remittances and gifts, or to justify unhappiness, because of a foster parent's mistreatment or a parent's insufficient remittances. As discussed in chapter 1, care is understood to take place through the provision of the necessities of life—clothing, food, and education—as well as in meeting demands or requests for certain items, like snacks or books. It is expressed through cash as well as gifts. Children developed a finely tuned calibration to what they thought adults could provide, given their resources, and thus the extent to which provision of clothes, school fees, and pocket money was a sign of deep affection.[4]

There are gendered differences in how parents are expected to share their resources: while fathers are expected to have more resources than mothers, mothers are expected to share the little they have with their children. One girl, living with her maternal aunt because her father had recently died and her mother was in desperate straits, suggested that because her mother would desire to give more than she could, she, the daughter, would be pleased with the little her mother could provide, knowing her mother loved her and cared for her well-being. With someone other than her mother, on the other hand, she might doubt whether he or she would be as generous with his or her resources.

A study by Ernestina Tetteh (2008), based on interviews with seventeen young people aged twelve to seventeen living in Accra and its suburbs who were left behind by both parents who had migrated abroad, highlights their general contentment with their situation because of the flow of remittances, the good care they receive from their foster parents, and the fact that they were young when their parents migrated. Because a parent is abroad, children can go to private school or pursue higher education through secondary school and university, pursuits difficult to do on a Ghanaian salary. I met a girl at an elite secondary school in Kumasi whose father had lived in the United States for the past five years and who lived with her mother. She spoke in a general way about the phenomenon as a way of describing her own situation indirectly:

> I don't have any problem with them [parents] going to stay there [abroad] to pay school fees and those things. But I think that when they go there, they will work a lot; they would work very hard to get the money over there. If parents are educated and they have jobs [in Ghana], I don't think that nobody [anybody] will wish to go there [abroad] and work [because they would rather stay in Ghana]. We have our own companies, and those people who own those companies, they can pay children's school fees. But we don't have many good jobs. The salaries are very low. Going there [abroad], it will help them to pay our school fees for us.

When I visited her mother, who lived near the school in Kumasi, she agreed with her daughter's assessment, adding that her two older children were attending university. Without her husband's remittances from the United States, her three children's tuitions would not be within their reach.

Furthermore, young people gain status and popularity among their peers and some adults if they are known to have a parent who is abroad, in part because they are seen as having money, which they are pressured to share with their friends and relations. Emmanuel, introduced in chapter 5, who had been sent back to an elite secondary school in Ghana from the United States, complained, "People treat you as if you're above another person if your parent is overseas, as if you receive more money than others," even though, he added, a parent abroad may be working in a lower-status occupation than a parent in Ghana.[5] Consumption of certain material goods, or wearing particular kinds of clothing, acts as a marker that one has a parent or relation abroad, and thus signals social status.[6] Kwabena, introduced above, said about the clothes that his mother sent him:

> *Aburokyiri de no yɛ tough sen ha de no. Watumi hu, sɛ wohwɛ ɛha ntaade a, ebi wɔ ha ɛnyɛ papa sɛ quality.*
> Clothes from abroad are stronger and more durable than clothes available here. Some of the clothes from here are not of good quality.

Young people were loath to talk about *themselves* as displaying having a lot of money, because of the stigma associated with aggrandizement. However, they described other children of international migrants as dressing in the latest fashions that could only have been brought from abroad, having new electronics, and acting in a self-important way. This style is known as "bolga," a term derived from "burgher" and that emerged in the 1980s to describe international migrants who were visiting from Hamburg, Germany (Van Hear 2002).

Two boys in their late teens who had attended two different secondary schools and were living in Akropong described this phenomenon in a joint discussion with my research companion, Joe Banson, and me. Charles, introduced earlier in this chapter, had felt lonely after his mother migrated to the United States. Richmond was living with a paternal uncle while his father worked as a teacher in Nigeria.

Charles: Everyone thinks if you have a parent abroad, then you have no problem, because definitely they [your parents] will come for you [to take you abroad with them]. You need not worry. You have no burden. That is what they say. . . . You are welcome to every place you go or something.
We all laugh.
Richmond: They respect you, an elderly person, you will be walking o, see? They will just call you, "Buy me this," sort of thing so.
Charles: They always bug you with money: "Buy this for me."
Joe: Because they think you have [it]. But let me also ask you, um, is it an impression that they have gathered from some other people, not necessarily you? Is there a way those who have parents outside have shown themselves up to give the impression that they have [money]?
Charles: It's like some people who have parents abroad are living very large. When I say large, it is like, they have no problem [in relation to financial matters].
Joe and Cati make sounds of affirmation.
Charles: Precisely. Because it is like they need not worry about money, clothes, or anything. All they need is to give one phone call [to a parent abroad] and then they are through.
Cati: They have it. They get the money that they ask for.
Charles says that the general impression is that if your parent is abroad, "you are rich or you have no problem." This impression overshadows children "who are suffering," those who are not receiving remittances.[7]
Richmond: Me too, how they behave, the kinds of friends they have, going to the party and buying the things for friends, to show—what?— they have it. But that is not the right way to behave.

Boys, more than girls, are prone to the negative assessment that they are acting "bolga" because they, more than girls, act like rich and important men who can gain popularity and status through sharing their wealth. The status they receive from being the children of those abroad can even overturn existing social hierarchies, such as the respect normally accruing to the elderly. Older teenagers, particularly young men, complain that their parents abroad are suspicious of their reasons for asking for money and deny them their requests, thinking that they are perhaps misusing the funds to live "high" or act "bolga," such as supporting girlfriends rather than concentrating on their studies.

To the extent that a parent's migration leads to better support for a child, a migrant parent can be a better parent than one who lives in Ghana. If parents send remittances regularly and foster parents treat children like their own children, as is the ideal, then children generally seem content with their parents' international migration. Knowing or suspecting that it is the migrant parent who is underwriting their living expenses and school fees, some children in fact feel closer to a migrant parent than to their foster parent. The greater the material connection with the migrant parent, the greater the longing on the part of the child to join a migrant parent abroad, even when they are satisfied with their life in Ghana. Furthermore, they do not experience the ordinary frustrations and tensions of sharing a household with the migrant parent, who comes for short visits, if at all. Other children are as appreciative of the foster parent as of the migrant parent, acknowledging that the foster parent has also contributed to their care, whether financially or through their daily needs. Much of the difference seems attributable to the age at which the child came to live with the foster parent, with younger children having more appreciation for the foster parent than for the migrant parent.

However, it is important to highlight that the evaluation of good care is dependent on the child's expectation of what a parent can provide, and here there are certain advantages and disadvantages to international migration. The allure of migration abroad means that migrant parents are expected to be able to provide more than parents who are living in Ghana. Migrant parents deal with this disadvantage of international migration by dampening these expectations through the constant refrain (as foster parents and children reported to me) that life abroad is difficult, reporting when they cannot find work or when they are too sick to work. Migrants make efforts to change their relatives' expectations that *Aburokyiri* is a land of milk and honey, trying to reconcile the distance between their relatives' imagining of abroad and its reality. The advantage of international migration is that these statements cannot be easily verified independently, unlike for a parent living in Ghana: one cannot see the wealth or poverty of migrants by visiting them at home or knowing their exact occupation.

As Charles and Richmond said about their own situations, some children of transnational migrants do not receive as much money as others imagine they do. Although *Aburokyiri* is usually viewed as a place where money is plentiful, migrants face periods of unemployment, insecure or low-paid work, or employment that is incommensurate with their credentials and abilities. Therefore, there may be periods of time when migrants cannot send money in the way their relatives at home expect. Some children do not even hear from migrant parents again (Coe 2011b). Even in cases where migrants do remain in touch, they may not provide as much as the children request.

However, a more common complaint by the children of migrants about material support is that foster parents are misusing the remittances migrant parents send by diverting it for their own use. One of the reasons this complaint emerges so frequently is that children usually do not know how much their parents are remitting to the foster parents and overestimate that amount because they, like others, believe their parents, as migrants abroad, can afford to send home quite a bit. Yet several foster parents, as discussed in the last chapter, told me they were subsidizing the children's care. Children's calibrations to what an adult is able to provide is not so finely tuned in these situations.

Children also seem to assume that the full sum of remittances is for their own care, whereas the parents assume the remittances are also going to support the foster parent, who is usually their own sibling or mother. Because of reciprocal relations built up over time, migrants consider themselves obligated to help their siblings and mother, especially if one is raising their children. Cecilia even treats all her siblings similarly, to alleviate any jealousy. As described in chapter 6, Cecilia's stepsister, Comfort, was taking care of Cecilia's three children in Ghana. Cecilia told me she was helping to pay for the education of Comfort's three children as well as her own, to prevent Comfort's jealousy of Cecilia's children and to thank her for her help. Cecilia told me she furthermore sent the monthly amount she sent Comfort to her other two siblings, so that they also would not be jealous of her own or Comfort's children, because, she worried, any conflicts between them would be painful and destructive to the next generation. Although parents certainly did not want their children to be neglected materially, they expected their remittances to provide for the foster parent's needs as compensation for their daily care and to ensure that the foster parent would treat their children well.

Because of the differences in parents' and children's expectations concerning the use of remittances, a complaint about the diversion of remittances was not commonly made by parents, although it was by young people. For example, Grace, who had been sent to a prestigious secondary school in Ghana from Canada, said,

> One of my friends, her mom went and her dad went; they left her with her mom's sister, and [she] always maltreats the girl. When they bring her clothes or money, instead of using it to cater for her, they use it for their [own] children. Oh—it was bad. So the girl had always [a] frown. So when she came there, even when you don't do anything to her—a serious face! Even when she smiles, you think she's angry.

Furthermore, children are concerned that a foster parent is less generous with financial support than a biological parent would be, because there is less affection in the relationship. In a separate group discussion, Daniel, attending secondary school, was living with a paternal aunt while his parents were in the United Kingdom. He said that the difficulties of staying with relatives "make you miss your parents too much." When I asked about the nature of those difficulties, he responded, "It is like maybe if your parents are there, that is what they will do for you, anything you need they will provide for you. But if your parents are away, there are petty, petty things," such as pocket money to buy snacks at school, which your relatives will not give you when you ask them. Richard, at the same school and also living with his aunt while his parents were abroad in the United States, agreed with Daniel's assessment: "The relative will not do what your parent will do. So it is not everything that you ask for that they can provide for you." Because relatives refuse children's requests for money, children feel constrained around them and stop asking for money, something they did not feel they would do with their own parents. Some put a positive spin on this characteristic of fosterage, as did many adults looking back at their fostered childhoods, suggesting that the hardship of being fostered made them more responsible and disciplined. "I know when to ask for something and I know when not to ask, when to say something and when not to say something, when to do something and when not to do it," said Edward, a secondary-school student, which he attributed to living with his aunt and uncle.

Because of the perceived injustice of the situation, some adolescents lobbied their parents to receive remittances directly, rather than through their foster parents. Once children reached their late teens, some parents began to acquiesce to these demands. Samuel, a young man in his early twenties, described living first with a family friend and then with his grandmother while waiting for his father to sort out his immigration papers. Toward the end of his time in Ghana, his father sent him money directly, convinced by his son that his guardian might be spending the remittances for other purposes:

> It was like, my dad felt—I didn't know though—he felt when he sent my guardian money, cause I write to him, "Dad, what is going on, I need money." . . . He thinks he sent my guardian money and I keep asking him for money, so why don't he give me the money myself and see what I can do with it? So when I move over [to my grandmother's house], he gives me the money in my name. So I go for it and open an account. I didn't know how to work for money. [For] a young boy [to] have a bank account in Ghana—oh [it is amazing]! I just go around and shop. I wasn't doing the bad things, though, but I was living like I was rich. But I wasn't. That was what happened. That was basically how I got into the spending money stuff [the habit of spending a lot of money].

When he came to the United States four years ago, Samuel found that he could no longer act "bolga"; he had to change his spending habits and began working—first in a restaurant and then in retail—while attending community college part-time.

As I have indicated, the idiom of material support can be used to indicate contentment or sadness with a parent's separation. Some children can be satisfied with the situation, because a parent's remittances allow them to continue with their schooling or gain status and popularity among their peers and adults. Some others, more dissatisfied, can use the discourse of diversion of remittances to complain about the mistreatment they receive from a foster parent. Others, however, used a very different idiom to describe their emotions, talking about the loss or gain of love and emotional intimacy, as I describe next. Although I separate these idioms from one another to discuss them more clearly, they probably reflect a similar set of emotions and feelings among the children left behind, because material care is taken (and given) as a sign of affection and closeness.

"They Lacked That Parental Love":
The Idiom of Emotional Intimacy

The idiom of love, like the idiom of material care, can be used to explain both happiness and unhappiness with the absence of a migrant parent. One marker of its class signification is that "love" as a term appeared only in English and was only used by secondary-school students who decided to speak English in their conversations with me.[8] Although many Ghanaians associate a particular style of family life and consumption patterns with the educated elite and the urban middle class in Ghana, the attitudes and ideals that support that way of life are available for those beyond these elite and middle-class circles to use, if they are familiar with it through their contacts and activities. Churches have encouraged their members, at all levels of the social strata, but particularly in the new Pentecostal and Pentecostal-inspired churches that serve those aspiring to middle-class status, to focus more on their spouse and children and sever ties to extended family kin (Meyer 1999; van Dijk 2002). The ideal family of a "caring husband, his loving wife, and their children, who all lead a Christian life" living in their own private house is regularly showcased in videos from Ghana and Nigeria that are readily available and are shown on TV (Meyer 2003, 212). In highlighting the class-based nature of these discourses, I do not want to overstate the differences between middle-class, urban residents and poorer, rural residents in Africa, given that many of the urban elite have poorer relatives whom they support. Urban middle-class and elite residents travel regularly to their more rural hometowns for celebrations and funerals. Furthermore, there is variation among the middle class and elite in the degree to which they subscribe to this model of family life.

Rather than seeing these classes as bounded units, it makes more sense to see "educated" or "elite" ways of life as a cultural style, a form of identity that can be deeply felt, but also flexibly deployed. These ways of life are cultivated in activities with other people over time.[9] Although I heard more talk of love and the nuclear family living together among secondary-school students who resided in metropolitan areas, some of them also talked about the importance of material care, particularly in relation to their foster parent. Most young people who lived in the smaller town of Akropong talked about how they were satisfied with remittances and gifts from migrant parents, but some expressed their dissatisfaction in terms of the loss of emotional intimacy, particularly those like Charles who had been to reputable secondary schools where students from more metropolitan areas predominated.

"Love" was often modified with another word like "maternal," "paternal," or "parental," to indicate that this kind of love was special and unique, something only such a person—mother, father, or parent—could give. However, one should not make too much of these adjectives. Some children of migrant parents used the idiom of love to say they missed their parents intensely and lacked the love they needed because of their parents' migration. Others, despite the modifying adjectives that seemed to indicate that this kind of love was something only a parent could provide, said they loved and were loved by their foster parents and were not troubled by a lack of emotional connection to their biological parents. Children who said this generally had gone to live with their foster parents at a young age, sometimes even before a parent's international migration. Because the parent migrated a long time ago and had little chance to visit, because of immigration regulations or the expense of travel, some of these children were more attached to their foster parents than to the migrant parent. Furthermore, although the idiom of material support posited gendered differences, the idiom of love did not. For example, there did not seem to be a sense that maternal love was more powerful or significant than paternal love.

For children who experience relative happiness living with their foster parents in Ghana, the emotional break can come when they eventually join the migrant parent abroad, a finding that supports other work based on interviews with children from Haiti, Mexico, China, and elsewhere who had recently joined their parents in the United States (Menjívar and Abrego 2009; Schulte 2005; Suárez-Orozco, Todorova, and Louie 2002). Jennifer, age twenty-one, had lived with her paternal grandparents, mother, and younger brother after her father migrated to the United States when she was eight years old.[10] It took ten years for her father to regularize his and his children's papers. Jennifer has now lived with her father for three years in a major city in the Midwest. Jennifer's father paid for her schooling during the years she was in Ghana and continues to do so, so that she does not have to combine work and schooling as many of her community-college peers do. Despite his material support, demonstrating that he is a responsible father, Jennifer says she does not feel close to him.

> In Ghana, it was great. I didn't really miss my dad, because I lived with my mom for a very long time. And I think I didn't really know my dad. He left when I was around six years old. So I was very attached to my mom. So even living here with him is hard. Because I don't have that father-daughter relationship like most people have. Because most people are like, "Oh, every-

thing, my dad, my dad, my dad." But I'm all like "my mom." It's not really easy living with him; it's hard. Like I don't ask him anything like I will ask my mother. It makes it difficult. Sometimes I cry. *She laughs.* I'm old, but I still cry.

Despite his ability to give, she feels constrained about asking him for things because of the lack of emotional connection. Some of her analysis and evaluation of her relationship with her father comes from a comparison with her present-day friends, other Ghanaian immigrants at her church and fellow students who are the children of South Asian and African immigrants, and how they express their attachment to their fathers in their interactions with her.

Felicia, a sixteen-year-old secondary-school student in Ghana, had a similar experience when her parents returned to Ghana from being migrants in Italy, where her mother worked in a factory.[11] Felicia had been born in Italy and was sent back to Ghana as a baby to live with her grandmother. Her parents returned from Italy to stay when Felicia was twelve years old.

It is like when they came back, I had rather more love for my grandmum. Although I liked them, but then, I was too close to my grandmum. I was uncomfortable with them. I tried to stay with them, but it wasn't working. Later, I had to decide: these are my parents and I have to stay with them. Now things are okay and I relate to them as a family.

She describes how she consciously attempted to control her emotions to bring them in line with what she considered appropriate for "a family," for instance, that she loved her parents and ought to live with them rather than being "too close" to her grandmother.

Edward also feels positively about his foster parents because he also went to live with them at an early age. Edward has lived with his maternal aunt and her husband since he was five years old, accompanying them whenever they are transferred by his uncle's job with a multinational brewing company. He is generally content with his situation, because his aunt and uncle treat him "as a son." His mother sends money regularly, providing for his needs. He said, "I love my mum" and "I can speak to her and stuff." At the same time, although his mother wants Edward to join her in the United States, he is "a little reluctant. Because I would say I have everything here."

Other children, who experienced more disruption in their care or who went to live with their foster parent later in life, felt their foster parents were unable to provide the love they received and expected from their parents. I had earlier introduced Afua, whose mother died shortly after Afua was able to overcome immigration hassles and join her parents in the United States. She described how she and her two brothers were taken care of by their maternal aunt after their mother and two younger siblings joined their father in the United States.

> Living with my aunt is not like living with your parents, you know. I would say that it really had much effect on my brothers. . . . They lacked that parental love. Before, my mom really loved us. That was almost the only thing she could do, like, call us and talk. Almost every Sunday, she would call. We've been so attached to her than to my dad [who had left earlier]. My dad and [her younger sister] Emma are really pretty close, but with the rest of us, it's like, Emma left [Ghana] when she was like four and a half years, and lucky for her, she came with both of them [their mother and father], so she got all the love from both parents. . . . My aunt wasn't so, so nice to us. We didn't really get all the *love* from her. It was more like each one for himself. You do whatever you have to do to survive. That was really hard.

For her, the key damage for her and her brothers was that rather than thinking about the family as a unit—close, together, thinking and caring about one another—they became more individual, thinking only about themselves. As an example, she said that she would finish up the food, not leaving any for her brothers, because she had difficulty getting enough food in her aunt's house. Although their mother called regularly, it was not enough to protect them from the lack of affection from their mother's sister. Afua experienced disruption in her living situation because she was an adolescent when her mother left, even though her mother tried to design the transition so that there would be elements of continuity and familiarity, such as bringing a favorite aunt to live with her children in their own house.

Afua's relating of her experiences brings up the third discourse, that of "living together" as a family; namely, a nuclear family where parents and children live together.

"As a Family": The Idiom of Living Together

Although the idioms of material care and love could be used to explain happiness or unhappiness with a parent's migration, images of a nuclear family living together were only used to express sadness. When children talked about living together "as a family," using the English word, they meant living with their parents and siblings, rather than living with members of their extended family, as many did in their daily lives. The young people who talked about living together "as a family" often contrasted the situation prior to the parent's migration when they "lived together" with the situation thereafter, speaking to a mode of life that is associated with the educated, urban middle-class. They often mixed the idiom about living together as a family with complaints about the loss of parental love *and* lack of material care, which a parent could best provide for them because of the affection he or she had, despite the fact that going abroad contributed to a parent's resources and ability to give.

Beatrice was a thirteen-year-old girl living in a house her father built in Kumasi and under the care of her maternal aunt; both her parents are in the United States. The younger sister of Beatrice's mother had come to live with Beatrice's mother, her older sister, when Beatrice's sister was about eleven years old, before Beatrice was born. At that time, Beatrice's mother was living alone and working as a trader, and her younger sister helped her with trading and household chores. When I met Beatrice's father and mother later in the United States, the father joked that his wife and her younger sister "came as a package": when he married Beatrice's mother, her sister also came to live in his house. Beatrice's father had been a migrant prior to his marriage, in neighboring Côte d'Ivoire, Spain, and Israel, before coming to the United States eleven years ago. Beatrice's mother joined him two years ago. Beatrice's aunt is now twenty-five years old, a seamstress, unmarried, without children, and Beatrice's foster parent. The chain of care—from Beatrice's mother to her younger sister, from her younger sister to Beatrice herself—proceeds in a stepwise fashion down the generations, similar to other fosterage situations described to me. Other relatives on both the father's and mother's side joined Beatrice and her aunt in the house, not as Beatrice's caregivers, but simply to live there, as one of the ways that Beatrice's father and mother can help out their siblings and family members.

Although Beatrice's father said that Beatrice knows her aunt better than her mother, Beatrice herself is less satisfied, saying that her aunt looks after her well, but not like her mother would. She said firmly,

Mepɛ sɛ me ne me papa ne me maame tena bom sen sɛ mete obi nkyɛn.
I want to live with my mother and father, rather than with someone else.

I asked why, surprised that she called her aunt by a term usually used to refer to someone who was not a relative. She replied,

Nea enti a mepɛ sɛ metena me maame ne me papa nkyɛn ne sɛ sɛ ebia me wɔ me
*maame nkyɛn a, me*feeli more comfortable *sɛn sɛ mete obi nkyɛn, esiane sɛ sɛ*
mete me maame nkyɛn a, nea mepɛ na me maame bɛyɛ ama me.
The reason I want to live with my mother and father is that if I live with my
mother, I will be more at ease than living with someone else. Because if I live
with my mother, my mother will do what I like for me.

Beatrice complained that her aunt did not give her all the money that her
mother sent, and that her relatives, mainly young adults, were too old to
play with her. Although her mother is not likely to do *all* that Beatrice
would like, as already described, a child may accept a mother's refusals
more readily than she would from someone who is not her mother, when
she may wonder if her request was refused out of lack of love. In other
words, Beatrice would have less doubt for her mother's love when her request for money is refused than she would with her aunt.

Later in our conversation, Beatrice reiterated her desire to live with her
parents, strikingly using the English words "one family" to emphasize the
nuclear unit in a statement otherwise made mainly in Twi:

Mepɛ sɛ yɛn nyinaa tena bom, saa no yɛn nyinaa na ɛbɛkɔ Aburokyiri anaasɛ me
papa na ɔbɛba ha sei na yɛn nyinaa ayɛ one family *na yeatumi atena.*
I want us all to live together. Whether we all are abroad or my father comes
here [to Ghana], we can live together as one family.

Beatrice, then, brought together all three idioms to express her dissatisfaction with her situation.

Mary's two daughters, aged sixteen and eighteen, similarly seemed upset that the family was not living together. They described how their family
had been scattered by divorce and both parents' separate international migrations, Mary to the United States and their father to southern Africa. In
their parents' absence, their elder brother had gone to live with a paternal
uncle, while they had stayed with their maternal grandparents. The elder
sister felt her parents' migration had made them lose "the motherly love"
they had for their children, focusing their attention on work and money
instead.

When they are far away from us, it is like, they lose this motherly affection. If
we are there with them, together with them, they know what we want, what
we don't want, and so they are able to provide it well.

Note how she connects living together to motherly love *and* ascertaining what a child needs and desires, without which a parent cannot provide well for her child. Material support and love are fused, in knowing what pleases another, a knowledge that is conditional on living together. Like Afua, she also felt sad that her siblings have been emotionally disconnected and physically separated from one another because of a parent's migration.

Mary's daughters have grown attached to a church as a surrogate family. In this particular church, gender roles within the nuclear family were emphasized, more so than in other Christian faiths. Mary's daughters were very aware of how their family did not meet this religious ideal, and they drew on the church's emphasis on a particular model of family life as a way to articulate their complaints about their situation. For instance, Mary's eldest daughter said that her father was not performing his role as head of the household, although he called regularly and assisted with their school fees. She explained why living together as a nuclear family was so important to her:

> Maybe I will say, ah, hope and faith in our family stems from the Bible. We know that every family owes its name to God. And so God has a purpose— and still, He has a purpose, He had and *He still has* that purpose—that our family should be together. And so we want to reach that purpose and then, give thanks to God, because our family owes its name to God. And then, being separated is keeping that purpose—should I say—it is making it latent, it is making it hidden. But then we want to bring that purpose out.

Living together as a nuclear family, no matter how imperfectly, was in her mind a religious imperative: she knew that even if the family reunited in the United States, their father and his new family would not join them. It caused these two deeply religious teenagers much pain that bringing their family together in accordance with their religious ideals was not in their power.

Some children expressed their unhappiness at their parents' migration by articulating particular expectations of family life associated with the urban, educated middle class. They expected "motherly" or "fatherly" love from their parents and an emotional attachment with them. They longed for similar closeness with their siblings. In their minds, these emotional bonds were generated through coresidence, preferably in a house where the nuclear family lived together. Material care flowed out of this closeness and affection. Children articulated these expectations when living apart from their migrant parents saddened them. However, it is not only the children left behind by transnational migrants who feel this way. Many of the friends and schoolmates of Mary's daughters were similarly living with someone other than their parents, such as their parents' friends, even if their parents were living and working in Ghana. As Mary's younger daughter said, "Most of them don't have their parents with them, and they are going through a lot, 'cause some stay with people [they] don't even know; they are not related to the people. They don't treat them [well]—they mistreat them." Her older daughter added to what her sister said, "Being with your parent is one thing you could never get anywhere. And then, people will see you as a burden; others might not have kids so they would want you to be there, but, no matter how hard they try, they can never treat you as your parents [would]. And so what I would say is that the feeling is similar everywhere, with people who have parents even not too far [away], but then not staying with them. They go through the same things [as we do]."

Continuities/Disruptions and Emotions

We come to know what another person is feeling when he or she tells us. Feelings are of course more than these idioms: feelings can be mixed-up, ambivalent, and change over time. Naming a feeling as one thing or another can help reify and fix a feeling, or cause greater internal turmoil because it becomes clear that one's language does not, in fact, describe the feeling (Reddy 2001). How children talked about their feelings gave me a sense of their habitual repertoire for talking about feelings, and what criteria they felt were appropriate to express in their conversations with me for evaluating a parent's actions.

Explaining why some children expressed unhappiness and others did not is more than I can do, made up of a host of complicated factors, including children's expectations for a particular relationship and the dynamics between personalities. One factor that I suspected played a role was the kind of disruption a child experienced, in two ways: the age at which his or her situation changed, and the degree to which his or her living situation changed as a result of a parent's migration. However, there was a great deal of variation in the degree of disruption and how it affected young people. At the high end of the disruption spectrum, some children, like Samuel, experienced a variety of foster parents, bouncing around from house to house, but did not seem to miss his parents much. Charles had been living with his mother before she migrated abroad, and when she left, he had to live with a foster parent he did not know very well, a relative of his father whom he disliked. In the midrange, Afua and her siblings received a foster parent, who had lived with them before, into her parents' house and missed their mother terribly. At the low end, Kwabena, who seemed content, went to live with his foster parents, his maternal aunt and her husband, when he was a baby and his mother was an urban migrant; when she went farther afield, his situation did not change. Yet Beatrice and Mercy, both unhappy, similarly experienced many continuities in their living situation, other than the loss of a parent, which perhaps further heightened what was missing: Mercy remained living with her mother and siblings after her father migrated, and Beatrice continued living with her maternal aunt, with whom she had lived since she was a baby. Beatrice, somewhat surprisingly, imagined living together as a nuclear family, a situation she had never experienced because her father had been a migrant throughout her lifetime. Continuity in a child's living situation explained some of the responses that children had to a parent's migration, but not entirely, as they also imagined different possibilities than those they had experienced, drawing on the discourses of family life that were available to them from their churches, peers, and relatives. Even those who experienced change at a young age are expecting further disruption in the future, perhaps when they are reunited with a migrant parent. For example, when Kwabena joins his mother, her husband, and his half-siblings abroad, he will probably leave his adored aunt behind in Ghana.

Conclusion

Like adults, children respond to their situation drawing on existing discourses in their repertoires, combining and articulating them to make sense of the situations they encounter and the feelings they experience. The dominant discourses of family life in Ghana—of material care, love, and living together—could be used to express either contentment or discontent.

In general, children seemed unhappier with separation than migrant parents were. Migrant parents felt ambivalence and frustration, confronted with choices, none of which seemed attractive and whose outcomes were uncertain, but the choices they made were, for the most part, their own. Children, on the other hand, felt a lack of agency, in which they could not control the situation—even their feelings—very easily. At the same time, they felt far more certainty than did their parents about what was right and what was wrong about their situation. Perhaps this speaks to the difference between those who are self-conscious about their repertoire (the parents) and those who assume that it is normal and commonsensical (their children).

Yet comparatively, children left behind in Ghana seemed more content than did similar children in other parts of the world, such as the Philippines or Mexico. One reason is that the idiom of material care allowed them to feel more attached to a migrant parent, rather than abandoned, and to express satisfaction with a relationship on that basis without being criticized for being materialistic or unloving. Secondly, traditions of fostering, and its prevalence, made them not stigmatized or unusual in living apart from their parents, with an uncle, aunt, or grandmother. For some, like Kwabena, but not for Beatrice, fostering and traditions of women's migration within Ghana lent continuity to their living situations so that they bonded closely to their foster parent *prior to* a parent's international migration. Furthermore, Mary's daughters did not feel alone in their suffering: other schoolmates, whose parents were elsewhere in Ghana, were also living with foster parents and feeling sad about it.

However, despite these discourses and practices that legitimate children's feelings of contentment and that reduce children's isolation and sense of strangeness in fosterage situations, there is a great deal of variation in Ghanaian children's responses to being separated from their parents, speaking not only to the fact that there is much individual variation, but also that they have not yet developed a consistent ideology to address the separations transnational migration causes. Capitalism affects family life not by imposing a particular emotional regime but as children transpose what is available to them in their repertoires—through their experiences and interactions with school friends, relatives, foster parents, parents, and church members—to evaluate the situation in which they find themselves and to explore and rationalize what they feel. I return to the larger issues about the relationship between capitalism, family life, and global inequality, that these children's responses to their scattered families pose, in the conclusion.

Barriers and Openings

Over the past thirty years, men and women in developing countries increasingly have worked abroad. In stagnant economies with few formal employment opportunities and a disappearing array of social services, parents face difficult choices in raising their children and taking care of their families. Many parents within these economies increasingly choose to migrate to work in another country in order to financially support their children and other relatives. In migrating, many leave their children behind or send their children back home. Global competition and trade seem to demand a new kind of worker, one not expecting a stable income or career: "The ideal image conveyed by the labour market is that of a completely mobile individual regarding him/herself as a functioning flexible work unit, competitive and ambitious, prepared to disregard the social commitments linked to his/her existence and identity" (Beck and Beck-Gernsheim 1995, 6). Within the United States, large and international companies may require workers to move across the country or to another country, leaving behind extended family and friends. More than five million American men and women, nearly 4 percent of the American workforce, relocate for work every year, to a new job after a layoff, to accept a high-ranking position, or to the next rung in a career (Uchitelle 2008). Almost four million married couples were living apart from each other in 2006, reported the US Census Bureau, and the poor economy may mean that more families are apart for the sake of a paycheck (Conlin 2009).

Much scholarship on families in this era of global mobility, particularly in the field of sociology, has assumed that the scattering of families is new, an indication of the ways that global capitalism has restructured how families raise children. As a result, it has focused on the stresses and strains in family life that emerge, particularly when women migrate. Women's migration usually separates mothers from their children across great distances, which opens them up to criticism that they are not good mothers. The new family arrangements that accompany women's labor migration, these scholars argue, do not match existing cultural norms for gender roles and parenting, generating pain on the part of children when their mothers are away and opportunities for new gendered notions and practices to emerge. Thus the new family arrangements are a sign of the suffering global capitalism inflicts.

My research with Ghanaian transnational families suggests a more complicated story. Rather than transnational migration challenging long-standing cultural traditions of family and gender, I instead see transnational migrants transposing their repertoires into the situations they find themselves. As discussed in chapters 1 and 2, their repertoires have been shaped through previous generations of migration within Ghana and by earlier periods of global capitalism, particularly through the production of palm oil and cocoa as export crops and by the expansion of cities due to global trade and colonial administration. They have been affected by middle-class norms closely associated with Christianity. Rather than family practices being the static products of history, this story reveals that their repertoires have always been changing in relation to these economic and political forces.

In migrating transnationally, Ghanaians rely on practices within their experience such as fosterage and modes of showing care through gifts of material goods. These practices highlight flexibility and pragmatism in responding to family members' individual needs and abilities to be supportive. In fact, international migration enhances some aspects of this repertoire. For example, transnational migrants seem to have revived the fostering-out of children, despite its current stigma among the middle class in Ghana. Three aspects of contemporary migration make fostering children out more likely than it is for nonmigrants. The first, discussed in chapter 3, involves the legal difficulty of migrating with young family members in tow. US immigration laws—with a narrow definition of family, expensive application fees, long waiting periods during which children may "age out" of priority categories, and an emphasis on formal documentation spelling out relationships and identities—make it difficult for migrants to bring their children to live with them, as Afua's story illustrated. The second reason, discussed in chapter 4, is that working mothers in the United States find it difficult to work and raise a family there, because of the lack of family support, the cost of day care relative to their wages, and the value of Ghanaian credentials in the US labor market. Sending US citizen children to Ghana, as Irene has done, is a way of combining work and child care. Finally, the topic of chapter 5, many Ghanaians have a belief that America is not the optimal place to raise a child. Oppositions between "America" as a place where children's good character is lost and "Africa" as a place where children are obedient and respectful, oppositions stimulated in discussions with other Ghanaians, lead some parents in the United States, like Emmanuel's father, to send their adolescents back to Ghana until they are old enough to attend college and work, when they will return to the United States.

Furthermore, parents' obligations to provide material care means that migrant parents can be good parents, sometimes even better than those who stay in Ghana and do not have the resources to provide care. While this might seem to be an example of the ways that transnational migration commodifies familial relations, as other studies have suggested, material exchanges between the generations were even more commodified in the past, for example, during the cocoa boom in Akuapem, as described in chapter 1.

Although the prevalence and normality of fosterage and the way that love can be signaled by material support would seem to make parent-child separation a much smoother process for Ghanaians than for many other transnational migrants, challenges and tensions do result. For one, urban, middle-class ideals of raising one's own children are increasingly given lip service, if not always practiced, by a wide swath of people in southern Ghana. Because international migrants are associated with the urban middle class, international migrants' fostering-out their children disrupts class ideals about parent-child arrangements, as discussed in chapter 6. Although many contemporary Ghanaians are increasingly ambivalent about child fosterage arrangements, transnational migrants ironically seem to be reinvigorating these practices. Moreover, international migrants are relying on some kinds of fosterage that have supported working mothers ("grandmother fosterage"). However, they are not able to foster-*in* their nieces and nephews, practices that have historically given children access to new, more modern locales that provide them with opportunities, education, and training. These changes generate tensions around fosterage within Ghanaian families, as the flows of children are reversed from wealthier to poorer households and from more urban (as "abroad" is conceived) to more rural areas (as Ghana is conceived, in comparison). In response, parents try to place their children with foster parents like themselves—middle-aged, formally employed, and resident in urban areas—rather than with grandmothers and poorer relatives. However, it is these preferred foster parents who feel the burden of caring for the children of transnational migrants most keenly and appreciate remittances the least. As a result of these fraught emotional and moral situations, some parents turn to hired help and boarding schools instead of relatives, in a hope that monetizing and professionalizing fostering relationships will make them more straightforward and less conflictual. International migration is thus causing changes in Ghanaian family life, against the shifting and varied backdrop of changes occurring in family life in Ghana independently of international migration.

These changes are significant because the care and fostering of children are so intimately tied to reciprocal exchanges between the generations. These reciprocal exchanges are material as well as emotional. We need to understand how migration and globalized capitalism are affecting the flows of resources that enable children to grow, and through their growth, for families, households, and society at large to be reproduced.

Global Inequalities in Social Reproduction

Where children are raised and by whom have implications not only for the relations between siblings or grandmothers and their grandchildren but also for the United States and Ghana as nation-states. Both countries devote considerable resources to the care of children, through their schools, health facilities, and other social services. From an economic perspective, governments help support workers throughout their lives, by training them in public schools and when they are not working because they are young, sick, disabled, or retired. Because governments take care of some of these costs that support individuals over their total life course, employers have less responsibility for paying the full cost of what it takes to produce their employees' labor—in other words, the cost of their employee from birth to death, including their socialization and training. The growing wage and price competition of the global economy has further caused American employers to reduce their investment in the training of workers, particularly at the low end of the wage scale (Aspen Institute 2002). Workers' demands regarding health care, education, and disability rights are therefore directed at the state rather than to employers.

Governments are not the only ones to absorb some of these costs, for so do families, by raising children or helping the sick and elderly through unpaid household labor (Katz 2001). As economist Nancy Folbre notes, "If parents don't create and nurture children, schools can't educate them, employers can't hire them, and governments can't tax them" (2008, 179). In documenting the costs American parents incur in raising children (averaging $20,000 per child per year in 2000), she argues that such costs should be treated as an investment by the whole society rather than part of a household's consumption.

It is because of these costs of maintaining people across their life course —not just when they are working—that some advocate against immigration. They argue that immigrants use social services like hospitals and schools disproportionately to their contribution to the taxes or revenue that support such services. Economists debate whether immigrants contribute more than they use or vice versa. However, one study estimated that an immigrant aged twenty-one with a high school education arriving in the United States in the mid-1990s contributed $126,000 more in taxes than he or she cost in terms of benefits, with a net positive effect over his or her lifetime, even if he or she remained in the United States through retirement (Smith and Edmonston 1997, 329). As previously discussed, most of the Ghanaian-born population in the United States is of working age, with disproportionately few children or elderly. Ghana therefore bears the cost of social reproduction of this population, at a great bargain to America, where they spend their working and productive lives.

That parents and children are separated from one another might seem strange given that family reunification is the easiest way to legally live and work in the United States; one would therefore expect that immigrants' children could accompany them. In guestworker programs, by contrast, such as in the Middle East or Hong Kong, only the adult with a work permit can migrate and has to leave his or her family behind. But US immigration law has perverse effects. The family reunification program is the most common way of living and working in the United States long term because other pathways to legal entry such as through asylum, visitor's visas, and temporary work permits (like H-1Bs) are very narrow corridors. The popularity of family reunification is a sign of how restrictive, in comparison, other legal modes of entry are.

The situation therefore is somewhat parallel to what was experienced in South Africa under apartheid or in contemporary China, in which legal mechanisms like pass laws or residency permits combine with business interests in outsourcing the full costs of labor to the rural villages of contemporary China or the homelands in apartheid South Africa (Hahamovitch 2011; Zolberg 1987). Historically, colonial and apartheid policies in South Africa constrained the mobility of labor, restricting Africans' residence to selected areas, called homelands, the least fertile wastelands. Only those with an employment contract were allowed to live and work outside those areas. This resulted in men in the prime of their working lives migrating to factories and mines in the industrial belt and urban areas of South Africa, leaving behind their dependents—their elderly parents, their wives, and children—in the reserves, to scratch out a living from farming in the poor soils.

The result was translocal families. Those on the reserves were dependent on remittances from the migrants in the mines and cities. At the same time, those working were dependent on the reserves, for the industrial and commercial enterprises in the cities and mines did not provide adequately for these workers' retirement or disability. As a result, when workers were too old or sick to work any longer, they lost their employment contracts and had to return to their "homelands"(Mamdani 1996; Meillassoux 1981; Murray 1981; Schapera 1947). Anthropologist Claude Meillassoux concludes, "Preservation of the relations with the village and the familial community is an absolute requirement for the wage-earners, and so is the maintenance of the traditional mode of production [farming] as the only one capable of ensuring survival" (1972, 103). Businesses in South Africa were relieved of the responsibility of sustaining an individual laborer over the course of his or her life and for developing the next generation of workers. Instead, some of the costs were realized by those who remained in the reserves who took care of the elderly and sick and raised the children who would grow up to be labor migrants like their fathers (see also Dei 1992). Furthermore, the costs of such a system remained less visible because they were geographically distant. As Cindy Hahamovitch describes with guestworker programs in the United States, "By hiring a young, male labor force, agricultural employers banished the most persistent and media-worthy problems that had plagued the nation's fields since the late nineteenth century—child labor and illiteracy, abysmal maternal health care, and aged former farmworkers. They did so not by solving these problems but by outsourcing them to the United States' poorest neighbors" (2011, 8–9).

Likewise, in today's China, the *hukou* system prevents rural migrants from establishing rights to live permanently in cities. Urban migrants lack residency permits that would allow their children to attend public schools where they live, which are generally better schools than those in the rural areas. Although some urban migrants who can afford to do so send their children to private urban schools, others leave their children behind in their home villages, raised by grandparents (*Economist* 2011).

These modes of regulating internal migration are similar to those states use to control people's movement across national borders. Both China and South Africa are cases of internal migration, and so the mechanisms by which the costs of care are outsourced are more visible than in immigration regimes in Western Europe and the United States. In the latter cases, the economic inequalities and repercussions immigration regimes generate are not visible due to nationalist and anti-immigrant sentiment. Because of the ways that nation-states have gained legitimacy and been normalized, permits to cross an international boundary seem commonsensical, while residency permits within a country appear, in contrast, to be an overreach of government authority, in which citizens become "foreigners in their own land" (Hahamovitch 2011, 17).

Through the restrictions on migrants' families, immigration regimes are consistent with new forms of neoliberal governance in which "states endeavor to govern more while spending less" (Merry 2001, 17). Neoliberal forms of governance accomplish this by outsourcing risk (Ho 2011). In particular, they rely on individuals to become autonomous market actors, who master and fulfill themselves through their choices, such that individual desires for self-advancement contribute to the economic growth of the state (Burchell 1996; Giddens 1991; Rose 1999). Immigrants in many ways exemplify the self-made, risk-taking individual neoliberal discourses tout, even as neoliberal policies states enact destabilize and weaken immigrants' full social belonging and political participation. When immigrants come to the United States as young adults, when they leave their dependents behind, when they bring their children to live with them only as young adults, the United States benefits because their expenses for care are reduced and tax revenues increase through the income and businesses that immigrants develop (Porter 2005).

As the social safety net in some countries in the developed world begins to unravel, the burden of care work can be shifted to the countries from which migrants come, rather than or in addition to the host country, as Barbara Ehrenreich and Arlie Russell Hochschild (2002) suggest. Like the health care workers who are trained at government expense in Africa but seek employment in other countries once they are qualified (Clemens and Pettersson 2007; Kaba 2009; Manuh 2006; Nyonator and Dovlo 2004), the practices of fosterage this book describes—the result of legal regulations, conditions of employment, and a reliance on kin connections—mean that the Ghanaian government and households in Ghana bear the costs of reproducing some of the next generation of the American workforce, since migrants and the children of migrants arrive in their late teens or early twenties. By bringing with them capabilities developed elsewhere, some have argued, immigrants are a form of capital that offsets US trade imbalances (Folbre 2008; Sider 1992). Will Ghana, like the "homelands" of South Africa, be the home of children and the elderly while an adult labor force travels abroad for work that does not provide wages sufficient to raise a family abroad? Because the proportion of migrants to the general population is still small, between 3 and 7 percent of the population, Ghana is not in such a situation at the moment. The effects of out-migration are, however, spread unevenly, with the southern and more urbanized areas of Ghana experiencing greater transnational migration than more rural and northern areas.

Even with more limited numbers, there is some indication of stresses and strains on those left behind, in particular in those situations when children have been left unexpectedly or for those middle-aged, single women with children who are also trying to balance work with domestic responsibilities, as discussed in chapter 6. Some, particularly those who are poorer, are grateful for migrants' remittances as a substitute for fostering their children, but such foster parents are the least preferable to migrants as caregivers for their children. This suggests that while remittances are touted as a factor in poverty reduction and an increasingly major source of revenue for African countries (e.g., Adams and Page 2005; Quartey 2006), we need to be cautious in evaluating their impact, because we need to take into account the care work that those in Ghana are using to support their relatives abroad (Mazzucato 2008) as well as that which migrants might have provided had they stayed in Ghana. To the extent that remittances are substituting for the care work migrants might otherwise provide, the value of the remittances from abroad may be less than initially perceived. Also, if more and more migrants go abroad, the pressure on those left behind may increase, and what may be appreciated now may seem like a burden in the future.

Transnational Migration and Changing Repertoires

This book supports William Sewell's and Ann Swidler's conclusions that repertoires change through their transposition into new contexts, contexts that may prove balky to those ideas and practices. Repertoires are flexible, with people picking up new solutions and strategies they encounter in their daily lives, through their contacts and networks. Sometimes, in the case of immigrant parents, this process makes them more self-conscious of their practices, as they make meaning of their experiences, or sense out of what seems incomprehensible and puzzling. Migration helps illuminate the ways repertoires change, but it is important to note that repertoires also change outside of the context of migration.

This research also highlights the dynamics of power that shape repertoires, and that repertoires can shape. Some ways of organizing knowledge and social life dominate and others do not. All repertoires generate social practices that organize valued resources and create hierarchies in particular ways, but some practices are more resistant to change. For Ghanaians in Ghana and the United States, US immigration law appears as an unwielding behemoth to which they have to adapt. Why are immigration laws not more responsive to immigrants' conceptions of families? Why are American legal frameworks more powerful than immigrants' kinship practices?

William Sewell proposes that some schemas—"generalizable procedures applied in the enactment/reproduction of social life" (2005, 131), a concept close to that of repertoire—are deeper and more powerful than others. By deep, he means they are pervasive and underlie "a wide range of institutional spheres, practices, and discourses" (146) and are more taken for granted, in that they are unquestioned and less available to consciousness. By power, he means they command more resources. Thus, using his rubric, Ghanaians have to adapt to US immigration laws because US immigration authorities wield considerably more power and resources, such as the legal, financial, and organizational resources to detain and deport people, and the resources used in these ways have become widely accepted, through the discourses of nationalism and national security.

As Ann Swidler (2001) points out, this is a bit of tautology: some practices and worldviews command more resources because they are considered more legitimate; their power comes not from the resources they command but from the fact that they are taken for granted. Instead, she proposes that social institutions are powerful at shaping action "because they define problems actors must solve. The various solutions then share common schemas (or common cultural logics) because they are solutions to the same institutionally structured problem" (209). There is much that is attractive about this theory: drawing on their respective repertoires, immigrants—whether from Ghana, China, Mexico, or the Philippines—leave behind or send back their children in response to institutional structures such as similar immigration laws and economic constraints. Still, Swidler also takes us into a dead end: if stable patterns like institutional structures are created by individuals transposing their repertoires, why then do the repertoires of some trump those of others? I do not have an answer to this question, although I think the question is worth posing. I am also aware that while to Ghanaians, immigration law seems all powerful, to many Americans, and particularly those in anti-immigrant movements, it seems the law is in danger of being invalidated by immigrants who ignore its procedures (e.g., Buchanan 2006).

Despite the power of immigration law over intimate relations (Boehm 2012), the disjuncture between immigrants' repertoires of family life and US immigration law may result in changes in the latter's definitions of family and its bureaucratic processes. In Sewell's words, "structures are at risk, at least to some extent, in all the social encounters they shape" because multiple structures are in operation in any single situation, the response to the enactment of a repertoire is unpredictable, and because material and symbolic resources, like "the American Dream," have multiple meanings that can be mobilized in immigrant struggles (2005, 143). What, then, might change look like?

A Way Forward for Immigration Laws?

Sometimes I imagine how the Ghanaian families I know would improve American immigration law if they could. At one point, I thought the manual I would write would not be a parenting manual, as the Ghanaians I talked to hoped, but one detailing how US immigration law should be reformed, as a way of imagining and laying the groundwork for legal pluralism (Clarke 2009). What Ghanaian migrant parents and their children would ask for, I think, is flexibility.

Maintaining separate households is not an issue for Ghanaians, because they have experienced such households for the purpose of work and schooling in their own family histories and childhoods, going back to the cocoa migrations of the early twentieth century. Relationships can be maintained through exchanges of material support, phone calls, and visits. No matter what immigration law allowed, some Ghanaians might maintain separate households and scattered families, even if just for a few years, because of economic and social reasons.

The difficulty with international migration is that social relationships are more difficult to keep up or reestablish if ties are broken. In particular, children, parents, and spouses cannot visit back and forth regularly across international boundaries to maintain emotional and financial commitments to one another across the geographical distance. International migration exacerbates the already common problems of paternal abandonment, sexual infidelity, and marital separation, which I have discussed more extensively elsewhere (Coe 2011b). If visitor's visas were more readily given out to relatives—to grandmothers or sisters to visit women who have just given birth, to children to stay with their parents for their school vacations, and to nieces and nephews to visit aunts and uncles—the arrangements of Ghanaian transnational families would look more like those of migrants within Ghana. Enabling immigrants like Rexford to keep alive transnational ties to their families would contribute to the familial network of support for orphans and neglected children.

Furthermore, Ghanaians would appreciate a more expansive definition of family, one that allows already fostered nieces and nephews to be included among a migrant's children and in which migrants can begin fostering their nieces and nephews if other relatives can no longer do so. Fostering nieces and nephews would give them access to high-status education and well-paid work (by Ghanaian standards) abroad and, in their own right, contribute to taking care of the family. Ghanaians would appreciate siblings, nieces, and nephews being included in priority lists of relatives of permanent residents. At the very least, the current immigration categories for extended relatives of citizens should be protected, and efforts taken to make sure they are made available to immigrants from countries in Africa and elsewhere that rely heavily on diversity admissions and therefore have relatively small coethnic communities in the United States.

Thinking about immigration laws in this way is a bit of a fantasy, since the American political environment is such that there is currently little hope of immigration laws being altered along these lines. Furthermore, some provisions are in place to prevent fraud and abuse such as the trafficking of children into domestic service. Flexibility runs up against a fundamental mistrust of immigrants, in which statements need to be proved through extensive documentation and DNA tests. Bureaucratic procedures are a way of ensuring fairness in the United States. These measures render the immigration system opaque and seemingly arbitrary to many Ghanaians; not only maddening, in many Ghanaians' eyes, it shows a fundamental lack of care and pity for human beings, as individuals with specific needs and in situations of crisis.

Global capitalism and neoliberal state policies have created an anxious and mobile labor force separated from family, but much could change to further destabilize these conditions. The current political climate in the United States and contemporary global capitalism are considerably unsettled at the moment, creating opportunities for change. Immigration laws could become more restrictive, or the desires to migrate could decline as the numbers of unemployed grow in developed countries and as migrants' own countries, particularly in Africa, experience economic growth. The fact that contemporary global capitalism is not accompanied by a particular family arrangement or emotional regime means it is not fully hegemonic. People have not been fully remade to suit it. This book has argued that although the contradictory pressures of global capitalism and the state have generated conditions that promote the separation of families, there is variation in how migrants and their kin respond to these conditions. Family separations—and the emotions necessary to sustain family ties in such conditions—have not been made to fit a particular economic or political structure. Instead, as this book documents, people creatively draw on their repertoires as they encounter the possibilities and constraints neoliberalizing states increasingly dependent on a mobile and fickle capital generate. The frictions and frustrations separated families experience create some hope for new directions. As the relationship between global capitalism and nation-states continues to shift, I expect that Ghanaian families will continue to adapt their repertoires to the barriers and openings those changes present.

NOTES

1. Home health work, I learned that afternoon and in other conversations with Ghanaian home health aide workers, is full of uncertainty. Not only is the work period dependent on the elderly person's vulnerable and potentially changing health status, but also the relationship between home health aide and elderly person is of a sensitive nature and can often fray because of differing employer-employee expectations and the intimacy of living together.
2. Ages given throughout are at the time of the interview.
3. In the survey, 59 percent came from Latin America, 19 percent from Asia, and 22 percent from other parts of the world.
4. The US age data are based on Catherine Andrzejewski's analysis of 2008 American Community Survey data.
5. The argument in this section elaborates on my discussion in Coe 2012a.
6. Alejandro Portes (2003) raises important questions about the prevalence of transnationalism, focusing on entrepreneurship in particular.
7. This argument was previously articulated in Coe 2008.
8. Like other Twi speakers from urban areas and in the United States, he mixed English and Twi. Similar sentiments were shared by a Dominican father who sent his son back to the Dominican Republic for high school, "This [the United States] is the strangest country in the world: the richest and most powerful but all twisted in knots as far as children are concerned" (Portes and Rumbaut 2001, 6).
9. According to the US Census of 2000, the top five states where Ghanaians lived were: New York (26 percent), New Jersey (11 percent), Maryland (10 percent), Virginia (9 percent), and Illinois (5 percent) (Migration Policy Institute Data Hub n.d.; see also Takyi 2009). However, like other African immigrants, Ghanaians live in many different parts of the country, including in Iowa, Texas, California, North Carolina, Massachusetts, and Louisiana (Kent 2007). For more detail, see table 4 in chapter 5.
10. On the significance of indirection in Ghanaian speech, see Yankah 1995.

ONE
1. This argument was more deeply developed in Coe 2012b.
2. The Guan may have arrived in the fifteenth century but, based on archaeological evidence, definitely by the end of the sixteenth century (Kwamena-Poh 1973).

3. For more on Guan families, see Gilbert 1988, 1994.
4. For more on Akan kingship in Akuapem, see Gilbert 1989, 1992, 1993, 1995, 1997.
5. For more on the process of "Akanisation" among the Okere Guan and relations between Guan and Akan towns, see Gilbert 1988, 1989, and 1997.
6. While inheritors could be any member of the matrilineage, the line of inheritance gradually narrowed to the matrilineal issue of a man's own mother and her sisters, a process that was speeded up by the cocoa migrations among the Aburi and Akropong people (Hill 1963, 135, drawing on Fortes's work among the Asante).
7. "While large exogamous matriclans served to incorporate and organize production for labor-intensive tasks like the felling of trees or the clearing of land, planting, weeding, and harvesting were largely accomplished by groups composed of a husband, a wife, and any dependent children, slaves, or pawns" (Allman and Tashjian 2000, 60; see also Austin 2005, 112).
8. Michelle Gilbert (1995) quotes from an Akropong elder who describes how slaves were killed when a chief had died: "People disappeared easily. We used strangers, people from outside. We would catch them, find out if their blood could be used for the [black] stool[s], and if so, throw the head away. During *Odwira* [the annual festival] in the old days, the double bell would be beaten warning people to look after their children because something serious was to happen. People from the north [slaves: *nnonkofo*] would be killed, not for the stool, but just to throw them away. They were killed and left in the streets" (354–55).
9. As one respected and wealthy man, Kwaku Sae, did in Akropong in the 1850s (Haenger 2000, 36).
10. There were two cases in 1915 in Akropong in which the husband was the first person the family turned to for a loan for married woman (*Anim Kofi v. Kofi Otuo*, April 6, 1915, and *Kwasi Defo v. Akosua Ayim*, April 30, 1915, both in ECRG 16/1/18). In another court case, the court ruled against a husband who complained when his wife was pawned to someone else, because the family had given him the opportunity to first provide them with a loan (*Ayeh Kwadjo v. Kwadjo Tettey*, May 19, 1921, ECRG 16/1/22).
11. See also the observation by the Basel missionary Josef Mohr in 1906, "The villages situated on the Akwapim range from Aburi northwards to Apirede are gradually emptying themselves and everything withdraws more and more into the plantation district between Akwapim and Akim and into the Densu valley, where these people now build themselves good houses and where new villages arise" (quoted in Hill 1963, 227n1).
12. The Basel Mission did not discourage pawning by Christians but had guidelines that pawns Christians held be paid a monthly wage.
13. In my analysis of Akuapem court cases, the average loan for which a pawn served increased slightly from nine pounds in 1900–1909 to eleven pounds in 1910–29.
14. It was the conflict in the following court cases, spanning 1908 to 1925: *Akrong Kwaben v. Addi Affua*, February 5, 1908, ECRG 16/1/2; *Ohene Yaw Bampo of Obom v. Kofi Manukure of Obom*, February 5, 1910, ECRG 16/1/5; *Ayitey Mensa v. Boneamaye*, October 8, 1914, ECRG 16/1/18; *Yao Mante v. Tekwor*, November 3, 1914, ECRG 16/1/18; *Ammo Kwao v. Kwadjo Mensa and Ohene Kwadjoe*, December 26, 1914, ECRG 16/1/20; *Ohene Kwaku v. Adwowa Asi*, January 12, 1925, and *Kwabena Atiemo v. Akua Baduwa*, February 16, 1925, both in ECRG 16/1/21.
15. This section draws on Coe et al. 2011.
16. This section draws on Coe 2011c.

TWO

1. These reasons are very similar to those among the Mende in Sierra Leone (Bledsoe and Isiugo-Abanihe 1989).
2. For a discussion and justification of using the language of social class in West Africa, see Cohen 1972 and Sanjek 1982.
3. The World Fertility Survey (1980) shows that 24.5 percent of surveyed children age 0–14 in the Eastern Region were not living with their mothers, with rates increasing from 17.1 percent of those age 0–4, to 31.7 percent of those age 10–14 (Page 1989).
4. Fiawoo (1978) found similar high rates of 45 percent among schoolchildren surveyed in Abokobi, on the Accra Plains, which he also attributed to their highly respected schools.
5. The original (in Twi) does not indicate the gender of the child.
6. Literally, she says that the girl is not scared of her mother; as I understand it, what she means is something like what Jean Briggs (1998) terms ~ilira among the Inuit, in which shyness and lack of familiarity with an adult lead to respectful and decorous behavior among children.
7. The 1948 Census in Larteh showed that the adult population was heavily skewed towards women: there were fifteen women (aged sixteen years or more) for every ten men (Census, the Polly Hill Papers, Box 4, Folder 7).
8. Middle school was unusual for girls in her generation growing up in the 1940s, but was common for those growing up in the 1960s.
9. Whereas in 1970 (a more difficult economic time), in Konkonnuru, an Akuapem village, only 70 percent of boys and 36 percent of girls age six to seventeen had had some schooling (Hardiman 2003).
10. Robertson (1984) describes how elderly women in Accra received help from a wider range of relatives than did elderly men, in part because women tended to live with their relatives or take care of their grandchildren. However, elderly women were generally poorer than elderly men (208–10). In one study of remittances, remittances—both from abroad and within Ghana—came first and foremost from grown children (38 percent) and then from siblings (23 percent) (Mazzucato, van den Boom, and Nsowah-Nuamah 2005).
11. A study of remittances on 1998–99 data found that the poorest 40 percent of households in Ghana were more likely to receive remittances in the form of food, as opposed to cash or gifts (Mazzucato, van den Boom, and Nsowah-Nuamah 2005).
12. Data from elsewhere in Ghana suggest that younger children remained in the hometown in the care of a grandmother, while older children moved farther afield, to urban areas and other relatives and nonrelatives. In 1973, in the Kwahu town of Obo (also in the Eastern Region), children of migrants were usually raised in the hometown, where they attended primary school, after which they migrated to various rural or urban host locations, often going to where their parents or other kin were already residing (Bartle n.d.). Data drawn from across Ghana in 1971 showed that as children grew up, they were more likely to be fostered in urban areas and more likely to go to nonrelatives (Isiugo-Abanihe 1983).
13. Gottlieb (2004) describes how carrying a child on one's back refers directly to taking care of a child. See also LeVine et al. 1996.
14. People in Ayacucho, Peru, put a similar emphasis on poverty as the reason why children circulate between households (Leinaweaver 2008).

THREE

1. The top ten immigrant-sending countries to the United States in 2002 were Mexico, India, China, the Philippines, Vietnam, El Salvador, Cuba, Bosnia-Herzegovina, the Dominican Republic, and the Ukraine (Wasem 2004). On the insufficiency of economic motives, see Portes 1976 and Sassen 1998.

2. Overall, 691,003 green cards were given out to the relatives of citizens and permanent relatives in 2010, representing 66 percent of all green cards (Office of Immigration Statistics 2011).

3. The Illegal Immigration Reform and Immigrant Responsibility Act of 1996 established that the sponsor must establish that they have an income at least 125 percent of the federal poverty line (US Citizenship and Immigration Services 2008). This was enacted to prevent legal immigrants from becoming eligible for means-tested social services. Sponsors' affidavits of support were also made legally enforceable, such that their assets and incomes could be garnished if sponsored relatives became poor (Zolberg 2006).

4. I do not know whether this was a temporary work permit or a green card. In either case, he could have brought over his wife and children; I am not sure why he did not. I also do not know why he did not apply for asylum, although it is very difficult to be granted asylum.

5. While there are no costs for applying, at the time of the visa interview at a US consular office, each applicant (the diversity visa entrant and any accompanying family members) is charged a $330 diversity lottery visa fee, recently reduced, as of April 13, 2012, from $440 (US Embassy, Accra, Ghana, 2012).

6. Their work is based on round four of the Ghana Living Standards Survey.

7. This is based on the filing fees for the forms I-130 and I-485, as of November 23, 2010. There may be additional fees for fingerprints, photographs, a birth certificate, a medical examination, and vaccinations.

8. Technically, citizens of any age can sponsor their children and spouses, but these conditions presuppose adulthood. Only those over the age of twenty-one can sponsor siblings and parents.

9. Immigration regulations define an adult as over the age of twenty-one years.

10. Almost twice as many Ghanaians received permanent residency status in 2008 as became citizens (4,001) (Office of Immigration Statistics 2011). The processing time for citizenship varies at different regional centers (US Citizenship and Immigration Services 2010b). Some Ghanaians think about trying to marry a US citizen in exchange for a large sum of money in order to change their status more quickly. Many are tempted but some decide it is too risky. Fantastic rumors and stories about such marriages, ending in disaster and death, circulate within the Ghanaian community.

11. I have decided to use the term *unauthorized* rather than *undocumented* because I am swayed by the arguments that many of the *undocumented* do have documents—driver's licenses, false social security cards, and matrícula consular cards given out at Mexican consular offices—just not the right ones for what they are doing (Haines and Rosenblum 1999; Hayworth 2006). The term *illegal* overly criminalizes lack of authorization.

12. After January 4, 2010, potential immigrants are no longer denied visas on the basis of their HIV status.

13. Five percent of children of the householder under the age of eighteen were stepchildren, and another 2.5 percent were adopted children (US Census Bureau 2003a).

14. Recent health care legislation recognizes adult children's dependency, allowing

adult children up to the age of twenty-six years to remain on their parents' health care coverage.

15. Of 105 million households the US Census Bureau recorded in 2000, married couples headed fifty-four million households, while five million were headed by unmarried partners, the majority of whom were of the opposite sex. Unmarried couples represented 9 percent of households headed by a couple (US Census Bureau 2003b).

16. The US Department of State (2010b) website on international adoptions reads: "According to the INA, a child must meet the following two conditions in order to be considered an orphan: 1) The child must have no parents; or 2) The child has a sole or surviving parent who is unable to care for the child and has, in writing, irrevocably released the child for emigration and adoption. In general, a child would be considered to have no parents if both are determined to have died, disappeared, deserted, abandoned or have been lost or separated from the child. Abandonment requires that the birth parents give up all parental rights, obligations and claims to the child, as well as all control over and possession of the child (without transferring these rights to any specific person). Under U.S. law, children may not be abandoned, relinquished, or released to a specific prospective adoptive parent for adoption."

17. Note that in many countries, children given to orphanages may also have parents who are alive and well but are struggling temporarily to take care of their children. Parents may remove their children when their circumstances improve, but some children get adopted in the interval (Leinaweaver 2008).

FOUR

1. A version of this chapter was published in Coe 2012c.

2. One study of African immigrants in Washington, DC, noted that one reason that African immigrants might be drawn to New York City and Washington, DC (as the two metropolitan areas with the most African immigrants) was for their high per capita incomes (Wilson and Habecker 2008).

3. A similar issue plagues Asian immigrants, who earn less on average than US whites, despite comparable levels of education. A study of Asian immigrants found that Asian-educated immigrants earned 16 percent less than US-born whites, US-born Asian-Americans, and US-educated Asian immigrants. Among the latter three groups, there were no substantial income differences (Zeng and Xie 2004).

4. More broadly, in developed countries as a whole, Ghanaians tend to work in the health sector (19 percent), followed by manufacturing (18 percent) and wholesale trade (12 percent) (International Organization for Migration 2009).

5. In contrast to the Moroccan women Zontini (2010) studied, who did not work in part because they did not find it satisfying.

6. Many Ghanaian immigrants feel the need to further their education, because their existing credentials do not lead to well-paid, stable employment in the United States.

7. A woman from Accra, Ghana, interestingly describes a similar situation of giving birth when she and her husband lived in Cameroon in the late 1920s or early 1930s. "My husband was also very helpful; he would go for water and sweep the rooms and the compound before going to work every day for the first week after my delivery. After that week I did everything" (Robertson 1984, 71).

8. For more on conflicts in Ghanaian marriages abroad, see Biney (2011) and Manuh

(1998). Cheikh Anta Babou (2008) also raises concerns about divorce among the Senegalese diaspora. For similar transformations in migrant households from Mexico, see Hirsch (2003), Hondagneu-Sotelo (1994), and Smith (2006).

9. The World Bank is a bit suspicious of its own figures but considers it the best estimate given what districts report, which is closer to 96 percent.

10. Eleven states have no state-funded prekindergarten for three- and four-year-olds: Arizona, Hawaii, Idaho, Indiana, Mississippi, Montana, New Hampshire, North Dakota, South Dakota, Utah, and Wyoming. An additional fifteen states, including Maryland, North Carolina, and Virginia, do not serve three-year-olds in their prekindergarten programs (Barnett et al. 2011).

FIVE

1. Such stories are also shared in the media, as in a story of British students of Ghanaian descent being educated in Ghanaian schools because they were becoming involved in gangs and drugs (McConnell 2007; see also Brulliard 2007).

2. For examples, see Bledsoe and Sow (2011) on West African parents in Europe; Shani (2010) on Ghanaian parents in New York City; Brulliard (2007) on Nigerian immigrants in Washington DC; Thorne et al. (2003) about Yemeni and Central American immigrant parents in the United States; Portes and Rumbaut (2001) and Guarnizo (1997) about Dominicans; Waters (1999) on West Indians; Loucky (2000) on Mayan Guatemalans; and Kasinitz et al. (2008), based on a survey of immigrants' children in New York City, mainly Dominicans, South Americans, West Indians, Chinese, and Russian Jews. Portes and Rumbaut (2001) also report on the growth of private schools in Belize and other Central American countries to cater for such children. Those who cannot send their children back to their country of origin might instead try to recreate aspects of the home country through the extended family, a religious organization, or a strong ethnic community. For example, in one study, the researchers met a Laotian Hmong family that was planning to move to another city where there was a larger Hmong community to try to rescue their eighteen-year-old son from gang membership (Portes and Rumbaut 2001, 93–94).

3. Coontz (2000) notes that welfare benefits do increase the likelihood of unmarried teenage mothers moving away from their parents' households, but do not seem to cause teenage pregnancy, as has been the perception (82).

4. However, a Guatemalan mother talked about how there was more freedom for her children in Guatemala because her concerns about children's safety in the United States kept them indoors (Thorne et al. 2003, 249; see also Smith 2006).

5. For similar concerns within the Somali community in Minnesota, see Holtzman 2000.

6. For other work on the use of physical punishment of children in West Africa, see Perry 2009 and Bledsoe 1990.

7. The Ghana Education Service prohibits teachers from caning students; only head teachers are allowed to, although physical punishment still occurs regularly in Ghanaian schools. Recent cases in which teachers have been taken into police custody when beating has resulted in the child's death have also been in the news, generating debate on this issue (*Ghanaian Times* 2009).

8. The youth group meetings in the church were disbanded for some time because the adult leaders were so frustrated by the experience, particularly the disconnect between their expectations and the children's responses, that they were not eager to

continue teaching. Instead, the youth began to take on roles in the church: as ushers, for instance, or musicians.

9. Speaking English at home is unusual among Ghanaians but is increasingly practiced by elite families.

10. Cookson and Persell (1985), writing about American elite boarding schools, comment how alumni focus on their classmates and the escapades rather than academic life. Boarding schools have also been discussed as significant to the sometimes-overlapping circles of Britain's business, media, and civil service elite after World War II (Sampson 1962).

11. The children of Mexican migrants to the United States also typically come to the United States in their mid- to late adolescence, but because they can begin working, not for college (Dreby 2010).

12. The woman making this comment did indeed "post" her daughter, at the age of eight or nine months old, to Ghana, in part so that she could work more easily.

13. *Abɔrofo* does not mean "American" per se, but rather non-African or "white." In this context, however, I think the best translation is American.

14. A Nigerian man and Senegalese woman, in separate interviews, similarly described their moves from New York City to Washington, DC. He called New York City "too wild" and "a *huge* urban jungle" (italics in original), and she called it "a crazy big city" (quoted in Wilson and Habecker 2008, 441).

SIX

1. Robertson (1984), discussing women's lives in Accra, says that multigenerational households help women with their labor, even though such households are often poor.

2. Seventy-three percent of remittances from abroad go to the wealthiest quintile of Ghanaian households, and only 1 percent to households in the poorest quintile (Mazzucato, van den Boom, and Nsowah-Nuamah 2005).

3. One study based on interviews with a range of African immigrants in South Africa found that many were young (average age of thirty-two years), 38 percent worked in the informal sector, and most were poor. African immigrants to South Africa were pleased with the employment opportunities and services like education, water, and health care, but were concerned about safety and the quality of life (McDonald, Mashike, and Golden 2000).

4. She was not particularly concerned about the health effects of his desire for sweet drinks and food, but rather the expense. She described feeding him *banku*, a starchy meal, with her fingers, the only way that he would eat it.

5. Kindergarten teachers are not paid well in Ghana.

SEVEN

1. This chapter represents a rethinking of Coe 2008.

2. Glenn Adams's work on Ghanaians' conceptions of friends and enemies supports this argument. In particular, more Ghanaians chose exchange of material support as a defining characteristic of a friend than emotional closeness and disclosure of information (Adams, Anderson, and Adonu 2004; Adams and Plaut 2003).

3. Richard Shweder (1988) also discusses how "a person's representations or descriptions of the nature of her suffering and its causes can be part of the suffering it describes" (486).

4. This section draws on Coe 2011c.
5. It was interesting that Emmanuel made this argument. Although I initially thought he was referring to his own situation, his parents worked in white-collar jobs in the United States.
6. For more on the role of fashion and consumption in the making of social class, see Liechty 2003.
7. His exact statement that I have summarized is, "So they that have [money] are more than people who have parents there and then they are suffering down here [because they are not, in fact, receiving remittances], so they have overshadowed people who are suffering [those that get money affect the overall image of children left behind], so the main idea [impression] is that if your parent is there [abroad], you are rich or you have no problem."
8. Dɔ (the Twi word for "love") is used interchangeably with pɛ n'asɛm, which is commonly translated as "liking." Dɔ is most commonly used in the Bible, and thus people are likely to reply to the question of "Who do you love?" with religious responses, such as "I love Jesus." Another way of asking this question is through the word tima, or "feeling," again, a word that is used in the Bible. Tima or feeling is felt deep in one's heart: someone really touches you. Love, particularly in its form of romantic love, seems to be a not very elaborated concept locally, although its influence is growing through local and foreign video productions and soap operas. Jennifer Cole and Lynn Thomas (2009) have an excellent collection of essays on romantic love in Africa. Several of the essays discuss the effect of videos and print media on conceptions of romantic love (Fair 2009; Masquelier 2009; Mutongi 2009; Spronk 2009). Stephanie Newell (2000) points out that "locally published romances have been in widespread circulation in West Africa for at least two generations," since the 1960s (151).
9. This discussion of cultural style is indebted to James Ferguson's masterful discussion regarding urban migrants in Zambia (1999, chapter 3). Thomas Turino (2000) uses a similar formulation in his analysis of popular music in Zimbabwe.
10. While her paternal grandparents stressed that Jennifer and her brother had stayed with them because of the mother's problematic behavior, Jennifer herself represented her time in Ghana as staying with her mother.
11. For more on the lives of African immigrants in Italy, see Calavita 2005, Carter 1997, and Riccio 2008.

REFERENCES

Aboderin, Isabella. 2004. "Decline in Material Family Support for Older People in Urban Ghana, Africa: Understanding Processes and Causes of Change." *Journal of Gerontology* 59B (3): S128–37.

Abu-Lughod, Lila. 1986. *Veiled Sentiments: Honor and Poetry in a Bedouin Society.* Berkeley: University of California Press.

Adams, Glenn, Stephanie L. Anderson, and Joseph K. Adonu. 2004. "The Cultural Grounding of Closeness and Intimacy." In *The Handbook of Closeness and Intimacy,* edited by Debra J. Maslak and Arthur Aron, 321–39. Mahwah, NJ: Lawrence Erlbaum Associates.

Adams, Glenn, and Victoria C. Plaut. 2003. "The Cultural Grounding of Personal Relationship: Friendship in North American and West African Worlds." *Personal Relationships* 10: 335–49.

Adams, Richard H., and John Page. 2005. "Do International Migration and Remittances Reduce Poverty in Developing Countries?" *World Development* 33 (10): 1645–69.

Adeku, J. 1995. "Ghanaians Outside the Country." In *Migration Research Study in Ghana,* edited by K. A. Twum-Baah, J. S. Nabila, and A. F. Aryee. Vol. 2, *International Migration,* 1–18. Accra: Ghana Statistical Service.

Ahearn, Laura. 2001. *Invitations to Love: Literacy, Love Letters, and Social Change in Nepal.* Ann Arbor: University of Michigan Press.

Alber, Erdmute. Forthcoming. "Negotiating Fosterage and Children's Life Courses: Baatombu Siblings in Intergenerational Relations." In *Siblingship: Shared Parentage, Experience, and Exchange,* edited by Erdmute Alber, Cati Coe, and Tatjana Thelen. New York: Palgrave.

Allman, Jean, and Victoria Tashjian. 2000. *"I Will Not Eat Stone": A Women's History of Colonial Asante.* Portsmouth: Heinemann.

Ametefe, Gertrude A. 2001. "A Micro Study of Fostering among Employed Mothers in Dansoman Estate community." MPhil thesis, Institute of African Studies, University of Ghana.

Amoa, Samuel. 1907. "Ayeforohyia ho asɛm" (About weddings). *Kristofo Sɛnkekafo* 2 (12): 145–46.

Amselle, Jean-Loup. 1971. "Parenté et commerce chez les Kooroko." In *The Development of Indigenous Trade and Markets in West Africa,* edited by Claude Meillassoux, 253–65. London: Oxford University Press for the International African Institute.

Amu, Nora Judith. N.d. *The Role of Women in Ghana's Economy*. Accra: Friedrich Ebert Foundation.

Anderson, Elijah. 1990. *Streetwise: Race, Class, and Change in an Urban Community*. Chicago: University of Chicago Press.

Appadurai, Arjun. 1996. *Modernity at Large: Cultural Dimensions of Globalization*. Minneapolis: University of Minnesota Press.

Arcelin, Jacques. 1983. *Bitter Cane*. New York: Cinema Guild. Film.

Ardayfio-Schandorf, Elizabeth, and Margaret Amissah. 1996. "Incidence of Child Fostering among School Children in Ghana." In *The Changing Family in Ghana*, edited by Elizabeth Ardayfio-Schandorf, 179–200. Accra: Ghana Universities Press.

Argenti, Nicolas. 2010. "Things That Don't Come by the Road: Folktales, Fosterage, and Memories of Slavery in the Cameroon Grasslands." *Comparative Studies of Society and History* 52 (2): 224–53.

Arthur, John A. 2008. *The African Diaspora in the United States and Europe: The Ghanaian Experience*. Burlington, VT: Ashgate.

Asare, N. V. 1917. "Amanne bɔne a ɛsɛ sɛ wogu" (Bad customs that we should get rid of). *Kristofo Sɛnkekafo* 12 (9): 100–101.

Aspen Institute. 2002. "Grow Faster Together; Or Grow Slowly Apart: How Will America Work in the Twenty-First Century?" Available at http://www.pwib.org/downloads/GrowFast.pdf, accessed June 21, 2010.

Austin, Gareth. 1987. "The Emergence of Capitalist Relations in South Asante Cocoa-Farming, c. 1916–33." *Journal of African History* 28 (2): 259–79.

———. 2005. *Labour, Land, and Capital in Ghana: From Slavery to Free Labour in Asante, 1807–1956*. Rochester, NY: University of Rochester Press.

Babou, Cheikh Anta. 2008. "Migration and Cultural Change: Money, 'Caste,' Gender, and Social Status among Senegalese Female Hair Braiders in the United States." *Africa Today* 55 (2): 3–22.

Bain, Susan E. 1974. *Child Socialisation in Twenty Educated Families in Accra: An Exploratory Study*. Guelph: University of Guelph.

Balcom, Karen. 2012. "Back Door In: Private Immigration Bills and Transnational Adoption in the U.S. in the 1940s and 1950s." Paper presented at the 4th Adoption and Culture Conference, Scripps College.

Barnett, W. Steven, Megan E. Carolan, Jen Fitzgerald, and James H. Squires. 2011. *The State of Preschool 2011*. New Brunswick, NJ: National Institute for Early Childhood Research. Available at http://nieer.org/sites/nieer/files/2011yearbook.pdf, accessed October 9, 2012.

Bartle, Philip F. W. N.d. "Who Looks After the Rural Children of West African Urban Migrants? Some Notes on Households and the Non-Family in a Dispersed Matrilineal Society." Leiden: Afrika-Studiecentrum.

Beck, Ulrich. 1992. *Risk Society: Towards a New Modernity*. Translated by Mark Ritter. Thousand Oaks, CA: Sage Publications.

———. 1999. *World Risk Society*. Malden, MA: Blackwell.

Beck, Ulrich, and Elizabeth Beck-Gernsheim. 1995. *The Normal Chaos of Love*. Translated by Mark Ritter and Jane Wiebel. Cambridge, MA: Blackwell.

Benneh, E. Yaw. 2004. "The International Legal Regime and Migration Policies of Ghana, the ECOWAS Sub-Region and Recipient Countries." In *At Home in the World? International Migration and Development in Contemporary Ghana and West Africa*, edited by Takyiwaa Manuh, 103–17. Legon: Sub-Saharan Publishers.

Bergquist, Kathleen Ja Sook. 2009. "Operation Babylife or Babyabduction? Implications of the Hague Convention on the Humanitarian Evacuation and 'Rescue' of Children." *International Social Work* 52 (5): 621–33.

Bernstein, Basil. 2000. *Pedagogy, Symbolic Control, and Identity: Theory, Research, Critique.* Lanham, MD: Rowman and Littlefield.

Biney, Moses O. 2011. *From Africa to America: Religion and Adaptation among Ghanaian Immigrants in New York.* New York: New York University Press.

Black, Dan, Jeffrey Smith, and Kermit Daniel. 2005. "College Quality and Wages in the U.S." *German Economic Review* 6 (3): 415–43.

Blanc, Ann K., and C. B. Lloyd. 1994. "Women's Work, Child-Bearing, and Child-Rearing over the Life Cycle in Ghana." In *Gender, Work, and Population in Sub-Saharan Africa,* edited by Aderanti Adepoju and Christine Oppong, 112–31. London: James Currey.

Bledsoe, Caroline H. 1990. "'No Success without Struggle': Social Mobility and Hardship for Foster Children in Sierra Leone." *Man* 25: 70–88.

Bledsoe, Caroline H., and Uche Isiugo-Abanihe. 1989. "Strategies of Child-Fosterage among Mende Grannies in Sierra Leone." In *Reproduction and Social Organization in Sub-Saharan Africa,* edited by Ron J. Lesthaeghe, 442–74. Berkeley: University of California Press.

Bledsoe, Caroline H., and Papa Sow. 2011. "Back to Africa: Second Chances for the Children of West African Immigrants." *Journal of Marriage and Family* 73 (4): 747–62.

Boehm, Deborah A. 2012. *Intimate Migrations: Gender, Family, and Illegality among Transnational Mexicans.* New York: New York University Press.

Boehm, Deborah A., Julia Meredith Hess, Cati Coe, Heather Rae-Espinoza, and Rachel R. Reynolds. 2011. "Children, Youth, and the Everyday Ruptures of Migration." In Coe et al., *Everyday Ruptures,* 1–22.

Bohr, Yvonne, and Connie Tse. 2009. "Satellite Babies in Transnational Families: A Study of Parents' Decisions to Separate from Their Infants." *Infant Mental Health Journal* 30 (3): 265–86.

Boni, Stefano. 2001. "Twentieth-Century Transformations in Notions of Gender, Parenthood, and Marriage in Southern Ghana: A Critique of the Hypothesis of 'Retrograde Steps' for Akan Women." *History in Africa* 28: 15–41.

Bourdieu, Pierre. 1977. *Outline of a Theory of Practice.* Translated by Richard Nice. New York: Cambridge University Press.

Bourdieu, Pierre, and Jean-Claude Passeron. 1990. *Reproduction in Education, Society, and Culture.* Translated by Richard Nice. 2nd ed. Newbury Park, CA: Sage Publications.

Briggs, Jean L. 1998. *Inuit Morality Play: The Emotional Education of a Three-Year-Old.* New Haven, CT: Yale University Press.

Brokensha, David. 1966. *Social Change at Larteh, Ghana.* Oxford: Clarendon Press.

———. 1972. "Society." In *Akwapim Handbook,* edited by David Brokensha, 75–79. Tema: Ghana Publishing Corporation.

Brown, Claude. 1965. *Manchild in the Promised Land.* New York: Macmillan.

Brown, Tamara Mose. 2011. *Raising Brooklyn: Nannies, Childcare, and Caribbeans Creating Community.* New York: New York University Press.

Brulliard, Karin. 2007. "To Africa, for Culture and Credits: U.S.-Born Students Are Going Back to Their Family Roots." *Washington Post,* September 23: C1, C12.

Brydon, Lynne. 1979. "Women at Work: Some Changes in Family Structure in Amedzofe-Avatime, Ghana." *Africa* 49 (2): 97–111.

Buchanan, Patrick J. 2006. *State of Emergency: The Third World Invasion and Conquest of America.* New York: St. Martin's Press.

Burawoy, Michael. 1976. "The Functions and Reproduction of Migrant Labor: Comparative Material from South Africa and the United States." *American Journal of Sociology* 81 (5): 1050–87.

Burchell, Graham. 1996. "Liberal Government and Techniques of the Self." In *Foucault and Political Reason: Liberalism, Neo-Liberalism, and the Rationalities of Government*, edited by Andrew Barry, Thomas Osborne, and Nikolas Rose, 19–36. Chicago: University of Chicago Press.

Bureau of Labor Statistics. 2010a. "Nursing and Psychiatric Aides." *Occupational Outlook Handbook, 2010–2011 Edition*. Available at http://www.bls.gov/oco/ocos327.htm, accessed April 12, 2012.

———. 2010b. "Occupational Employment Statistics: Occupational Employment and Wages, May 2011: Nursing Aides, Orderlies, and Attendants." Available at http://www.bls.gov/oes/current/oes311012.htm, accessed April 12, 2012.

Calavita, Kitty. 1992. *Inside the State: The Bracero Program, Immigration, and the INS*. New York: Routledge.

———. 2005. *Immigrants at the Margins: Law, Race, and Exclusion in Southern Europe*. New York: Cambridge University Press.

Caldwell, John C. 1969. *African Rural-Urban Migration: The Movement to Ghana's Towns*. Canberra: Australian National University Press.

Campbell, Bebe Moore. 1989. *Sweet Summer: Growing Up with and without My Dad*. New York: Putnam.

Capps, Randy, Kristen McCabe, and Michael Fix. 2011. *New Streams: Black African Migration to the United States*. Washington, DC: Migration Policy Institute.

Carsten, Janet. 1997. *The Heat of the Hearth: The Process of Kinship in a Malay Fishing Community*. Oxford: Clarendon Press.

Carter, Donald Martin. 1997. *States of Grace: Senegalese in Italy and the New European Immigration*. Minneapolis: University of Minnesota Press.

Casper, Lynne M., and Kenneth R. Bryson. 1998. "Co-Resident Grandparents and Their Grandchildren: Grandparent Maintained Families." Population Division Working Paper No. 26. Washington, DC: US Census Bureau. Available at http://www.census.gov/population/www/documentation/twps0026/twps0026.html, accessed February 5, 2010.

Cervantes, Wendy. 2011. "Improving the Wellbeing of Children of Immigrants: Priorities for the 112th Congress." Washington, DC: First Focus. Available at http://www.firstfocus.net/library/fact-sheets/improving-the-wellbeing-of-children-of-immigrants-priorities-for-the-112th-congr.html, accessed May 8, 2012.

Children's Defense Fund. 2010. "The State of America's Children." May. "Early Childhood Development" section. Available at http://www.childrensdefense.org/child-research-data-publications/data/the-state-of-americas-children-2010-report-early-childhood-development.pdf, accessed June 21, 2010.

Chua, Amy. 2011. *Battle Hymn of the Tiger Mother*. New York: Penguin.

Clark, Gracia. 1999. "Mothering, Work, and Gender in Urban Asante Ideology and Practice." *American Anthropologist* 101 (4): 717–29.

———. 2001. "'Nursing Mother Work' in Ghana: Power and Frustration in Akan Market Women's Lives." In *Women Traders in Cross-Cultural Perspective: Mediating Identities, Marketing Wares*, edited by Linda J. Seligmann, 103–28. Stanford, CA: Stanford University Press.

Clarke, John. 2002. "Turning Inside Out? Globalization, Neo-Liberalism, and Welfare States." Paper presented at the joint Society of the Anthropology of North America and Canadian Association for Social and Cultural Anthropology meeting, Ontario, Canada.

Clarke, Kamari Maxine. 2009. *Fictions of Justice: The International Criminal Court and the Challenge of Legal Pluralism in Sub-Saharan Africa*. New York: Cambridge University Press.

Clemens, Michael A., and Gunilla Pettersson. 2007. "New Data on African Health Professionals Abroad." Working Paper No. 95, Center for Global Development, Washington, DC. Available at http://www.cgdev.org/content/publications/detail/9267, accessed December 29, 2009.

Coe, Cati. 2005. *The Dilemmas of Culture in African Schools: Youth, Nationalism, and the Transformation of Knowledge*. Chicago: University of Chicago Press.

———. 2008. "The Structuring of Feeling in Ghanaian Transnational Families." *City & Society* 20 (2): 222–50.

———. 2011a. "How Children Feel about Their Parents' Migration: A History of the Reciprocity of Care in Ghana." In Coe et al., *Everyday Ruptures*, 97–114.

———. 2011b. "What Is the Impact of Transnational Migration on Family Life? Women's Comparisons of Internal and International Migration in a Small Town in Ghana." *American Ethnologist* 38 (1): 148–63.

———. 2011c. "What Is Love? The Materiality of Care in Ghanaian Transnational Families." *International Migration* 49 (6): 7–24.

———. 2012a. "Growing Up and Going Abroad: How Ghanaian Children Imagine Transnational Migration." *Journal of Ethnic and Migration Studies* 38 (4): 913–31.

———. 2012b. "How Debt Became Care: Child Pawning and Its Transformations in Akuapem, the Gold Coast, 1874–1929," *Africa* 82 (2): 287–31.

———. 2012c. "Transnational Parenting: Child Fostering in Ghanaian Immigrant Families." In *Young Children of Black Immigrants in America: Changing Flows, Changing Faces*, edited by Randy Capps and Michael Fix, 265–96. Washington DC: Migration Policy Institute.

Coe, Cati, and Bonnie Nastasi. 2006. "Stories and Selves: Managing the Self through Problem-Solving in School." *Anthropology and Education Quarterly* 37 (2): 180–98.

Coe, Cati, Rachel R. Reynolds, Deborah Boehm, Julia Meredith Hess, and Heather Rae-Espinoza, eds. 2011. *Everyday Ruptures: Children, Youth, and Migration in Global Perspective*. Nashville: Vanderbilt University Press.

Cohen, Robin. 1972. "Class in Africa: Analytical Problems and Perspectives." *Socialist Register* 231–55.

Cole, Jennifer. 2009. "Love, Money, and the Economics of Intimacy in Tamatave, Madagascar." In Cole and Thomas, *Love in Africa*, 109–34.

Cole, Jennifer, and Lynn M. Thomas, eds. 2009. *Love in Africa*. Chicago: University of Chicago Press.

Comaroff, Jean. 1985. *Body of Power, Spirit of Resistance: The Culture and History of a South African People*. Chicago: University of Chicago Press.

Comaroff, Jean, and John L. Comaroff. 1991. *Of Revelation and Revolution: Christianity, Colonialism, and Consciousness in South Africa*. Vol. 1. Chicago: University of Chicago Press.

Conlin, Jennifer. 2009. "Living Apart for the Paycheck." *New York Times*, January 2. Available at http://www.nytimes.com/2009/01/05/business/worldbusiness/05iht-commuter.4.19095939.html?scp=1&sq=living%20apart%20for%20the%20paycheck&st=cse, accessed July 16, 2010.

Constable, Nicole. 2003. *Romance on a Global Stage: Pen Pals, Virtual Ethnography, and "Mail-Order" Marriages*. Berkeley: University of California Press.

———. 2007. *Maid to Order in Hong Kong: Stories of Migrant Workers*. 2nd ed. Ithaca, NY: Cornell University Press.

Cookson, Peter W., Jr., and Caroline Hodges Persell. 1985. *Preparing for Power: America's Elite Boarding Schools*. New York: Basic Books.

Coontz, Stephanie. 2000. *The Way We Never Were: American Families and the Nostalgia Trap*. New York: Basic Books.

Cooper, Frederick. 2001. "What Is the Concept of Globalization Good For? An African Historian's Perspective." *African Affairs* 100: 189–213.

Coutin, Susan Bibler. 2000. *Legalizing Moves: Salvadoran Immigrants' Struggle for U.S. Residency*. Ann Arbor: University of Michigan Press.

———. 2003. "Illegality, Borderlands, and the Space of Nonexistence." In *Globalization under Construction: Governmentality, Law, and Identity*, edited by Richard Warren Perry and Bill Maurer, 171–20. Minneapolis: University of Minnesota Press.

D'Alisera, JoAnn. 2004. *An Imagined Geography: Sierra Leonean Muslims in America*. Philadelphia: University of Pennsylvania Press.

Debrunner, Hans W. 1967. *A History of Christianity in Ghana*. Accra: Waterville Publishing.

De Genova, Nicholas P. 2002. "Migrant 'Illegality' and Deportability in Everyday Life." *Annual Review of Anthropology* 31: 419–47.

Dei, George J. Sefa. 1992. "A Ghanaian Town Revisited: Changes and Continuities in Local Adaptive Strategies." *African Affairs* 91 (362): 95–120.

Dodoo, F. Nii-Amoo. 1997. "Assimilation Differences among Africans in America." *Social Forces* 76 (2): 527–46.

Douglas, Mary. 1971. "Is Matriliny Doomed in Africa?" In *Man in Africa*, edited by Mary Douglas and Phyllis M. Kaberry, 123–37. Garden City, NY: Anchor Books.

Dow, Mark. 2004. *American Gulag: Inside U.S. Immigration Prisons*. Berkeley: University of California Press.

Dreby, Joanna. 2006. "Honor and Virtue: Mexican Parenting in a Transnational Context." *Gender and Society* 20: 32–59.

———. 2010. *Divided by Borders: Mexican Migrants and Their Children*. Berkeley: University of California Press.

Duster, Troy. 1990. *Backdoor to Eugenics*. New York: Routledge.

Ebron, Paulla. 2002. *Performing Africa*. Princeton, NJ: Princeton University Press.

Economist. 2011. "School's Out: Beijing's Migrant Workers." September 3: 40.

Ehrenreich, Barbara, and Arlie Russell Hochschild, eds. 2002. *Global Woman: Nannies, Maids, and Sex Workers in the New Economy*. New York: Metropolitan Books.

Empez Vidal, Núria. 2011. "The Transnationally Affected: Spanish State Policies and the Life-Course Events of Families in North Africa." In Coe et al., *Everyday Ruptures*, 174–87.

Erickson, Frederick. 1987. "Transformation and School Success: The Politics and Culture of Educational Achievement." *Anthropology and Education Quarterly* 18: 335–56.

Eriksen, Thomas Hylland, ed. 2003. *Globalisation: Studies in Anthropology*. London: Pluto Press.

Etienne, Mona. 1979. "Maternité sociale, rapports d'adoption et pouvoir des femmes chez les Baoulé (Côte d'Ivoire)." *L'Homme* 19 (3–4): 63–107.

Fahim, Kareem, and Matthew Sweeney. 2006. "Bronx 13-Year-Old Is Held and 2nd Is Sought in Killing." *New York Times*, March 3: B5.

Fair, Laura. 2009. "Making Love in the Indian Ocean: Hindi Films, Zanzibari Audiences, and the Construction of Romance in the 1950s and 1960s." In Cole and Thomas, *Love in Africa*, 58–82.

Ferguson, James. 1999. *Expectations of Modernity: Myths and Meanings of Urban Life on the Zambian Copperbelt*. Berkeley: University of California Press.

Fiawoo, D. K. 1978. "Some Patterns of Foster Care in Ghana." In *Marriage, Fertility, and Parenthood in West Africa*, edited by C. Oppong, G. Adaba, M. Bekombo-Priso, and J. Mogey, 273–88. Canberra: Australian National University Press.

Fleischer, Annett. 2008. "Marriage over Space and Time among Male Migrants from Cameroon to Germany." MPIDR Working Paper WP 2008-006. Max Planck Institute for Demographic Research, Germany.

Folbre, Nancy. 2001. *The Invisible Heart: Economics and Family Values*. New York: New Press.

———. 2008. *Valuing Children: Rethinking the Economics of the Family*. Cambridge, MA: Harvard University Press.

Foner, Nancy. 2005. *In a New Land: A Comparative View of Immigration*. New York: New York University Press.

———. 2009. "Introduction: Intergenerational Relations in Immigrant Families." In *Across Generations: Immigrant Families in America*, 1–20. New York: New York University Press.

Fong, Vanessa L. 2011. *Paradise Redefined: Transnational Chinese Students and the Quest for Flexible Citizenship in the Developed World*. Stanford, CA: Stanford University Press.

Forde, Maarit. 2011. "Modes of Transnational Relatedness: Caribbean Migrants' Networks of Childcare and Ritual Kinship." In Coe et al., *Everyday Ruptures*, 79–94.

Fortes, Meyer. 1971. "Some Aspects of Migration and Mobility in Ghana." *Journal of Asian and African Studies* 6 (1): 1–20.

Fouron, Georges E., and Nina Glick Schiller. 2002. "The Generation of Identity: Redefining the Second Generation within a Transnational Social Field." In *The Changing Face of Home: The Transnational Lives of the Second Generation*, edited by Peggy Levitt and Mary C. Waters, 168–208. New York: Russell Sage Foundation.

Foxen, Patricia. 2007. *In Search of Providence: Transnational Mayan Identities*. Nashville: Vanderbilt University Press.

Gamburd, Michele Ruth. 2000. *The Kitchen Spoon's Handle: Transnationalism and Sri Lanka's Migrant Housemaids*. Ithaca, NY: Cornell University Press.

García Canclini, Néstor. 1995. *Hybrid Cultures: Strategies for Entering and Leaving Modernity*. Translated by Christopher L. Chiappari and Silvia L. López. Minneapolis: University of Minnesota Press.

Georges, Eugenia. 1990. *The Making of a Transnational Community: Migration, Development, and Cultural Change in the Dominican Republic*. New York: Columbia University Press.

Georgetown University's Center on Education and the Workforce. 2010. "College Is Still the Best Option." Available at http://cew.georgetown.edu/resources/presentations/, accessed March 18, 2010.

Getz, Trevor R. 2004. *Slavery and Reform in West Africa: Towards Emancipation in Nineteenth-Century Senegal and the Gold Coast*. Athens: Ohio University Press.

Geurts, Kathryn Linn. 2002. *Culture and the Senses: Bodily Ways of Knowing in an African Community*. Berkeley: University of California Press.

Ghana National Commission on Children. 1997. "State of the Child Report: Akuapem North District, Eastern Region, Ghana." Accra: Ghana National Commission on Children.

Ghana Statistical Service. 1998. *Ghana Demographic and Health Survey, 1998*. Accra: Ghana Statistical Service.

———. 2005. "Ghana 2003: Results from the Demographic and Health Survey." *Studies in Family Planning* 36 (2): 158–62.

Ghana Statistical Service, Ghana Health Service, and ICF Macro. 2009. *Ghana Demographic and Health Survey 2008*. Accra: GSS, GHS, and ICF Macro.

Ghanaian Times. 2009. "Pupil Dies after Caning, Should Caning Be Banned?" March 15. Available at http://discussions.ghanaweb.com/viewtopic.php?t=99090&sid=78cb1cd d4ac5d73793373d1f6aaa5f77, accessed March 26, 2010.

Gibson, Margaret A. 1988. *Accommodation without Assimilation: Sikh Immigrants in an American High School*. Ithaca, NY: Cornell University Press.

Giddens, Anthony. 1991. *Modernity and Self-Identity: Self and Society in the Late Modern Age*. Stanford, CA: Stanford University Press.

———. 2000. *Runaway World*. New York: Routledge.

Gilbert, Michelle. 1988. "The Sudden Death of a Millionaire: Conversion and Consensus in a Ghanaian Kingdom." *Africa* 58 (3): 291–313.

———. 1989. "The Cracked Pot and the Missing Sheep." *American Ethnologist* 16 (2): 213–29.

———. 1992. "The Person of the King: Ritual and Power in a Ghanaian State." In *Rituals of Royalty: Power and Ceremonial in Traditional Societies*, edited by David Cannadine and Simon Price, 298–330. Cambridge: Cambridge University Press.

———. 1993. "The Cimmerian Darkness of Intrigue: Queen Mothers, Christianity, and Truth in Akuapem History." *Journal of Religion in Africa* 23 (1): 2–43.

———. 1994. "Vengeance as Illusion and Reality: The Case of the Battered Wife." *Man* 29 (4): 853–73.

———. 1995. "The Christian Executioner: Christianity and Chieftaincy as Rivals." *Journal of Religion in Africa* 25 (4): 347–86.

———. 1997. "'No Condition Is Permanent': Ethnic Construction and the Use of History in Akuapem." *Africa* 67 (4): 501–33.

Gilbertson, Greta. 2009. "Caregiving across Generations: Aging, State Assistance, and Multigenerational Ties among Immigrants from the Dominican Republic." In *Across Generations: Immigrant Families in America*, edited by Nancy Foner, 135–59. New York: New York University Press.

Gindling, T. H., and Sara Poggio. 2008. "Family Separation and Reunification as a Factor in the Educational Success of Immigrant Children." Report, Maryland Institute for Policy Analysis and Research, University of Maryland, Baltimore County.

Glenn, Evelyn Nakano. 1983. "Split Household, Small Producer, and Dual Wage Earner: An Analysis of Chinese-American Family Strategies." *Journal of Marriage and Family* 45 (1): 35–46.

Glick Schiller, Nina, Linda Basch, and Cristina Blanc-Szanton, eds. 1992. *Towards a Transnational Perspective on Migration: Race, Class, Ethnicity, and Nationalism Reconsidered*. New York: New York Academy of Sciences.

Godelier, Maurice. 1977. *Perspectives in Marxist Anthropology*. Translated by Robert Brain. New York: Cambridge University Press.

———. 1986. *The Mental and the Material: Thought, Economy, and Society*. Translated by Martin Thom. London: Verso.

Goffman, Erving. 1986. *Frame Analysis: An Essay on the Organization of Experience*. Boston: Northeastern University Press.

Gonzales, Patrick, Trevor Williams, Leslie Jocelyn, Stephen Roey, David Kastberg, and Summer Brenwald. 2009. "Highlights from TIMSS 2007: Mathematics and Science Achievement of U.S. Fourth- and Eighth-Grade Students in an International Context." National Center for Education Statistics. Available at http://nces.ed.gov/pubs2009/2009001 .pdf, accessed March 18, 2010.

Goody, Esther N. 1966. "The Fostering of Children in Ghana: A Preliminary Report." *Ghana Journal of Sociology* 3: 26–33.

———. 1982. *Parenthood and Social Reproduction: Fostering and Occupational Roles in West Africa*. Cambridge: Cambridge University Press.

Goody, Jack. 2000. *The European Family: An Historico-Anthropological Essay*. Malden, MA: Blackwell.

Gottlieb, Alma. 2004. *The Afterlife Is Where We Come From: The Culture of Infancy in West Africa*. Chicago: University of Chicago Press.

Greenhouse, Steven. 2007. "Justices to Hear Case on Wages of Home Aides: Worker's Overtime Plea Has Broad Implications." *New York Times*, March 25: 31, 35.

Grewal, Inderpal. 2005. *Transnational America: Feminisms, Diasporas, Neoliberalisms*. Durham, NC: Duke University Press.

Griffith, David C. 1985. "Women, Remittances, and Reproduction." *American Ethnologist* 12 (4): 676–90.

Guarnizo, Luis Eduardo. 1997. "'Going Home': Class, Gender, and Household Transformation among Dominican Return Migrants." In *Caribbean Circuits: New Directions in the Study of Caribbean Migration*, edited by Patricia R. Pessar, 13–60. New York: Center for Migration Studies.

Guarnizo, Luis Eduardo, and Michael Peter Smith. 1998. "The Locations of Transnationalism." In *Transnationalism from Below*, edited by Michael Peter Smith and Luis Eduardo Guarnizo, 3–34. New Brunswick, NJ: Transaction Publishers.

Gutiérrez, Kris D., and Barbara Rogoff. 2003. "Cultural Ways of Learning: Individual Traits or Repertoires of Practice." *Educational Researcher* 32 (5): 19–25.

Gyimah, Stephen Obeng. 2006. "Migration and Fertility Behavior in Sub-Saharan Africa: The Case of Ghana." *Journal of Comparative Family Studies* 37 (2): 235–52.

Haenger, Peter. 2000. *Slaves and Slave Holders on the Gold Coast: Towards an Understanding of Social Bondage in West Africa*. Edited by J. J. Shaffer and Paul Lovejoy. Basel: P. Schlettwein.

Hagan, Jacqueline Maria. 1994. *Deciding to Be Legal: A Maya Community in Houston*. Philadelphia: Temple University Press.

The Hague Conference on Private International Law. 2007. "The Convention on the International Recovery of Child Support and Other Forms of Family Maintenance, Concluded 23 November 2007." Available at http://www.hcch.net/index _en.php?act=conventions.text&cid=131, accessed March 20, 2009.

Hahamovitch, Cindy. 2011. *No Man's Land: Jamaican Guestworkers in America and the Global History of Deportable Labor*. Princeton, NJ: Princeton University Press.

Haines, David W., and Karen E. Rosenblum. 1999. "Introduction: Problematic Labels, Volatile Issues." In *Illegal Immigration in America: A Reference Handbook*, edited by David W. Haines and Karen E. Rosenblum, 1–12. Westport, CT: Greenwood Press.

Hamann, Edmund T., and Víctor Zúñiga. 2011. "Schooling and the Everyday Ruptures: Transnational Children Encounter in the United States and Mexico." In Coe et al., *Everyday Ruptures*, 141–60.

Hannerz, Ulf. 1969. *Soulside: Inquiries into Ghetto Community and Culture*. New York: Columbia University Press.

Hansen, Karen V. 2005. *Not-So-Nuclear Families: Class, Gender, and Networks of Care.* New Brunswick, NJ: Rutgers University Press.

Hardiman, Margaret. 2003. *Konkonuru: Life in a West African Village.* Accra: Ghana Universities Press.

Hays, Sharon. 1996. *The Cultural Contradictions of Motherhood.* New Haven, CT: Yale University Press.

Hayworth, J. D. 2006. *Whatever It Takes: Illegal Immigration, Border Security, and the War on Terror.* Washington, DC: Regency Publishing.

Heidbrink, Lauren. Forthcoming. "Recasting the Agency of Unaccompanied Youth." In *Emerging Perspectives on Children in Migratory Circumstances: Selected Proceedings of the Working Group on Childhood and Migration June 2008 Conference,* edited by Rachel R. Reynolds, Cati Coe, Deborah Boehm, Julia Meredith Hess, Heather Rae-Espinoza, and Joanna Dreby. Philadelphia: Drexel University College of Arts and Sciences and the Drexel iDea Repository.

Heintz, James. 2005. "Employment, Gender, and Poverty in Ghana." Working Paper Series, No. 92. Political Economy Research Institute, University of Massachusetts.

Hernandez, Donald J. 2012. *Changing Demography and Circumstances for Young Black Children in African and Caribbean Immigrant Families.* Washington, DC: Migration Policy Institute.

Hernandez, Donald J., and Wendy D. Cervantes. 2011. *Children in Immigrant Families: Ensuring Opportunity for Every Child in America.* Washington, DC: First Focus.

Heyman, Josiah McC. 1995. "Putting Power in the Anthropology of Bureaucracy: The Immigration and Naturalization Service at the Mexico–United States Border." *Current Anthropology* 36 (2): 261–87.

Hill, Polly. 1958. "The Acquisition of Land by Larteh Cocoa Farmers." Cocoa Research Series No. 14. Economics Research Division, University College of Ghana, November. Available in Box 6 (Folder 4) of the Polly Hill Papers, Africana Library, Northwestern University.

———. 1960. "Two Akropong Cocoa Estates: Bepoase and Omenako." Cocoa Research Series No. 19. Legon: Economics Research Institute, University College of Ghana. Available in Box 6 (Folder 6) of the Polly Hill Papers, Africana Library, Northwestern University.

———. 1963. *The Migrant Cocoa-Farmers of Southern Ghana: A Study in Rural Capitalism.* Cambridge: Cambridge University Press.

Hintzen, Percy Claude, and Jean Muteba Rahier, eds. 2003. *Problematizing Blackness: Self-Ethnographies by Black Immigrants to the United States.* New York: Routledge.

Hirsch, Jennifer S. 2003. *A Courtship after Marriage: Sexuality and Love in Mexican Transnational Families.* Berkeley: University of California Press.

Ho, Karen. 2011. "Comment to Ilana Gershon's 'Neoliberal Agency.'" *Current Anthropology* 52 (4): 548–49.

Hochschild, Arlie Russell. 2002. "Love and Gold." In *Global Woman: Nannies, Maids, and Sex Workers in the New Economy,* edited by Barbara Ehrenreich and Arlie Russell Hochschild. New York: Metropolitan Books.

———. 2003. *The Managed Heart: Commercialization of Human Feeling.* 2nd ed. 1983; Berkeley: University of California Press.

Holme, Jennifer J. 2002. "Buying Homes, Buying Schools: School Choice and the Social Construction of School Quality." *Harvard Educational Review* 72 (2): 177–205.

Holtzman, Jon D. 2000. *Nuer Journeys, Nuer Lives: Sudanese Refugees in Minnesota.* Boston: Allyn and Bacon.

References / 225

Hondagneu-Sotelo, Pierrette. 1994. *Gendered Transitions: Mexican Experiences of Immigration*. Berkeley: University of California Press.

Hondagneu-Sotelo, Pierrette, and Ernestine Avila. 1997. "'I'm Here, but I'm There': The Meanings of Latina Transnational Motherhood." *Gender & Society* 11 (5): 548–71.

Illouz, Eva. 2007. *Cold Intimacies: The Making of Emotional Capitalism*. Malden, MA: Polity Press.

International Labour Organization. 2006. "Table 3: Status in Employment (by Sex) in Ghana." Key Indicators of the Labour Market, 7th ed. Available at http://kilm.ilo.org/kilmnet/, accessed May 9, 2012.

International Organization for Migration. 2009. "Migration in Ghana: A Country Profile, 2009." Available at http://www.iom.int/jahia/Jahia/about-migration/lang/en, accessed December 23, 2009.

Isaac, Barry L., and Shelby R. Conrad. 1982. "Child Fosterage among the Mende of Upper Bambara Chiefdom, Sierra Leone: Rural-Urban and Occupational Comparisons." *Ethnology* 21 (3): 243–57.

Isiugo-Abanihe, Uche Charlie. 1983. "Child Fostering in West Africa: Prevalence, Determinants, and Demographic Consequences." PhD diss., Demography, University of Pennsylvania.

———. 1985. "Child Fostering in West Africa." *Population and Development Review* 11 (1): 53–73.

Jenkins, Paul. 1970a. "Asante, Mohr and Werner on Slave Emancipation Commission, dd 26 Jun 1875." In "Abstracts from the Correspondence of the Basel Mission Archives, 1852–1898." Master's thesis, University of Ghana, Legon.

———. 1970b. "Dieterle to Basel, dd. Aburi 22 Jun 75." In "Abstracts from the Correspondence of the Basel Mission Archives, 1852–1898." Master's thesis, University of Ghana, Legon.

Johnson, Marion. 1972. "The Migration." In *Akwapim Handbook*, edited by David Brokensha, 58–63. Tema: Ghana Publishing Corporation.

Jones, Delmos. 1992. "Which Migrants? Temporary or Permanent?" In *Towards a Transnational Perspective on Migration*, edited by Nina Glick Schiller, Linda Basch, and Cristina Blanc-Szanton, 217–24. New York: New York Academy of Sciences.

Joseph, Suad. 1994. "Brother/Sister Relationships: Connectivity, Love, and Power in the Reproduction of Patriarchy in Lebanon." *American Ethnologist* 21 (1): 50–73.

Kaba, Amadu Jacky. 2009. "Africa's Migration Brain Drain: Factors Contributing to the Mass Emigration of Africa's Elite to the West." In *The New African Diaspora*, edited by Isidore Okpewho and Nkiru Nzegwu, 109–26. Bloomington: Indiana University Press.

Kane, Ousmane Oumar. 2011. *The Homeland Is the Arena: Religion, Transnationalism, and the Integration of Senegalese Immigrants in America*. New York: Oxford University Press.

Kasinitz, Philip, John Mollenkopf, Mary Waters, and Jennifer Holdaway. 2008. *Inheriting the City: The Children of Immigrants Come of Age*. New York: Russell Sage Foundation.

Katz, Cindi. 2001. "Vagabond Capitalism and the Necessity of Social Reproduction." *Antipode* 33 (4): 709–28.

Kaye, Barrington. 1962. *Bringing Up Children in Ghana: An Impressionistic Survey*. London: George Allen and Unwin.

Kent, Mary Mederios. 2007. "Immigration and America's Black Population." *Population Bulletin* 62 (4) (December). Washington, DC: Population Reference Bureau.

Kertzer, David I., and Marzio Barbagli, eds. 2001. *The History of the European Family*. New Haven, CT: Yale University Press.

Kibria, Nazli. 1993. *Family Tightrope: The Changing Lives of Vietnamese Americans*. Princeton, NJ: Princeton University Press.

Kingdon, Geeta, and Måns Söderbom. 2008. "Education, Skills, and Labor Market Outcomes: Evidence from Ghana." May. The World Bank. Available at http://siteresources .worldbank.org/EDUCATION/Resources/278200-1099079877269/547664-1208379 365576/EWPS11_Labor_Market_Outcomes_Ghana.pdf, accessed June 29, 2010.

Klingshirn, Agnes. 1964. "Some Aspects of Socialisation in a Ghanaian Town: A Descriptive Study of Child Rearing Practices at Larteh." Master's thesis, University of Ghana.

Klomegah, Roger. 2000. "Child Fostering and Fertility: Some Evidence from Ghana." *Journal of Comparative Family Studies* 30 (1): 107–15.

Konadu-Agyemang, Kwadwo. 2001. *The Political Economy of Housing and Urban Development in Africa: Ghana's Experience from Colonial Times to 1998*. Westport, CT: Praeger.

Korboe, David. 1992. "Family-Houses in Ghanaian Cities: To Be or Not to Be?" *Urban Studies* 29 (7): 1159–72.

Kwamena-Poh, Michael A. 1973. *Government and Politics in the Akuapem State, 1730–1850*. Evanston, IL: Northwestern University Press.

———. 2005. *Vision and Achievement: A Hundred and Fifty Years of the Presbyterian Church in Ghana, 1828–1978*. Accra: Presbyterian Church of Ghana Press.

Lareau, Annette. 2003. *Unequal Childhoods: Class, Race, and Family Life*. Berkeley: University of California Press.

Le Espiritu, Yen. 1999. "Disciplines Unbound: Notes on Sociology and Ethnic Studies." *Contemporary Sociology* 28 (5): 510–14.

———. 2009. "Emotions, Sex, and Money: The Lives of Filipino Children of Immigrants." In *Across Generations: Immigrant Families in America*, edited by Nancy Foner, 47–71. New York: New York University Press.

Leinaweaver, Jessaca B. 2008. *The Circulation of Children: Kinship, Adoption and Morality in Andean Peru*. Durham, NC: Duke University Press.

LeVine, Robert, Suzanne Dixon, Sarah LeVine, Amy Richman, P. Herbert Leiderman, Constance H. Keefer, and T. Berry Brazelton. 1996. *Child Care and Culture: Lessons from Africa*. Cambridge: Cambridge University Press.

Levitt, Peggy. 2001. *The Transnational Villagers*. Berkeley: University of California Press.

Liechty, Mark. 2003. *Suitably Modern: Making Middle-Class Culture in a New Consumer Society*. Princeton, NJ: Princeton University Press.

Loucky, James. 2000. "Maya in a Modern Metropolis: Establishing Lives and Livelihoods in Los Angeles." In *The Maya Diaspora: Guatemalan Roots, New American Lives*, edited by James Loucky and Marilyn M. Moors, 214–22. Philadelphia: Temple University Press.

MacLeod, Jay. 1995. *Ain't No Makin' It: Aspirations and Attainment in a Low-Income Neighborhood*. Boulder, CO: Westview Press.

Malkki, Liisa H. 1995. *Purity and Exile: Violence, Memory, and National Cosmology among Hutu Refugees in Tanzania*. Chicago: University of Chicago Press.

Mamdani, Mahmood. 1996. *Citizen and Subject: Contemporary Africa and the Legacy of Late Colonialism*. Princeton, NJ: Princeton University Press.

Manuh, Takyiwaa. 1998. "Migrants and Citizens: Economic Crisis in Ghana and the Search for Opportunity in Toronto, Canada." PhD diss., Indiana University.

———. 2006. *An 11th Region of Ghana? Ghanaians Abroad*. Accra: Ghana Academy of Arts and Sciences.

Martin, Douglas. 2009. "Evelyn Coke, Home Care Aide Who Fought Pay Rule, Is Dead at 74." *New York Times*, August 9. Available at http://www.nytimes.com/2009/08/10/nyregion/10coke.html?scp=1&sq=evelyn%20coke&st=cse, accessed July 16, 2010.

Masquelier, Adeline. 2009. "Lessons from *Rubí*: Love, Poverty, and the Educational Value of Televised Dramas in Niger." In Cole and Thomas, *Love in Africa*, 204–28.

Mauss, Marcel. 2006. "Techniques of the Body (1935)." In *Techniques, Technology, and Civilisation*, edited by Nathan Schlanger, 77–96. New York: Durkheim Press/Berghahn Books.

Mazzucato, Valentina. 2008. "Informal Insurance Arrangements in Ghanaian Migrants' Transnational Networks: The Role of Reverse Remittances and Geographic Proximity." *World Development* 37 (6): 1105–15.

Mazzucato, Valentina, Bart van den Boom, and N. N. N. Nsowah-Nuamah. 2005. "Origin and Destination of Remittances in Ghana." In *At Home in the World? International Migration and Development in Contemporary Ghana and West Africa*, edited by Takyiwaa Manuh, 139–52. Accra: Sub-Saharan Publishers.

Mba, Chucks J., Stephen O. Kwankye, Delali M. Badasu, Clement Ahiadeke, and John Anarfi. 2009. "Child Poverty and Disparities in Ghana." UNICEF Global Study on Child Poverty and Disparities, 2007–2008. Available at http://www.unicef.org/social policy/files/Child_Poverty_and_Disparitites_in_Ghana.pdf, accessed June 11, 2010.

McConnell, Tristan. 2007. "African Cane Tames Unruly British Pupils." *Sunday Times*. Available at http://www.timesonline.co.uk/tol/news/world/africa/article2800904.ece, accessed March 29, 2010.

McDonald, David A., Lephophotho Mashike, and Celia Gordon. 2000. "The Lives and Times of African Migrants and Immigrants in Post-Apartheid South Africa." In *On Borders: Perspectives on International Migration in Southern Africa*, edited by David A. McDonald, 168–95. New York: St. Martin's Press.

McPhee, Allan. 1926. *The Economic Revolution in British West Africa*. London: Routledge.

McWilliam, H. O. A., and Kwamena-Poh, M. A. 1975. *The Development of Education in Ghana: An Outline*. 3rd ed. London: Longman.

Meillassoux, Claude. 1972. "From Reproduction to Production." *Economy and Society* 1: 95–105.

———. 1981. *Maidens, Meal, and Money: Capitalism and the Domestic Community*. New York: Cambridge University Press.

Menjívar, Cecilia, and Leisy Abrego. 2009. "Parents and Children across Borders: Legal Instability and Intergenerational Relations in Guatemalan and Salvadoran Families." In *Across Generations: Immigrant Families in America*, edited by Nancy Foner, 160–89. New York: New York University Press.

Menjívar, Cecilia, and Victor Agadjanian. 2007. "Men's Migration and Women's Lives: Views from Rural Armenia and Guatemala." *Social Science Quarterly* 88 (5): 1243–62.

Merry, Sally Engle. 2001. "Spatial Governmentality and the New Urban Social Order: Controlling Gender Violence through Law." *American Anthropologist* 103 (1): 16–29.

Meyer, Birgit. 1999. *Translating the Devil: Religion and Modernity among the Ewe of Ghana*. Trenton, NJ: Africa World Press.

———. 2003. "Ghanaian Popular Cinema and the Magic In and Of Film." In *Magic and Modernity: Interfaces of Revelation and Concealment*, edited by Birgit Meyer and Peter Pels, 200–222. Stanford, CA: Stanford University Press.

Middleton, John. 1979. "Home-Town: A Study of an Urban Centre in Southern Ghana." *Africa* 49 (3): 246–57.

Migration Policy Institute Data Hub. n.d. "Who's Where in the United States?" Results for search on country of origin = Ghana. Available at http://www.migrationinformation.org/datahub/whoswhere.cfm, accessed June 24, 2010.

Mintz, Sidney. 1960. *Worker in the Cane: A Puerto Rican Life History.* New Haven, CT: Yale University Press.

Moe, Karine, and Dianna Shandy. 2010. *Glass Ceilings and 100-Hour Couples: What the Opt-Out Phenomenon Can Teach Us about Work and Family.* Athens: University of Georgia Press.

Moore, Henrietta L. 1988. *Feminism and Anthropology.* Minneapolis: University of Minnesota Press.

Moran, Mary H. 1992. "Civilized Servants: Child Fosterage and Training for Status among the Glebo of Liberia." In *African Encounters with Domesticity*, edited by Karen Tranberg Hansen, 98–115. New Brunswick, NJ: Rutgers University Press.

Moran-Taylor, Michelle J. 2008. "When Mothers and Fathers Migrate North: Caretakers, Children, and Child Rearing in Guatemala." *Latin American Perspectives* 35 (4): 79–95.

Muncie, John. 1999. "Exorcising Demons: Media, Politics, and Criminal Justice." In *Social Policy, the Media, and Misrepresentation*, edited by Bob Franklin, 174–89. New York: Routledge.

Murray, Colin. 1981. *Families Divided: The Impact of Migrant Labour in Lesotho.* New York: Cambridge University Press.

Mutongi, Kenda. 2009. "'Dear Dolly's' Advice: Representations of Youth, Courtship, and Sexualities in Africa, 1960–1980." In Cole and Thomas, *Love in Africa*, 83–108.

Nazario, Sonia. 2006. *Enrique's Journey.* New York: Random House.

Newell, Stephanie. 2000. *Ghanaian Popular Fiction: "Thrilling Discoveries in Conjugal Life" and Other Tales.* Athens: Ohio University Press.

Niane, D. T. 1965. *Sundiata: An Epic of Old Mali.* Harlow: Longman.

Nkrumah, Kwame. 1957. *Ghana: The Autobiography of Kwame Nkrumah.* New York: Thomas Nelson and Sons.

Notermans, Catrien. Forthcoming. "Kinship Dynamics: Considering Life-Course and Changing Household Compositions in Fosterage Studies." In *Child Fosterage in West Africa: New Perspectives on Theories and Practices*, edited by Erdmute Alber, Jeannett Martin, and Catrien Notermans. Leiden: E. J. Brill.

Nyarko, Philomena E. 1995. "Female-Headed Households: Roles and Consequences of Migration." In *Migration Research Study*, edited by K. A. Twum-Baah, J. S. Nabila, and A. F. Aryee. Vol. 1, *Internal Migration*, 293–332. Accra: Ghana Statistical Service.

Nyonator, Frank, and Delanyo Dovlo. 2004. "The Health of the Nation and the Brain Drain in the Health Sector." In *At Home in the World? International Migration and Development in Contemporary Ghana and West Africa*, edited by Takyiwaa Manuh, 227–49. Legon: Sub-Saharan Publishers.

Oben, W. 1895. "III. Nnɛɛma horow a etumi siw yɛn adwuma kwan" (Different things which are obstacles to our work). *Kristofo Sɛnkekafo* 1 (1–3) (January–March): 105–10.

Odotei, Irene K. 2003. *Migration, Fishing, and Development: A Case Study of Ningo.* Legon: Institute of African Studies, University of Ghana.

Office of Immigration Statistics. 2011. "2010 Yearbook of Immigration Statistics." Available at http://www.dhs.gov/xlibrary/assets/statistics/yearbook/2010/ois_yb_2010.pdf, accessed May 7, 2012.

Office of Management and Budget. 2010. "The Federal Budget, Fiscal Year 2011: Depart-

ment of Health and Human Services." The White House. Available at http://www
.whitehouse.gov/omb/factsheet_department_health/, accessed July 28, 2010.

Ofori, I. 1907. "So anyamesɛm no renya nkɔso wɔ Akuapem asase so akyɛn aman a edi
n'akyi no ana?" (Is Christianity progressing in Akuapem more than in kingdoms that
came to Christianity later?). *Kristofo Sɛnkekafo* 2 (1) (January): 7–9.

Ogbu, John U. 1978. *Minority Education and Caste: The American System in Cross-Cultural
Perspective.* New York: Academic Press.

Olaniyan, Tejumola. 2003. "Economies of the Interstice." In *Problematizing Blackness: Self-
Ethnographies by Black Immigrants to the United States,* edited by Percy Claude Hintzen
and Jean Muteba Rahier, 53–64. New York: Routledge.

Olwig, Karen Fog. 1999. "Narratives of the Children Left Behind: Home and Identity
in Globalised Caribbean Families." *Journal of Ethnic and Migration Studies* 25 (2):
267–84.

———. 2007. *Caribbean Journeys: An Ethnography of Migration and Home in Three Family
Networks.* Durham, NC: Duke University Press.

Ong, Aihwa. 1999. *Flexible Citizenship: The Cultural Logic of Transnationality.* Durham, NC:
Duke University Press.

Oppong, Christine. 1974. *Marriage among a Matrilineal Elite: A Family Study of Ghanaian
Senior Civil Servants.* Cambridge: Cambridge University Press.

Orozco, Manuel, with Micah Bump, Rachel Fedewa, and Katya Sienkiewicz. 2005.
"Diasporas, Development, and Transnational Integration: Ghanaians in the U.S.,
U.K., and Germany." Report for Citizen International and USAID.

Ortner, Sherry B. 1999. Introduction to *The Fate of "Culture": Geertz and Beyond,* 1–13.
Berkeley: University of California Press.

———. 2006. *Anthropology and Social Theory: Culture, Power, and the Acting Subject.* Durham, NC: Duke University Press.

Ɔsabo, B. 1916. "Letter." *Kristofo Sɛnkekafo* 11 (5): 59.

Page, Hilary. 1989. "Childrearing versus Childbearing: Coresidence of Mother and Child
in Sub-Saharan Africa." In *Reproduction and Social Organization in Sub-Saharan Africa,*
edited by Ron J. Lesthaeghe, 401–41. Berkeley: University of California Press.

Parreñas, Rhacel Salazar. 2001. "Mothering from a Distance: Emotions, Gender, and Intergenerational Relations in Filipino Transnational Families." *Feminist Studies* 27 (2):
361–90.

———. 2002. "The Care Crisis in the Philippines: Children and Transnational Families
in the New Global Economy." In *Global Woman: Nannies, Maids, and Sex Workers in
the New Economy,* edited by Barbara Ehrenreich and Arlie Russell Hochschild, 39–54.
New York: Metropolitan Books.

———. 2004. *Children of Global Migration: Transnational Families and Gendered Woes.* Stanford, CA: Stanford University Press.

Pellow, Deborah. 2002. *Landlords and Lodgers: Socio-Spatial Organization in an Accra Community.* Chicago: University of Chicago Press.

Perry, Donna. 2009. "Fathers, Sons, and the State: Discipline and Punishment in a Wolof
Hinterland." *Cultural Anthropology* 24 (1): 33–67.

Phillips, Adam. 2011. "Stag at Bay." *London Review of Books* 33 (16) (August 25): 26–29.

Plange Rhule, Gyakua. 2005. "The Posted Babies Syndrome." *Daily Graphic,* August 11.

Polak, Barbara. 2012. "Peasants in the Making: Bamana Children at Work." In *African
Children at Work: Working and Learning in Growing Up for Life,* edited by Gerd Spittler
and Michael Bourdillon, 87–112. Zurich: Lit Verlag.

Porter, Eduardo. 2005. "Illegal Immigrants Are Bolstering Social Security with Billions." *New York Times*, April 5. Available at http://www.nytimes.com/2005/04/05/ business/05immigration.html?scp=9&sq=stephen+goss&st=nyt, accessed July 23, 2010.

Portes, Alejandro. 1976. "Determinants of the Brain Drain." *International Migration Review* 10 (4): 489–508.

———. 2003. "Theoretical Convergences and Empirical Evidence in the Study of Immigrant Transnationalism." *International Migration Review* 37 (3): 814–92.

Portes, Alejandro, and Rubén G. Rumbaut. 2001. *Legacies: The Story of the Immigrant Second Generation*. Berkeley: University of California Press.

Power, Michael. 1997. *The Audit Society: Rituals of Verification*. New York: Oxford University Press.

Pribilsky, Jason. 2007. *La Chulla Vida: Gender, Migration, and the Family in Andean Ecuador and New York City*. Syracuse, NY: Syracuse University Press.

Pugh, Allison. 2009. *Longing and Belonging: Parents, Children, and Consumer Culture*. Berkeley: University of California Press.

Quartey, Peter. 2006. "The Impact of Migrant Remittances on Household Welfare in Ghana." AERC Research Paper No. 158. Nairobi: African Economic Research Consortium.

Radner, Joan Newlon, ed. 1993. *Feminist Messages: Coding in Women's Folk Culture*. Urbana: University of Illinois Press.

Rae-Espinoza, Heather. 2011. "The Children of Émigrés in Ecuador: Narratives of Cultural Reproduction and Emotion in Transnational Social Fields." In Coe et al., *Everyday Ruptures*, 115–38.

Rattray, R. S. 1969 [1911]. *Ashanti Law and Constitution*. New York: Negro Universities Press.

Rebhun, Laura A. 1999. *The Heart Is Unknown Country: Love in the Changing Economy of Northeast Brazil*. Stanford, CA: Stanford University Press.

Reddy, William M. 2001. *The Navigation of Feeling: A Framework for the History of Emotions*. Cambridge: Cambridge University Press.

Reynolds, Pamela. 1991. *Dance Civet Cat: Tongan Children and Labour in the Zambezi Valley*. Athens: Ohio University Press.

Reynolds, Rachel. 2002. "An African Brain Drain: Nigerian (Igbo) Decisions to Immigrate to the U.S." *Review of African Political Economy* 29 (92): 273–84.

———. 2006. "Child Fostering and Child Labor in the African Novel." Paper given at the African Studies Association annual meeting, San Francisco.

Riccio, Bruno. 2008. "West African Transnationalisms Compared: Ghanaians and Senegalese in Italy." *Journal of Ethnic and Migration Studies* 34 (2): 217–34.

Robertson, Claire C. 1984. *Sharing the Same Bowl: A Socioeconomic History of Women and Class in Accra, Ghana*. Bloomington: Indiana University Press.

Roediger, David R. 2005. *Working toward Whiteness: How America's Immigrants Became White, the Strange Journey from Ellis Island to the Suburbs*. New York: Basic Books.

Rosaldo, Renato. 1989. *Culture and Truth: The Remaking of Social Analysis*. Boston: Beacon.

Rosaldo, Renato, ed. 2003. *Cultural Citizenship in Island Southeast Asia: Nation and Belonging in the Hinterlands*. Berkeley: University of California Press.

Rose, Nikolas. 1999. *Powers of Freedom: Reframing Political Thought*. Cambridge: Cambridge University Press.

Sahlins, Marshall. 2004. *Apologies to Thucydides: Understanding History as Culture and Vice Versa*. Chicago: University of Chicago Press.

———. 2010. "What Kinship Is (Part One)." *Journal of the Royal Anthropological Institute* 17: 2–19.

———. 2011. "What Kinship Is (Part Two)." *Journal of the Royal Anthropological Institute* 17: 227–42.

Sampson, Anthony. 1962. *Anatomy of Britain*. London: Hodder and Stoughton.

Sanders, Todd. 2011. "Comment to Ilana Gershon's 'Neoliberal Agency.'" *Current Anthropology* 52 (4): 549–50.

Sanjek, Roger. 1982. "The Organization of Households in Adabraka: Toward a Wider Comparative Perspective." *Comparative Studies in Society and History* 24 (1): 57–103.

Sassen, Saskia. 1996. *Losing Control? Sovereignty in an Age of Globalization*. New York: Columbia University Press.

———. 1998. *Globalization and Its Discontents*. New York: New Press.

———. 2006. *Territory, Authority, Rights: From Medieval to Global Assemblages*. Princeton, NJ: Princeton University Press.

Schapera, Isaac. 1947. *Migrant Labour and Tribal Life: A Study of Conditions in the Bechuanaland Protectorate*. Oxford: Oxford University Press.

Schildkrout, Enid. 1973. "The Fostering of Children in Urban Ghana." *Urban Anthropology* 2: 48–73.

Schmalzbauer, Leah. 2004. "Searching for Wages and Mothering from Afar: The Case of Honduran Transnational Families." *Journal of Marriage and Family* 66: 1317–31.

Schneider, David Murray. 1968. *American Kinship: A Cultural Account*. Englewood Cliffs, NJ: Prentice-Hall.

Schulte, Brigid. 2005. "Go Ask Your Mother: Rosemary Payne and Obaya Achiah." *Washington Post Magazine*, May 8: 12.

Scott, James. 1985. *Weapons of the Weak: Everyday Forms of Peasant Resistance*. New Haven, CT: Yale University Press.

Sewell, William H. 2005. *Logics of History: Social Theory and Social Transformation*. Chicago: University of Chicago Press.

Shabaya, Judith. 2006. "English Language Acquisition and Some Pedagogical Issues Affecting the Adaptation of African Immigrant Children." In *The New African Diaspora in North America: Trends, Community Building, and Adaptation*, edited by Kwadwo Konadu-Agyemang, Baffour K. Takyi, and John Arthur, 257–72. Lanham, MD: Lexington Books.

Shani, Serah. 2010. "'I will not lose my children': The New York City Ghanaian Network Village and Their Academic Success Pursuits." PhD diss., Columbia University.

Shipton, Parker. 2007. *The Nature of Entrustment: Intimacy, Exchange, and the Sacred in Africa*. New Haven, CT: Yale University Press.

Shore, Cris, and Susan Wright. 2000. "Coercive Accountability: The Rise of Audit Culture in Higher Education." In *Audit Cultures: Anthropological Studies in Accountability, Ethics, and the Academy*, edited by Marilyn Strathern, 57–89. New York: Routledge.

Shweder, Richard A. 1988. "Suffering in Style." *Culture, Medicine, and Psychiatry* 12: 479–97.

Sider, Gerald. 1992. "The Contradictions of Transnational Migration: A Discussion." In *Towards a Transnational Perspective on Migration*, edited by Nina Glick Schiller, Linda Basch, and Cristina Blanc-Szanton, 225–40. New York: New York Academy of Sciences.

Small, Cathy. 1997. *Voyages: From Tongan Villages to American Suburbs*. Ithaca, NY: Cornell University Press.

Smetherham, Claire. 2006. "Firsts among Equals? Evidence on the Contemporary Relationship between Educational Credentials and the Occupational Structure." *Journal of Work and Family* 19 (1): 29–45.

Smith, James, and Barry Edmonston, eds. 1997. *The New Americans: Economic, Demographic, and Fiscal Effects of Immigration.* Washington, DC: National Academy Press.

Smith, Robert Courtney. 2006. *Mexican New York: Transnational Lives of New Immigrants.* Berkeley: University of California Press.

Soto, Isa Maria. 1987. "West Indian Child Fostering: Its Role in Migrant Exchange." In *Caribbean Life in New York City: Sociocultural Dimensions,* edited by Constance R. Sutton and Elsa M. Chaney, 131–49. Staten Island, NY: Center for Migration Studies of New York.

Spronk, Rachel. 2009. "Media and the Therapeutic Ethos of Romantic Love in Middle-Class Nairobi." In Cole and Thomas, *Love in Africa,* 181–203.

Stearns, Peter, and Mark Knapp. 1993. "Men and Romantic Love: Pinpointing a 20th-Century Change." *Journal of Social History* 26 (4): 768–795.

Stepick, Alex, Guillermo Grenier, Max Castro, and Marvin Dunn. 2003. *This Land Is Our Land: Immigrants and Power in Miami.* Berkeley: University of California Press.

Stoller, Paul. 2002. *Money Has No Smell: The Africanization of New York City.* Chicago: University of Chicago Press.

Strathdee, Rob. 2009. "Reputation in the Sociology of Education." *British Journal of Sociology of Education* 30 (1): 83–96.

Strathern, Marilyn. 1985. "Kinship and Economy: Constitutive Orders of a Provisional Kind." *American Ethnologist* 12: 191–209.

———. 2000. "Introduction: New Accountabilities." In *Audit Cultures: Anthropological Studies in Accountability, Ethics, and the Academy,* 1–18. New York: Routledge.

Suárez-Orozco, Carola, Irina L. G. Todorova, and Josephine Louie. 2002. "Making Up for Lost Time: The Experience of Separation and Reunification among Immigrant Families." *Family Process* 41 (4): 625–43.

Sutton, Inez. 1983. "Labour in Commercial Agriculture in Ghana in the Late Nineteenth and Early Twentieth Centuries." *Journal of African History* 24 (4): 461–83.

Swidler, Ann. 1986. "Culture in Action: Symbols and Strategies." *American Sociological Review* 51 (April): 273–86.

———. 2001. *Talk of Love: How Culture Matters.* Chicago: University of Chicago Press.

Táíwò, Olúfẹ́mi. 2003. "This Prison Called My Skin: On Being Black in America." In *Problematizing Blackness: Self-Ethnographies by Black Immigrants to the United States,* edited by Percy Claude Hintzen and Jean Muteba Rahier, 35–52. New York: Routledge.

Takyi, Baffour K. 2009. "Africans Abroad: Comparative Perspectives on America's Postcolonial West Africans." In *The New African Diaspora,* edited by Isidore Okpewho and Nkiru Nzegwu, 236–54. Bloomington: Indiana University Press.

Tanaka, Greg. 2009. "The Elephant in the Living Room That No One Wants to Talk About: Why U.S. Anthropologists Are Unable to Acknowledge the End of Culture." *Anthropology and Education Quarterly* 40 (1): 82–95.

Taylor, Diana. 2003. *The Archive and the Repertoire: Performing Cultural Memory in the Americas.* Durham, NC: Duke University Press.

Taylor, Janelle S. 2003. "The Story Catches You and You Fall Down: Tragedy, Ethnography, and 'Cultural Competence.'" *Medical Anthropology Quarterly* 17 (2): 159–81.

Terray, Emmanuel. 1972. "Historical Materialism and Segmentary Lineage-Based Societies." In *Marxism and "Primitive" Societies,* 93–186. Translated by Mary Klopper. New York: Monthly Review Press.

Tetteh, Ernestina. 2008. "Voices of Left Behind Children: A Study of International Families in Accra, Ghana." Master's thesis, University of Ghana, Legon.

Thorne, Barrie, Marjorie Faulstich Orellana, Wan Shun Eva Lam, and Anna Chee. 2003. "Raising Children, and Growing Up, across National Borders: Comparative Perspectives on Age, Gender, and Migration." In *Gender and U.S. Immigration: Contemporary Trends*, edited by Pierrette Hondagneu-Sotelo, 241–62. Berkeley: University of California Press.

Trager, Lilian. 2005. *Migration and Economy: Global and Local Dynamics*. Walnut Creek, CA: AltaMira Press.

Transportation Center. 1964. *Patterns of Labor Migration in Ghana*. Evanston, IL: Transportation Center, Northwestern University

Trawick, Margaret. 1990. *Notes on Love in a Tamil Family*. Berkeley: University of California Press.

Turino, Thomas. 2000. *Nationalists, Cosmopolitans, and Popular Music in Zimbabwe*. Chicago: University of Chicago Press.

Twum-Baah, K. A. 2005. "Volume and Characteristics of International Ghanaian Migration." In *At Home in the World? International Migration and Development in Contemporary Ghana and West Africa*, edited by Takyiwaa Manuh, 55–77. Accra: Sub-Saharan Publishers.

Twum Baah, K. A., J. S. Nabila, and A. F. Aryee, eds. 1995. *Migration Research Study in Ghana*. Accra: Ghana Statistical Service.

Uchitelle, Louis. 2008. "Unsold Homes Tie Down Would-Be Transplants." *New York Times*, April 3. Available at http://www.nytimes.com/2008/04/03/business/03labor .html?scp=1&sq=unsold%20homes&st=cse, accessed July 16, 2010.

United Nations, Population Division, Department of Economic and Social Affairs. 2003. *World Fertility Report*. Geneva: United Nations.

UNESCO, Institute for Statistics. 2010. "Trends in Tertiary Education: Sub-Saharan Africa." UIS Fact Sheet, December, no. 10. Available at http://www.uis.unesco.org/Fact Sheets/Documents/fs10-2010-en.pdf, accessed May 7, 2012.

———. N.d. "Ghana Profile." Available at http://stats.uis.unesco.org, accessed May 7, 2012.

UNESCO, International Bureau of Education. 2006. *Ghana: Early Childhood Care and Education (ECCE) Programmes*. Geneva: UNESCO International Bureau of Education.

US Census Bureau. 2003a. "Adopted Children and Stepchildren: 2000." Available at http://www.census.gov/prod/2003pubs/censr-6.pdf, accessed February 5, 2010.

———. 2003b. "Married-Couple and Unmarried-Partner Households: 2000." Available at http://www.census.gov/prod/2003pubs/censr-5.pdf, accessed February 5, 2010.

———. 2008. "The Living Arrangements of Children in 2005. Population Profile of the United States (Dynamic Version): 2000 (Internet Release)." Available at http://www .census.gov/population/www/pop-profile/files/dynamic/LivArrChildren.pdf, accessed February 5, 2010.

US Citizenship and Immigration Services. 2008. "How Do I . . . Financially Sponsor Someone Who Wants to Immigrate?" August. Available at http://www.uscis.gov/ USCIS/New%20Structure/3rd%20Level%20(Left%20Nav%20Children)/Resources -3rd%20level/How%20Do%20I%20Guides/F3en.pdf, accessed July 9, 2010.

———. 2010a. "Green Card through the Diversity Lottery Program." Available at http:// www.uscis.gov/portal/site/uscis/menuitem.eb1d4c2a3e5b9ac89243c6a7543f6d1a/?v gnextoid=2df93a4107083210VgnVCM100000082ca60aRCRD&vgnextchannel=2df93 a4107083210VgnVCM100000082ca60aRCRD, accessed February 11, 2010.

234 / References

———. 2010b. "USCIS Processing Time Information." Available at https://egov.uscis.gov/cris/processTimesDisplay.do;jsessionid=bac585, accessed February 11, 2010.

———. 2012a. "Check Filing Fees." Available at http://www.uscis.gov/portal/site/uscis/menuitem.eb1d4c2a3e5b9ac89243c6a7543f6d1a/?vgnextoid=b1ae408b1c4b3210Vg nVCM100000b92ca60aRCRD&vgnextchannel=b1ae408b1c4b3210VgnVCM100000b 92ca60aRCRD, accessed October 9, 2012.

———. 2012b. "USCIS Processing Time Information for Our Vermont Service Center." Available at https://egov.uscis.gov/cris/processingTimesDisplay.do, accessed May 7, 2012.

US Department of State. 2010a. "Visa Bulletin for March 2010." 10 (18). Available at http://travel.state.gov/visa/frvi/bulletin/bulletin_4659.html, accessed February 11, 2010.

———. 2010b. "Who Can Be Adopted." Available at http://adoption.state.gov/about/how/childeligibility.html, accessed February 6, 2010.

US Embassy, Accra, Ghana. 2012. "Press Release: Visa Processing Fees to Change on April 13, 2012." Available at http://ghana.usembassy.gov/pr_040212.html, accessed May 7, 2012.

van der Geest, Sjaak. 1997. "Money and Respect: The Changing Value of Old Age in Rural Ghana." *Africa* 67 (4): 534–59.

———. 2002. "Respect and Reciprocity: Care of Elderly People in Ghana." *Journal of Cross-Cultural Gerontology* 17: 3–31.

Vandermeesch, Céline. 2002. "Les enfants confiés âgés de moins de six ans au Sénégal en 1992–1993." *Population* 57 (4–5): 661–88.

Vanderpuye-Orgle, Jacqueline. 2004. *Economy and Poverty in Ghana in the 1990s: A Review.* Discussion Paper No. 29. Legon: Institute of Statistical, Social, and Economic Research, University of Ghana.

Van Dijk, Rijk. 2002. "Religion, Reciprocity, and Restructuring Family Responsibility in the Ghanaian Pentecostal Diaspora." In *The Transnational Family*, edited by Deborah Bryceson and Ulla Vuorela, 173–96. New York: Berg.

Van Hear, Nicholas. 2002. "Sustaining Societies under Strain: Remittances as a Form of Transnational Exchange in Sri Lanka and Ghana." In *New Approaches to Migration? Transnational Communities and the Transformation of Home*, edited by Nadje Al-Ali and Khalid Koser, 202–23. London: Routledge.

Wadler, Joyce. 2009. "Caught in the Safety Net." *New York Times*, May 13. Available at http://www.nytimes.com/2009/05/14/garden/14return.html?_r=1&scp=7&sq=adult%20 children%20living%20with%20their%20parents&st=cse, accessed June 29, 2010.

Waldinger, Roger, and Michael I. Lichter. 2003. *How the Other Half Works: Immigration and the Social Organization of Labor.* Berkeley: University of California Press.

Wall, Karin, and José São José. 2004. "Managing Work and Care: A Difficult Challenge for Immigrant Families." *Social Policy and Administration* 38 (6): 591–621.

Warr, Mark. 2009. "Safe at Home." *Contexts* 8 (3): 46–51.

Wasem, Ruth Ellen. 2004. "U.S. Immigration Policy on Permanent Admissions." CRS Report for Congress, February 18. Available at http://fpc.state.gov/documents/organization/31352.pdf, accessed June 24, 2010.

Waters, Mary C. 1999. *Black Identities: West Indian Immigrant Dreams and American Realities.* New York: Russell Sage Foundation.

Waters, Mary C., and Jennifer Sykes. 2009. "Spare the Rod, Ruin the Child? First- and Second-Generation West Indian Child-Rearing Practices." In *Across Generations: Im-*

migrant Families in America, edited by Nancy Foner, 72–97. New York: New York University Press.

Wegner, Daniel M., and Laura Smart. 1997. "Deep Cognitive Activation: A New Approach to the Unconscious." *Journal of Consulting and Clinical Psychology* 65: 984–95.

Weiner, Myron. 1987. "International Emigration and the Third World." In *Population in an Interacting World*, edited by William Alonso, 173–200. Cambridge, MA: Harvard University Press.

———. 1998. "Opposing Visions: Migration and Citizenship Policies in Japan and the United States." In *Temporary Workers or Future Citizens: Japanese and U.S. Migration Policies*, edited by Myron Weiner and Tadashi Hanami, 1–28. New York: New York University Press.

Welch, Michael, and Liza Schuster. 2005. "Detention of Asylum Seekers in the U.K. and U.S.: Deciphering Noisy and Quiet Constructions." *Punishment and Society: An International Journal of Penology* 74 (4): 397–417.

West, Andy. 1999. "They Make Us Out to Be Monsters: Images of Children and Young People in Care." In *Social Policy, the Media, and Misrepresentation*, edited by Bob Franklin, 253–68. New York: Routledge.

Whitehouse, Bruce. 2009. "Bridging the Distance: A Comparison of Domestic and Transnational Split Households in Bamako, Mali and Brazzaville, Congo." Paper presented at the annual American Anthropological Association meeting, Philadelphia.

Wilcox, Kathleen. 1982. "Differential Socialization in the Classrooms: Implications for Equal Opportunity." In *Doing the Ethnography of Schooling*, edited by George Spindler, 269–305. New York: Holt, Reinhart, and Winston.

Wilks, Ivor. 1993. "Land, Labor, Gold, and the Forest Kingdom of Asante: A Model of Early Change." In *Forests of Gold: Essays on the Akan and the Kingdom of Asante*, 41–90. Athens: Ohio University Press.

Williams, Paul, and Julie Dickinson. 1993. "Fear of Crime: Read All about It? The Relationship between Newspaper Crime Reporting and Fear of Crime." *British Journal of Criminology* 33 (1): 22–41.

Williams, Raymond. 1977. *Marxism and Literature*. Oxford: Oxford University Press.

Wilson, Jill H., and Shelly Habecker. 2008. "The Lure of the Capital City: An Anthro-Geographical Analysis of Recent African Immigration to Washington, DC." *Population, Space, and Place* 14: 433–48.

Wolf, Diane L. 1997. "Family Secrets: Transnational Struggles among Children of Filipino Immigrants." *Sociological Perspectives* 40: 457–82.

Wolf, Margery. 1972. *Women and the Family in Rural Taiwan*. Stanford, CA: Stanford University Press.

World Bank. 2011. *Migration and Remittances Factbook 2011*, 2nd ed. Washington, DC: World Bank.

———. N.d. "World Development Indicators." Available at http://data.worldbank.org/indicator/SE.PRE.ENRR, accessed May 8, 2012.

Yankah, Kwesi. 1995. *Speaking for the Chief: Ōkyeame and the Politics of Akan Royal Oratory*. Bloomington: Indiana University Press.

Yoshikawa, Hirokazu. 2011. *Immigrants Raising Citizens: Undocumented Parents and Their Young Children*. New York: Russell Sage Foundation.

Zelizer, Viviana A. 1985. *Pricing the Priceless Child: The Changing Social Value of Children*. New York: Basic Books.

———. 2005. *The Purchase of Intimacy*. Princeton, NJ: Princeton University Press.

Zeng, Zhen, and Yu Xie. 2004. "Asian-Americans' Earnings Disadvantage Reexamined: The Role of Place in Education." *American Journal of Sociology* 109 (5): 1075–108.

Zhang, Liang. 2005. "Do Measures of College Quality Matter? The Effect of College Quality on Graduates' Earnings." *Review of Higher Education* 28 (4): 571–96.

Zhou, Min. 2009. "Conflict, Coping, and Reconciliation: Intergenerational Relations in Chinese Immigrant Families." In *Across Generations: Immigrant Families in America*, edited by Nancy Foner, 21–46. New York: New York University Press.

Zhou, Min, and Carl L. Bankston III. 1998. *Growing Up American: How Vietnamese Children Adapt to Life in the United States*. New York: Russell Sage Foundation.

Zolberg, Aristide R. 1987. "Wanted but Not Welcome: Alien Labor in Western Development." In *Population in an Interacting World*, edited by William Alonso, 36–73. Cambridge, MA: Harvard University Press.

———. 2006. *A Nation by Design: Immigration Policy in the Fashioning of America*. New York: Russell Sage Foundation.

Zontini, Elisabetta. 2010. *Transnational Families, Migration, and Gender: Moroccan and Filipino Women in Bologna and Barcelona*. New York: Berghahn Books.

ARCHIVAL SOURCES

Basel Mission Archives, Basel, Switzerland
D-20.4. Description: Manuscript in Twi, ca. 600 pages. Title: "Akwapim, Land und Leute, Religion." Ferner: eine Art Tagebuch, 1860–65.

Eastern Regional Archives, Koforidua, Ghana
ECRG 16/1/2. Civil Record Book, Omanhene's Court, Akwapim, October 17, 1907–December 29, 1908.

ECRG 16/1/5. Civil Record Book, Omanhene's Court, Akwapim, January 8, 1910–September 17, 1910.

ECRG 16/1/18. Civil Record Book, Native Tribunal of Akropong, April 7, 1914–November 27, 1915.

ECRG 16/1/20. Civil Record Book, Nifahene of Akwapim, December 23, 1914–January 14, 1916.

ECRG 16/1/21. Civil Record Book, Akwapim, Superior Court of Omanhene of Akwapim, Akropong, May 23, 1919–March 23, 1925.

ECRG 16/1/22. Civil Record Book, Native Tribunal of the Nifahene, Akwapim, February 25, 1921–May 4, 1923.

NATIONAL ARCHIVES, ACCRA, GHANA

SCT 2/5/16. Supreme Court, Accra, Criminal Record Book, April 6, 1905–July 20, 1907, National Archives, Accra, Ghana.

THE POLLY HILL PAPERS, AFRICANA LIBRARY, NORTHWESTERN UNIVERSITY, EVANSTON, ILLINOIS, UNITED STATES

Box 3, Folder 2. Visit to Kofi Pare, May 18, 1959.

Box 4, Folder 7. Larteh: Interview with E. R. Lattey.

———. Notes on the Manuscript Book by James Lawrence Tete.

———. 1948 Census of Larteh.

———. Information given by E. O. Walker, October 7, 1958.

Box 5, Folder 1. Interview with Okra Kwame Donkor, aged 81, in Akropong, April 5, 1958.

Box 19, Folder 6a. Mampong: Interview with Kwame Adu, February 24, 1960.

Avatime, Volta Region, 73. *See also* Amedzofe

Basel mission: and family ideals, 81; and fosterage, 66; history of, in Akuapem, 46; and migration, 49–50; and pawning, 46, 208n12; and schooling, 52, 66, 67; and slavery, 46, 47
Beck, Ulrich, 23, 195
Berekum, as destination for Akuapem migrants, 69
Berekuso, and pawning, 51
Bernstein, Basil, 17
Bledsoe, Caroline: on fosterage, 28, 74, 75, 209n1; on hardship, 136, 212n6; on West African migrants in Europe, 212n2
Boehm, Deborah, 9, 13, 21, 204
bolga, as style associated with migrants, 180–81, 184
Boni, Stefano, 53–54
Botswana, Ghanaian migration to, 90, 103
Bourdieu, Pierre, and habitus, 15–16, 22
Bronx, Ghanaian immigration to, 145, 146, 148
Brown, Claude, 9
Brydon, Lynne, 73, 74, 75

Calavita, Kitty, 105, 214n11
Cameroon: fosterage in, 61; Ghanaian migration to, 211n7
Campbell, Bebe Moore, 9
Canada, Ghanaian immigration to, 137, 183
Cape Coast, migration to, 49
capitalism: and cocoa farming, 29, 40, 48–54; definition, 12 ; as dependent on noncapitalist kinship, 11–12, 48–54; and emotional regimes, 12–13, 29, 174, 194; and family arrangements, 4, 11–14, 48–54; and hegemony, 205–6; and migration, 3–4, 7–10, 29, 92, 173; and separation of families, 4, 11–14, 29, 35, 195–98; and the state, 4, 29; and transnationalism, 9–10
care: commercial arrangements for, 155, 168–78; commodification of, 56–59, 197; distribution of costs of, 126, 155–56, 160, 198–202; through house-building, 40 (*see also* houses); and indebtedness, 40–42, 54–57; materiality of, 28, 57–58, 175–84, 194,

197; temporal dimensions of, 7, 9, 11, 61–63, 198–99
caregivers: experiences of, 155–71; paid, 168–69
children: as childcare providers, 132–33; in detention, representations of, 143–44; and eldercare, 55–56, 73, 75, 107; and household labor, 45–46, 67, 80, 128, 167; left behind, status of, 165–68, 171, 179–81; left behind, suffering of, 26–27, 99–102, 173–94; significance of having, 45, 55, 71, 116; as source of labor for cocoa, 51–52. *See also* adolescents; infants
China, *hukou* system in, 199, 200–201
Christianity: charismatic, 81–82; and "civilization," 67; and family ideals, 64, 81–82, 185; and good behavior, 148–51; and migration for work, 81. *See also* Basel Mission; church
church: in immigrant communities, 129–30, 142; and repertoire, 116, 129–31, 142–44, 152, 187; as research site, 30–32
"civilization": and fosterage, 28, 67, 68; and urbanization, 72, 88
Clarke, Kamari, 106, 204
class, social: cultures, 64, 185; in West Africa, 209n2. *See also* middle class
clothing: as care, 45–46, 56, 58, 177, 178; as sign of international connections, 179
cocoa farming: in Akuapem, 49–51, 64, 68–69; and capitalism, 29, 40, 48–54; changes in, 54, 64, 68–69; and pawning, 42, 50–51
commodification: of care, 56–59, 197; of kin relations, 48–49
communication, long-distance: and ease of remittances, 180; and parenting, 2, 121, 169, 175, 188; and transnationalism, 8, 204
Comaroff, Jean, 16, 23, 81
Comaroff, John, 16, 23
Conrad, Shelby R., 74
Côte d'Ivoire: fosterage in, 74; as stepping stone to further migration, 189
Coutin, Susan Bibler, 98, 103–4, 110
crime, in America, 128, 145, 152
cultural capital: definition, 15; and fosterage, 66; and the middle class, 82, 156

Made in United States
North Haven, CT
27 December 2021